Guides to Wines & To

Languedoc-Roussillon

2022 Edition

Benjamin Lewin MW

ISBN: 9781090144577

Vendange Press

www.vendangepress.com

Preface

This guide discusses the wines of Languedoc and Roussillon, both AOPs and IGPs. The first part discusses the region, and explains the character and range of the wines. The second part profiles the producers. There are detailed profiles of the leading producers, showing how each winemaker interprets the local character, and mini-profiles of other important estates.

In the first part, I address the nature of the wines made today and ask how this has changed, how it's driven by tradition or competition, and how styles may evolve in the future. I show how the wines are related to the terroir and to the types of grape varieties that are grown, and I explain the classification system. For each region, I suggest reference wines that illustrate the character and variety of the area.

In the second part, there's no single definition for what constitutes a top producer. Leading producers range from those who are so prominent as to represent the common public face of an appellation to those who demonstrate an unexpected potential on a tiny scale. The producers profiled in the guide represent the best of both tradition and innovation in wine in the region. In each profile, I have tried to give a sense of the producer's aims for his wines, of the personality and philosophy behind them—to meet the person who makes the wine, as it were, as much as to review the wines themselves.

Each profile gives contact information and details of production, followed by a description of the producer and the range of wines. For major producers (rated from 1 to 3 stars), I suggest reference wines that are a good starting point for understanding the style. Most of the producers welcome visits, although some require appointments: details are in the profiles. Profiles are organized geographically, and each group of profiles is preceded by maps showing the locations of producers to help plan itineraries.

The guide is based on visits to the region over recent years. I owe an enormous debt to the many producers who cooperated in this venture by engaging in discussion and opening innumerable bottles for tasting. This guide would not have been possible without them.

Benjamin Lewin

Contents

Tables

Appellation Maps

Producer Maps

Overview of the Languedoc

If the Languedoc were an independent country, it would be in fifth place in the world for wine production (more or less equal with Argentina and after the United States). It accounts for a third of all wine produced in France. Languedoc-Roussillon is a vast area, stretching around the Mediterranean from near the Rhône to the Pyrenees at the west. Roussillon is the southernmost part adjacent to Spain.

The name has been constantly changing, from Languedoc-Roussillon, to separating the two regions, to the latest incarnation in 2016 of the administrative region of Occitanie, which includes Languedoc, Roussillon, and the Midi-Pyrénées in the Southwest. In terms of wine production, it's easiest to think about Languedoc and Roussillon separately. Indeed, producers in Roussillon are proud of their Catalan heritage, and can become somewhat indignant at being bundled with Languedoc.

To say that the history of wine production is chequered would be kind. Together with Provence, immediately to its east, the region used to be known as the Midi, famous for providing the bulk of Europe's wine lake, a vast quantity of characterless wine from high-yielding varieties. But things are different today. Overall production has decreased sharply, and production of Vin de Table has been reduced to a small proportion. Unlike other areas of France, where most production is AOP, here the IGP is predominant, although there are some AOPs establishing good reputations. Most of the wine is red.

Rich is the word that first comes to mind to describe the style. The warm climate makes this a fertile area for growing grapes, but until recently, quantity ruled over quality. At the start of the nineteenth century, the focus was on producing wine for distillation; the Languedoc made about 40% of all spirits in France. After the railway connected Montpellier to Paris in 1845, producers switched to making cheap table wine that could be sent to the industrial cities in the north.

Phylloxera wiped out the vineyards here as elsewhere—there were riots in Montpellier in 1907 to protest cheap imports of wine from Algeria—but by the second decade of the twentieth century, recovery was under way. Production still focused on price; wine was produced as cheaply as possible, often blended with foreign imports, and sold in bulk. Almost all was Vin de Table, and as the demand for plonk declined, this surplus became the largest single contributor to Europe's wine lake. At its peak around 1970, Languedoc-Roussillon had 450,000 hectares of vineyards.

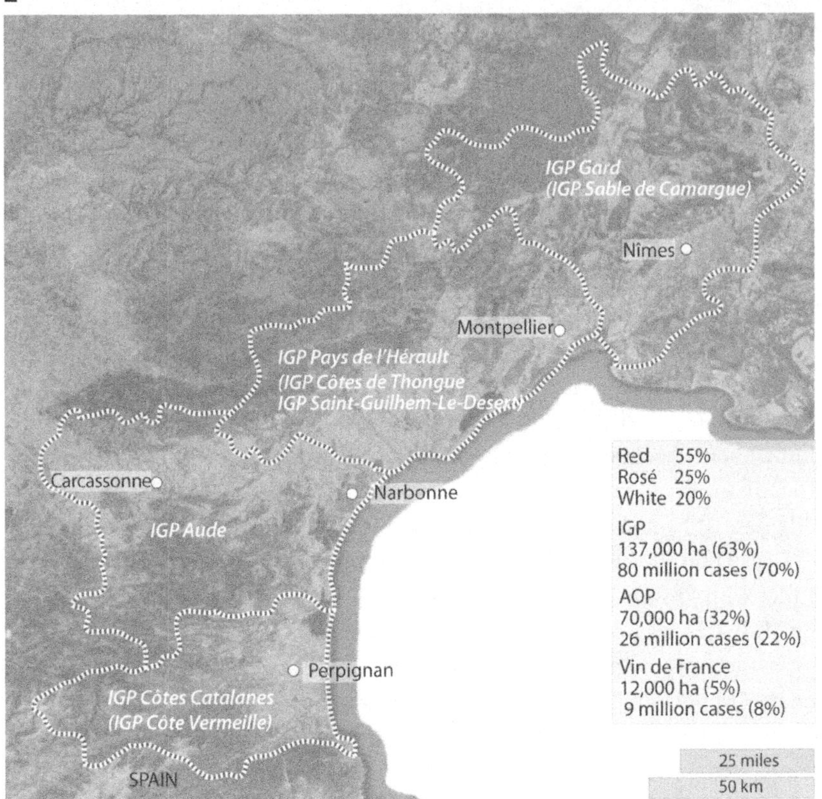

Languedoc-Roussillon stretches from Nîmes to the Spanish border. The IGP Pays d'Oc covers the whole region, and includes several departmental IGPs. IGP Aude and IGP Pays d'Hérault are the heart of Languedoc. IGP Gard extends from Languedoc into the Rhône. IGP Côtes Catalanes corresponds to Roussillon. Some of the better known zonal IGPs are named in parentheses.

Economic difficulties, combined with incentives to abandon production, led to a substantial decline in vineyards. Over the past forty years, production has declined by about half. In fact, subsidies for pulling up vineyards became a significant part of the income of the Languedoc. Today there are about 220,000 ha. The number of growers has declined, and in spite of a move by the more enterprising to bottle their own wine, cooperatives are more important here than anywhere else in France. Of the 700 cooperatives in France, around 500 are in the Languedoc, where the struggle of the past twenty years has been to improve quality. Overall, 72% of production goes through coops.

Decline in production has been accompanied by a move to quality. A major change has been the collapse of Vin de Table production, now less than

10% of its peak, and alone responsible for most of the decline in the category in France. Even so, almost half of France's remaining Vin de Table (now named Vin de France) still comes from the Languedoc. IGP has increased about three fold; the Languedoc is by far France's most important producer of wine at the IGP level. Of course, the change is partly cosmetic: the vast increase in IGP has come from vineyards that used to be Vin de Table.

Accounting for more than three quarters of production, the IGP Pays d'Oc is the prominent face of the Languedoc, covering the whole region. Within the generic IGP are several Départemental IGPs: IGP de Gard, IGP Pays d'Hérault, IGP d'Aude. In the far south, IGP Côtes Catalanes represents the Pyrénées-Oriéntal département, effectively equivalent to Roussillon. There are also many zonal IGPs, varying from single communes to broader swatches of the area, but almost none has established any typicity or made any particular reputation.

The AOP system is very much a work in progress, presently with more than 30 AOPs, varying in size from Corbières, which produces more than 4 million bottles annually, to several smaller AOPs with less than 100,000. (This is to ignore the catch-all AOP Languedoc which covers more or less the whole of the region.)

The majority of production is red, although over recent years it ahs dropped from two thirds to just over half of production. Most of the change has been to an increase in rosé, although there's also been a smaller increase in white production.

The name "Midi" somehow conjures up an impression of a vast plain of vines, but actually much of the Languedoc is distinctly mountainous. From Pic St. Loup, north of Montpellier, to La Clape just inland from Narbonne, massive calcareous cliffs overlook the vineyards. Syrah is more dominant in the north and Carignan is more dominant in the west, but the common focus across the region on GSM (Grenache-Syrah-Mourvèdre) blends with or without Carignan means that differences between appellations should be due more to terroir or climatic variations than to changes in varieties. So how distinctive are the appellations?

Some of the appellations are relatively homogeneous with regards to soil types, while others vary quite extensively, so there is no simple rule. While there are some differences in temperatures and rainfall, depending on proximity to cliffs, elevation of vineyards, and exposure to maritime influence, the fact is that the Languedoc is a hot, dry climate prone to make powerful wines. Skillful winemaking is key in restraining the reds and keeping freshness in the whites: the producer is the most important variable.

It is relatively rare for wines from Languedoc to need aging. The combination of the warm climate and relatively forward grape varieties means that most wines are ready to drink on release. The general attitude is captured by Tim Ford at Domaine Gayda. "People are drinking wines straight away now, they are not cellared, they are not decanted, the bottle is opened and it's straight down the hatch. We as winemakers have to make wine that is ready to drink." One the other hand, some wines have. "People have forgotten that wines of the south can age—it's a pity. You can forget about the wine for 8-10 years and then drink it. But people think they need to drink the wines of the south straight away," says Frédéric Pourtalié at Domaine de Montcalmès.

Grape Varieties in AOPs and IGPs

For several decades the Languedoc was plagued by the characterless wines produced by the infamous trio of Carignan, Cinsault, and Aramon; today these are only a quarter of black plantings. A drive to improve quality a few years back focused on "cépage amelioration," replacing poor quality varieties with better ones. Its success is indicated by the fact that Syrah (introduced relatively recently) and Grenache (a traditional variety of the region) overtook Carignan as the most planted varieties in 2009. In fact, there is now more Syrah and Grenache in Languedoc-Roussillon than in the Rhône. Newcomers Merlot and Cabernet Sauvignon are now among the leading black varieties. White varieties are less than a quarter of all plantings, with Chardonnay and Sauvignon Blanc as the leading varieties.

A major distinction between IGPs and AOPs is that international varieties are grown in the IGPs, whereas they are mostly not allowed in the AOPs. This means there tends to be a difference in character as well as quality, with the AOP more traditional, and the IGP more "international" in the choice of varieties. "In the Midi you can cultivate all the cépages, although their characters may be different from elsewhere. It's really a matter of deciding what type of wine you want to provide," says Serge Martin-Pierrat at Château les Hospitaliers.

There is continuing debate as to whether concentrating on making wines from the traditional varieties in the AOPs, or producing international varieties in the IGPs, is the best way forward. There's some criticism of INAO for its insistence on maintaining the original Southern varieties as the exclusive basis for AOP wines.

IGP is flexible about the composition of wines, which can be monovarietal or blended from multiple varieties. However, most IGP wines carry varietal

Major Black Grape Varieties in Capsule

The Old Varieties

Carignan originated in Spain (under the name of Mazuelo) and came to the Languedoc after phylloxera. The current tendency is to pull it out as the wine tends to lack fruit concentration and can be bitter. Carbonic maceration is often used to soften it. It is usually blended, but vines from the original plantings are among the oldest in the Languedoc, and there has been something of a revival in producing dedicated cuvées of old vines Carignan.

Cinsault is one of the oldest varieties of the region. Plantings increased through the 1970s but now it is being pulled out. Its tendency to high yields means the wine is soft but characterless. What is left is mostly used to make rosé.

The GSM Trio

GSM stands for Grenache-Syrah-Mourvèdre and is a blend in which usually Grenache but sometimes Syrah is the major component.

Grenache is soft and fruity, relatively low in acidity, prone to high alcohol, and has a tendency to oxidization. It's the fruit-driven component of the GSM blend. As it was often planted after phylloxera, there are still old vines, and it is sometimes used for monovarietal old vines cuvées, although more in the Rhône than Languedoc. It's the major component of the sweet dessert wines.

Lledoner Pelut is a relative of Grenache and in some appellations can be used instead of it, although it's becoming rare.

Syrah is the most refined member of the trio, bringing structure and precision with taut fruits. It's the sole black grape of the northern Rhône. Plantings have greatly increased in the Languedoc in recent years.

Mourvèdre is a powerful grape, structured, spicy, and deeply colored. It is usually a minor component in the blend, although it's the major component of Bandol in Provence.

labels; in fact, the Languedoc is the largest source of varietal-labeled wines in France. The grape varieties that dominate varietal wines look quite different from tradition: Merlot, Cabernet Sauvignon, Syrah, and Chardonnay scarcely existed in the region twenty years ago. By contrast, the AOPs are blended wines, and carry identification only of origin. Because all of the AOPs in Languedoc require wines to be blended from at least two or three grape varieties, producers who want to make monovarietal wines, even from traditional varieties, are forced to declassify them to IGP or even to Vin de France.

The generic Languedoc AOP requires a minimum 50% of the GSM trio (Grenache, Syrah, and Mourvèdre) for red or rosé (which in effect means Syrah and Grenache as there is relatively little Mourvèdre). Each individual AOP has its variations on this theme. Chardonnay and Sauvignon Blanc are not allowed in white AOPs; the use of Viognier is restricted, so it also tends to be found only in the IGPs.

Major White Grape Varieties in Capsule
Traditional Varieties
Rolle is the same as Vermentino, popular because it does well in dry conditions, not very acid or concentrated.
Grenache Blanc is one of the most common white varieties, reliable but not very varied in flavor. Grenache Gris is a variant, but is less common.
Clairette was a major component of whites of the Midi, but has largely been uprooted as it tends to high alcohol, low acidity, and not much flavor.
Macabeu (Macabeo) comes from Spain and is found in the western part of the region. It's faintly floral.
Varieties from the Rhône
Roussanne is a high quality grape, fine, complex, sometimes a little spicy. It's often blended with Marsanne to get more body.
Marsanne is the other quality grape, not as refined as Roussanne, and with a tendency to bitterness. It's usually blended.
Viognier is an aromatic variety, made as a monovarietal in the Rhône, that has become more popular in Languedoc, where it's more often used to bring aromatic lift to a blend.
Specialized Varieties
Piquepoul Blanc makes dry, tight, wine. It's the sole grape of Picpoul de Pinet and elsewhere is used in blends.
Mauzac is the traditional white grape of Limoux, and tend to aromas of pears and apples, but can have low acidity and become soft and almost soapy.
Muscat actually smells and tastes of grapes. The more refined form of Muscat à Petit Grains is used for the vin doux naturel of Languedoc. Muscat d'Alexandrie is grown in Rivesaltes. There's a recent tendency to make dry Muscat or to include a little in a blend.

Modernism elsewhere in France tends to imply a move towards a more "international" style, usually meaning greater extraction to make more powerful wines. In the Languedoc, it has almost the opposite meaning; a move away from the old, heavy, extracted alcoholic styles to finer, more elegant wines (although there will always be alcohol in Languedoc). Innovation at the top level does not so much take the direction of trying new varieties, but more on moving in a more refined direction with the varieties (Grenache, Carignan, Cinsault, and more recently Syrah) that were previously known for producing powerful alcoholic wines.

There is definite progress, with excess production diminishing, and plantings of better varieties increasing, but no clear regional leader has emerged. With its (relatively) reliably hot climate, Languedoc-Roussillon better resembles the wine-producing regions of the New World than any other part of France. Today you meet many thoughtful, intelligent winemakers in Languedoc who are rethinking what they can do with the region, the very antithesis of the old view of the Midi as a bulk producer of rustic wines. Many are young winemakers for whom one attraction is that the Languedoc is one of the last places where they can still afford to buy vineyards.

The Fall and Rise of Carignan

In spite of its evident deficiencies—most notably the tendency to over produce—Carignan remains a major variety. Its history is not encouraging: "Carignan was introduced from Spain and was planted everywhere to make Vin de Table. It eliminated all the traditional cépages," says Jean Orliac at Domaine de l'Hortus. Reality is recognized in the AOP rules by allowing it to be included, but often restricting the maximum proportion. Carignan's tendency to show bitterness without fruitiness is sometimes counteracted by using carbonic maceration (similar to Beaujolais), but the result does not show much typicity. My general marker for a wine made from Carignan, or containing a large proportion of it, is a certain flatness, a lack of liveliness, on the palate.

But because almost no one is planting Carignan any more, what's left tends to be old vines. Some committed producers regard the old Carignan as the glory of the Languedoc. "Carignan is the great classic vine of the Languedoc, it's the Pinot Noir of the Languedoc. Why doesn't it have a better reputation? It's been a victim of its success. It's been planted everywhere, and because it's a productive variety, people have made wine at very high

Even Vieilles Vignes Carignan produces large bunches.

Reference Wines for Vieilles Vignes Carignan	
Faugères	Château de La Liquière, Nos Racines
IGP Hauterive (Corbières region)	Château La Baronne, Pièce de Roche
IGP du Mont Baudile (Hérault)	Domaine d'Aupilhac, Le Carignan
IGP Côtes Catalanes (Roussillon)	Domaine Olivier Pithon, Le Pilou Domaine du Mas Amiel, Val de Nuits Domaine Roc Des Anges, Vignes Centenaires Carignan
Côtes du Roussillon Village	Clos del Rey, l'Aragone
Vin de France (Corbières region)	Domaine Ledogar, La Mariole
Vin de France (Saint Christol)	Terre Inconnue, Cuvée Léonie

yields. But at low yields it is perfectly adapted to the terroir," says Rémy Pédréno at Roc L'Anglade.

My own view is that vines have to be a century old before the wine comes into an elegant balance that lets the fruit become the dominant note. Granted that the fruit profile of Carignan will always be flatter compared with the exuberance of Grenache or the freshness of Syrah, you can certainly find some Vieilles Vignes Carignans that are elegant, smooth, and seamless.

Languedoc AOPs

AOP regions make up a third of the area, and AOP production has been reasonably constant at just under a quarter of all volume for several years, but there are continuing changes in the organization of the AOPs. The region was divided into different appellations in the early 1980s, and since then a significant part of the effort to improve wine production in the Languedoc has focused on refining the list to make more specific AOPs.

The region is too large to have any geographical integrity, and falls into several parts, with climate varying from Mediterranean along the coast to Continental inland at the mountains. There are vineyards all along the coastal region from Montpellier to south of Narbonne. In the northeast corner, the mountain zone has quite rugged terroir. The major AOPs are located in the center and south, extending to Roussillon. To the west, around Carcassonne, there are some Atlantic influences.

The area from Montpellier to Narbonne used to be covered by a catch-all AOC called Coteaux du Languedoc. This was replaced in 2007 by the regional Languedoc AOP, which essentially includes all of the AOP areas, all the way from Montpellier to the Spanish border. The stated objective is to "define the

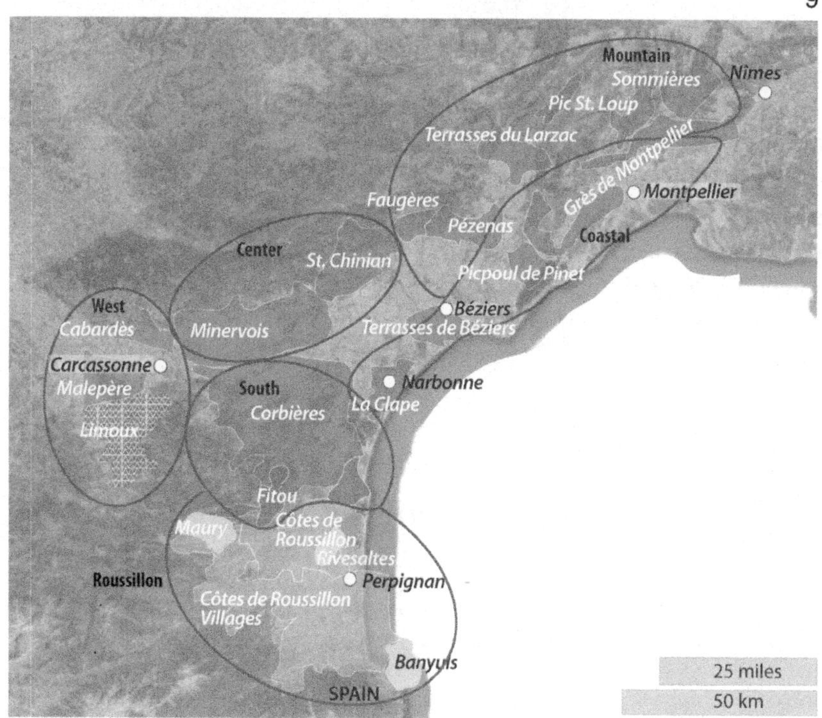

The AOPs of Languedoc-Roussillon extend from Montpellier to the Spanish border. The eastern part is divided into the inland mountain regions and the coastal regions. The heart of Languedoc is the center inland and the south running towards Roussillon. To the west there are Atlantic influences and sparkling wine. Roussillon runs in the far south to the Spanish border.

typical characteristics of the Languedoc region and grapes," but the creation of such a broad appellation seems retrogressive, since it's really impossible for it to have any coherence. Most of the wines in the Languedoc AOP are the same wines that used to be labeled as Coteaux du Languedoc, but there are some from additional areas, and others from within sub-regional AOPs that for one reason or another do not fit the requirements of their particular AOP.

The heart of the Languedoc is a large semicircle of AOPs radiating around Narbonne—the producers' organization likes to talk about the amphitheater of AOPs. Languedoc now includes around thirty AOPs, but the core AOPs are Faugères, St. Chinian, Minervois, Fitou, and Corbières (this last being about the size of all the others combined). The reputations of the appellations really pertain to their red wines: in fact, some of them allow only red wine, with the whites labeled simply as Languedoc AOP.

The local trade body, the CIVL, decided in 2010 to develop a hierarchy of appellations. Not a bad idea in itself, given the large number of appellations and wide variation in quality, but the scheme was not based on looking at terroirs, but on more diffuse commercial considerations. Appellations were divided into levels according to the average price for their wines, but these were so low as to cast doubt on the value of the exercise: €3-4, €4-7, and over €10 for the top tier. To qualify for the top level, a significant proportion of the wine must be sold in bottle rather than in bulk (which effectively excludes appellations where cooperatives are more important).

The CIVL wanted to call the top tier Grand Crus, but INAO refused to allow the Languedoc to have grand crus. Instead they are called Crus de Languedoc, the second level are Grand Vins de Languedoc, and the base is simple Languedoc. In the event, the criteria for classification have been more

Appellations and Classification of the Languedoc
The classification scheme announced by the CIVL in 2010 remains confusing. The CIVL says it has defined 7 Crus, but the list of Crus varies according to different sources. It's perhaps more useful to define three groups of appellations: the major individual AOPs (which the CIVL calls Grand Vins du Languedoc); the unquestioned top AOPs, which are genuine Crus in the sense that they lie within the original appellations; and a group of recent AOPs that are reliable in part because they are relatively small.
The Old Appellations (Grand Vins du Languedoc)
Minervois
Corbières
Faugères
Saint Chinian
Fitou
Saint Jean de Minervois
Limoux
Malepère
Cabardès
The Original Crus
Minervois La Livinière
Corbieres Boutenac
St. Chinian Roquebrun
St. Chinian Berlou
Recent Appellations (promoted from Coteaux du Languedoc)
La Clape
Terrasses du Larzac
Grès de Montpellier
Pic St. Loup
Pézenas
Limoux (Blanc)

nominal than real. Some Crus have established clear reputations, but the second level of Grand Crus has not really achieved much distinction from the base.

Four Crus which are relatively uncontroversial, each representing a sub area within one of the major appellations, are Minervois La Livinière, Corbières Boutenac, St. Chinian Berlou, and St. Chinian Roquebrun. All are for red wine only. Others that are appellations recently promoted out of Coteaux du Languedoc to become independent are more varied in their reputations.

There is a certain scepticism among producers about the usefulness of a detailed hierarchical classification. "Languedoc is a vast region. It's very heterogeneous. What matters is the quality of the work, rather than the label or the AOP. There are really only twenty or so domains of interest, in my opinion. For me the appellation has no importance, it's the work on the terroir that counts," says Paul Lignères at Château La Baronne in Corbières.

There's a feeling that the process has been rushed. "For me arriving at a cru means a high quality, it must really be better. But it takes time to do that. We haven't got the microclimates that Burgundy has. With a young appellation you can't divide into crus in only thirty years, it takes time to know the terroir," says Jean-François Orosquette at Château La Grave in Minervois.

Nearby at Château La Tour Boisée, Jean-Louis Poudou believes the process is too political. "You can't decree a cru just like that—it's an INAO-esque method that irritates me. There are producers who are increasing the quality of the Languedoc. The organization of crus in the Coteaux du Languedoc, is more of an administrative matter: it's all a political issue. The two appellations that genuinely have independence are St. Chinian and Faugères. There are really only two Crus—La Livinière and Boutenac," he says.

Terrasses du Larzac – Pic St. Loup

Appellations around Montpellier are mountainous.

Terrasses du Larzac	5 cooperatives 87 producers	2,000 ha	92,000 cases red: GSM >60%
Pic St. Loup	3 cooperatives 53 producers	1,100 ha	48,000 cases red/rosé: Syrah >50%
Grès de Montpellier	5 cooperatives 48 producers	1,000 ha	56,000 cases red: GSM >70%
Sommières	3 cooperatives 18 producers	1,971 ha	87,000 cases red: GSM >50%

All of the appellations around Montpellier make wines based on the GSM trio with other traditional varieties (Carignan, Cinsault, Counoise, Morrastel) as a minor part. The exact details vary with the appellation.

The best parts of the old Coteaux du Languedoc are the new appellations of Terrasses du Larzac and Pic St. Loup. The soil is poor, the sun is hot in summer, there can be dramatic rainstorms off the mountains, and the cold wind from the north dries everything out. Larzac describes an extensive chalk plateau to the north, and the Terrasses amalgamate a series of areas running up to it. Montpeyroux is a small area on its eastern side, with vineyards in the foothills of the Larzac range, at 120-350m, compared with those in the Terrasses which go up to more than 600m. A few miles farther east, Pic St. Loup is a plateau surrounded by calcareous cliffs spreading out from the base of Mont Hortus.

Terrasses du Larzac became a separate AOP in 2014. Vineyards are at 80-200m elevation on slopes with soils of clay and limestone. Wines must have at least three varieties, and are often blends of all five Languedoc varieties. Climate is Continental, as cool air coming down from the Larzac plateau creates a microclimate with very high diurnal variation, up to 20 degrees, the highest in Languedoc: "That's what preserves acidity and gives the elegance," says Frédéric Pourtalié at Domaine de Montcalmès. Vineyards are at elevations from 80m to 200m on the slopes of two valleys. A tasting of Grenache barrel samples from different terraces in the eastern part of the appellation shows a range from jammy impressions where there are galets (large pebbles), to broad flavors from the calcareous terroir at the base of the slope, to more mineral overtones from vineyards at higher altitude. The wines can be more restrained here (relatively speaking).

A little farther west and at lower elevation in Jonquières, Mas Cal Demoura divides its vineyards into those with more clay (planted with black varieties) and the more pebbly and calcareous (planted with white varieties). "Terrasses de Larzac has a balance between traditional generosity of Langue-

Calcareous cliffs loom over the vineyards of Pic St. Loup.

doc with an additional liveliness and freshness," says Vincent Goumard at Cal Demoura. There's enough variation across the AOP to find places that are suitable for each grape variety.

Pic St. Loup was promoted to an independent AOP in 2017. North of Montpellier on the Cevennes foothills, it has soils of clay- and marl-limestone. Between the mountains of Pic St. Loup and l'Hortus, the closest AOP to the Rhône, it is the most northern and coolest, and has the highest rainfall. The Mistral and Tramontane winds keep humidity down, however. Soil types are very varied. It produces rosé as well as red (rosé is about 15% of production).

Grès de Montpellier and Sommières have been named parts of Languedoc AOP since 2003. To the west of Montpellier, Grès de Montpellier is one of the driest AOPs. Sommières is the Languedoc's most easterly appellation (the only one to be entirely in the Gard Département.) The climate is Mediterranean and the Mistral is a strong effect.

Two other appellations in the Gard have what you might call mixed allegiances. On the one hand, they can make wines under IGP Gard, which is part of the IGP d'Oc. On the other hand, their appellations are classified as part of the southern Rhône. Costières de Nîmes, to the east of Montpellier and south of Nîmes was in fact part of the Languedoc, until its producers asked for reclassification as part of the Rhône (see *Guide to Southern Rhône*). Duché Uzès is a relatively new appellation, north of Nîmes, with its eastern border close to the Rhône, but stretching all the way west to due north of Montpellier. It's common for producers to make AOP wines in

Duché d'Uzès (classed as Southern Rhône) but IGP wines in IGP du Gard or its zonal IGPs (classed as Languedoc). Its producers are in this guide as they are close to other producers in the Languedoc.

Faugères and Saint Chinian

Faugères is on schist, St. Chinian varies from schist to calcareous. Mountains are never far away

Faugères	1 cooperative 57 producers	1,943 ha	710,000 cases 84% red, 14% rosé , 2% white
Saint Chinian	8 cooperatives 100 producers	3,300 ha	1,280,000 cases 89% red, 10% rosé, 1% white red: GSM >70% , Grenache >20%, Syrah >10%, Carignan <40%
Saint Chinian Berlou	1 cooperative 7 producers	250 ha	13,000 cases red: Carignan >30%, Syrah >20%
Saint Chinian Roquebrun	2 cooperatives 40 producers	400 ha	60,000 cases red: GSM >70%, Carignan <30%

Visiting Faugères in the autumn, a week or so after the harvest, the road climbs up steadily for miles, and by the time you arrive, the vineyards on the slopes can be shrouded in a mist so thick you can scarcely see from vine to vine. Faugères seems to be floating in the clouds. Terroir is relatively homogeneous, based on very friable gray and violet schist, typically 6-7m deep. The most important variation is the altitude of the vineyards, higher than most AOPs.

A tasting at Jean-Michel Alquier, a leading producer who helped build up the appellation, shows wines in a variety of styles: fresh and light for La Première, the GSM entry level wine from the base of the slope; fruity with a touch of piquancy for Maison Jaune, a Grenache-dominated wine from the middle of the slope; and massive black fruits for Le Bastide, a Syrah-dominated wine from the top of the hill, developing very slowly indeed over a

Faugères has thin topsoil based on a deep layer of schist.

decade. The range of styles has become more sophisticated in the past decade. "There was a period when everyone used new wood and the wines tended to taste the same, but now we have taken a step back," explained Jean-Michel.

There's a similar philosophy and range at Château de La Liquière. "At the start of the 2000s, people were trying to make wines that were very powerful. In Languedoc it's very easy to make wines that are very powerful. But public taste began to change and vignerons realized that great concentration reduces expression of terroir. People started to use less aggressive methods, including short maceration," says winemaker François Vidal. The entry level wine, Les Amandiers, classified as Languedoc, comes from the vines at lower elevation, while Cistus, the top Faugères, comes from vines higher up. "It's generally true—for both reds and whites—that more complexity and elegance, length and finesse, come from vines at high altitudes," says François. So in this sense the top wines are wines of altitude.

Faugères was reportedly denied cru status because more than half of its production is vinified by cooperatives and sold at prices that are felt to be too low for a cru, but it was considered one of the more promising appellations when the AOCs were first established. That promise is fulfilled by the top producers even if it isn't a Cru.

Adjacent to Faugères, Saint Chinian is sometimes said to make harder wines than Faugères. It is divided in two by the rivers Orb and Vernazobre. To the north, the vein of schist extends from Faugères, mixed with subsoil of grès (gravelly marl, a sort of muddy limestone). The vineyards in this part of the appellation are on the hills, whereas those in the south are on the plain below, where the soil is calcareous with clay. There's a view that wines coming from schist are more mineral, whereas those from the clay-chalk soils of the south are firmer. Cooperatives make two thirds of the wine.

The two crus, Berlou and Roquebrun, occupy scattered areas in the north, with soils marked by schist, and an interesting difference in their grape varieties: Roquebrun must have less than 30% Carignan, whereas Berlou has a minimum of 30% Carignan. A series of cuvées from different terroirs produced at Borie La Vitarèle shows more obvious structure in Les Schistes, coming from terroir like Faugères, and more rounded, forceful fruits, in Les Crès, coming from terroir with round galet pebbles.

Minervois and Corbières

Minervois and Corbières are the heart of the old Languedoc. La Livinière in Minervois is a top Cru; Corbières Boutenac is another.

Minervois	30 cooperatives 222 producers	5,000 ha	1,700,000 cases 94% red, 4% rosé. 2% white red: > 60% GSM, Carignan <40%
Minervois La Livinière	2 cooperatives 40 producers	350 ha	70,000 cases red: GSM >60%
Corbières	33 cooperatives 289 producers	13,500 ha	6,000,000 cases 90% red: Carignan <50% rosé, white
Corbières Boutenac	4 cooperatives 18 producers	1,429 ha	64,000 cases red: GSM + >30% Carignan
Fitou	3 cooperatives 35 producers	2,300 ha	84,000 cases red: Carignan + GSM
La Clape	3 cooperatives 25 producers	768 ha	300,000 cases red: GSM >70% white: Bourboulenc >40%

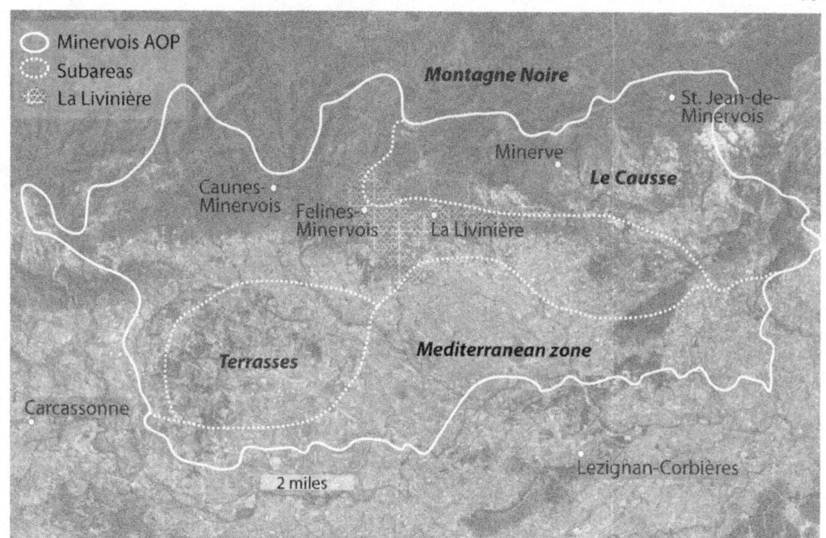

Minervois is east of Carcassonne, south of the Montagne Noire, and north of Corbières. La Causse in the northeast is the driest and highest area at 200-500m, La Livinière is in the center with south-facing exposure, the Terrasses is the Central, most temperate zone, and the southern zone is the most Mediterranean.

Minervois is one of the best established appellations, with one of the most notable Crus, La Livinière. A relatively large area to the east of the ancient city of Carcassonne, Minervois has a variety of terroirs and climates. Soil types, elevations, and climatic exposure are quite varied, including the characteristic grès (sandstone), as well as calcareous soils, schists, marble, and large pebbles. This makes it hard to get a bead on typicity.

In the northern part, the dominant feature is the Montagne Noire, running down into the northeast quadrant of Le Causse. This has the highest vineyards, a semi-mountain climate with the most diurnal variation, calcareous terroir, and is the last to harvest. At the northeast corner, Saint-Jean-de-Minervois is a small appellation focused on fortified sweet wines.

The southern zone, with the Canal du Midi running through, has a more Mediterranean climate (it is only 20 miles from the ocean), higher temperatures, more even distribution of rainfall, and harvests around three weeks earlier than the other areas.

The tendency in Minervois is to make cuvées from different terroirs, giving interesting variety, but making it difficult to define any single character for the appellation. The common feature is a focus on the GSM grape trio, supplemented by Carignan and Cinsault.

Corbières is hilly and rugged. Courtesy Jean-Luc Raby.

Just below the Montagne Noire, the cru of La Livinière has 350 ha of vineyards, at altitudes from 100-300m; only 5% of Minervois, it is restricted to red wines at slightly lower yields than Minervois. Even in this restricted area, there is significant heterogeneity, a sort of recapitulation in miniature of the entire area of Minervois. Wines may be dominated by either Syrah or Grenache; the GSM blend must include at least 40% Syrah or Mourvèdre, making for more structured wines than elsewhere. Cool winds from the Montagne Noir give good diurnal variation, and make the wines fresher than Minervois. The growers have asked for it to be called simply La Livinière instead of Minervois-La Livinière.

If Minervois is heterogeneous, then adjacent Corbières can verge on incoherence. The largest individual AOP in Languedoc (accounting for close to half of AOP production), it extends from the Toulouse-Narbonne autoroute in the north to Roussillon in the south. It is dry and hot, the very center of the Languedoc. Its four general areas are Corbières d'Alaric (near Mont Alaric at the northwest near Carcassonne), the heart of the AOP in Corbières Centrales, the highest areas of Hautes-Corbières, and Corbières Méditerranée near the coast.

Corbières-Boutenac is the cru, running around the Pinada, a small mountain with terroir of round pebbles. It's known as the "Golden Crescent" for its sunny, south-southeast-facing slope. Plantings are characterized by a good proportion of very old Carignan vines (often dating back more than a century). All wines must have 30-50% Carignan, and at least one other local variety. Here the proportion of Syrah is limited to 30%, so if there is anywhere that will make the case for Carignan, this is it.

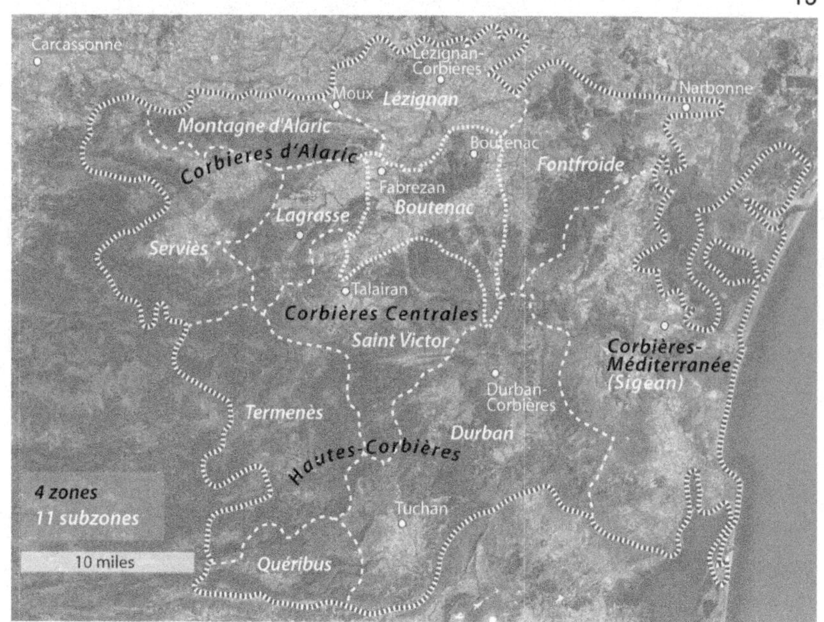

Corbières' four general zones are divided into 11 subzones. In Corbières d'Alaric vineyards extend from the plain onto the slopes of the mountain. Hautes Corbieres is the highest area, with vineyards up to 500m, mostly on schist. In Corbières Centrales, Boutenac is a Cru. To the east in Corbières Méditerranée, the climate is moderated by the Mediterranean, but there is less diurnal variation as the vineyards are lower.

It may be difficult for the outsider to obtain a clear bead on Corbières, but the AOP has a firm view of its typicity, or rather, of what isn't its typicity. A producer of natural wines, Domaine Ledogar has a mix of wines in the AOP and Vin de France. "All my parcels are in Corbières-Boutenac, I present my wines for approval because I was born here, but some do not conform. Why? Because I don't add yeast, I don't add tannins, I don't acidify... so my wines don't conform! They are true wines of terroir" says Xavier Ledogar. "And because Corbières must be a blend, I don't present my monocépages."

Xavier's wines encapsulate the continuing controversy about the true character of AOPs in Languedoc. La Mariole is a cuvée from century-old Carignan; precise and refined, it is the very model of a modern Languedoc. Tout Nature is a classic blend showing the broader flavors of what you might call old Languedoc, but that did not get approval to be labeled as Corbières. So here are two of the best wines of the appellation, respectively representing more modern and traditional styles, which in fact are labeled as Vin de France without any indication that they come from Corbières!

Reference Wines for Red Languedoc	
Languedoc	Domaine Peyre Rose, Clos Léone
Corbières	Domaine Ledogar, Tout Natur (Vin de France)
Faugères	Jean-Michel Alquier, La Maison Jaune Château de La Liquière, Cistus
La Clape	Château De Pech Redon, Centaurée
Montpeyroux	Domaine d'Aupilhac
Minervois	Château La Tour Boisée, Marie-Claude
Pézenas	Domaine les Aurelles, Solen Prieuré St. Jean de Bébian
Pic St. Loup	Domaine de L'Hortus, Grand Cuvée Clos Marie, Metairies du Clos
Saint Chinian	Borie La Vitarèle, Les Crès
Terrasses du Larzac	Mas Cal Demoura, Feu Sacré Mas Jullien, Carlan
IGP de Gard	Roc d'Anglade
IGP Pays d'Hérault	Mas de Daumas Gassac Domaine de la Grange des Pères Domaine d'Aupilhac, Les Plôs de Baumes

Further compounding the absence of clear identity, a major part of production goes to negociants or cooperatives (where the giant Val d'Orbieu cooperative is predominant). The result is that only a small proportion of Corbières is actually bottled by growers.

Carved out of the southern end of Corbières, Fitou consists of two completely separated areas. It's not obvious why it's a separate appellation as opposed to a cru of Corbières, or perhaps crus since the two areas are quite separate, one at the mountains, which is essentially an extension of Corbières with schist terroir, and the other by the Mediterranean with calcareous clay. Fitou produces only red wine.

To the east of Corbières, La Clape is a relatively small AOP, but somewhat varied. Just inland from Narbonne, it seems more like the appellations at the northern extremes of Languedoc: massive calcareous cliffs loom over the area, contrasting with the surrounding plains. This is the driest part of Languedoc—it rains less than forty days per year—but the climate is softened by humidity from the ocean, although winds can be very strong. By the coast vineyards run down almost to the water. The only rule for red wines is that Carignan and Cinsault together are limited to 70%; whites are based on Bourboulenc.

Malepère, Cabardès, and Limoux

At the western boundary of Languedoc, the appellations are a little different. Just north of Carcassonne, the small appellations of Malepère and Cabardès have just enough exposure to the Atlantic climate to be allowed to include the Bordelais varieties (Merlot, Cabernet Sauvignon, and Cabernet Franc), not to mention Malbec and Fer Servadou, as well as Syrah and Grenache.

Malepère requires reds to have more than 50% Merlot; the character is light and fresh rather than lush. Cabardès requires plantings to be half Atlantic varieties and half Mediterranean varieties, and there must be at least 40% of each in the blend. The best wines are based on combinations of Syrah and Cabernet Sauvignon.

Just to the south is Limoux, where the focus is on sparkling wines. Limoux claims to be the oldest region in France for producing sparkling wine, with its traditional style, the Blanquette de Limoux, made by a single fermentation that stops in the bottle. Based on the Mauzac variety, it is supposed to showcase notes of apples and pears, but can convey a slightly soapy impression.

Producers are now moving towards Crémant de Limoux, which allows Chardonnay and Chenin Blanc. The wines have got much better since Crémant was introduced, but it is somewhat of a misnomer to call them "grand vins." The AOP was allowed to make still wine from Mauzac, Chenin Blanc, and Chardonnay, in 2017.

IGP Pays d'Oc

The label of IGP Pays d'Oc is by far and away the single largest category of wine in France, accounting for two thirds of all IGP production and 90% of all varietal-labeled wines. It represents a third of all vineyards in the Languedoc. Altogether 58 varieties are authorized in IGP Pays d'Oc, but actual use of varieties is much more concentrated. In red wines, 90% include Merlot, Cabernet Sauvignon, Syrah or Grenache, in rosé 80% use Cinsault or Syrah, and for whites 80% are Chardonnay or Sauvignon Blanc. Two thirds of production is represented by varietal wines coming from only five international varieties. Brands from large negociants (and cooperatives) are a significant proportion of production.

The boundaries of the IGPs follow the political and administrative borders, so there is little consistency of terroir within any IGP. Within the four departments included in the region, the Hérault is the most important, essentially providing the engine of the Languedoc. With more than 90,000 hectares of plantings (three quarters in IGP), its vineyards make it the second most important department in France for wine production. (The Gironde is first, with just over 100,000 ha in Bordeaux.) The Hérault accounts for more than a third of wine produced in the Languedoc, and after the catch-all IGP Pays d'Oc, the IGP Pays d'Hérault is the best known of the region's IGPs.

For the most part, IGP wines are a notch lower than AOP wines, as they are elsewhere in France, but there are exceptions, mostly due to producers in AOPs who want to do something that is not allowed by the appellation. These mostly fall into two extremes. Monovarietals cannot be AOP, so the cuvées of very old vines Carignan, which many people really feel exemplify the Languedoc, are IGP. And international varieties, of which Cabernet Sauvignon is the most notable at the highest quality level, must be IGP. Of course, there are also some wines that are declassified because of disagreements with the AOP.

The Iconoclasts of the Hérault

The Hérault is home to some of the top wines of the Languedoc; denied AOP status because they do not conform to the rules for varietal blending, these are simply labeled as IGP Pays d'Hérault. Just to the west of Montpellier, Aniane is home to two of the producers, Mas de Daumas Gassac and Domaine de la Grange des Pères, who completely defied tradition in the area when they created their wines.

The pioneer for Cabernet Sauvignon in the Languedoc was Mas de Daumas Gassac, where winemaking began in 1972 as the result of an accidental encounter. Aimé Guibert had bought a house and land at Aniane, near Montpellier, as a country residence. The family was considering what sort of agricultural use they might find for the land when a family friend, the famous geographer Henri Enjalbert, remarked during a visit that the terroir reminded him of Burgundy's Côte d'Or and would make a remarkable vineyard. Aniane is a special place, not only for its red glacial soils, but also for the protected microclimate in the Gassac Valley, where cool night winds give greater diurnal variation than elsewhere in the vicinity.

The Guiberts were not much impressed with the local grape varieties. They did not feel that the climate was right for Pinot Noir, and as Bordeaux drinkers they naturally gravitated towards Cabernet Sauvignon. As Aimé recounts, "I consulted all the great oracles in Languedoc, asking them, 'How do you make great wine?' And these great professionals invariably answered, 'If it were possible to make great wine in Languedoc, we would already know about it.' They made fun of me." But by 1978, Emile Peynaud, the doyen of Bordeaux oenologists, became an advisor, and Mas de Daumas Gassac produced its first vintage, a blend based on Cabernet Sauvignon.

The blend has changed over the years, but has generally consisted of around 80% Cabernet Sauvignon with the remainder coming from a wide range of varieties, some Bordelais, others more exotic: initially they were mostly Malbec, Tannat, Merlot, and Syrah; by 1990 they were described as Cabernet Franc, Syrah and Merlot; and today the label just says "several other varieties."

One reason for adjusting the blend may have been to calm down the tannins, as some criticism had been expressed of rustic tannins, and current winemaker Samuel Guibert says freely that the wines could be tough and tight for the first few years. In the mid nineties, the young wines started to show more elegance and finesse, he says, probably as a result of increasing vine age.

The avowed intention is to produce a "grand cru" of the Languedoc, but these are not always obvious wines to characterize in the context of Cabernet Sauvignon. "We don't make a Cabernet wine; we make Daumas Gassac. The wine is no more typical of Bordeaux than it is of Languedoc," Samuel says. Perhaps the character of the wine depends on whether Atlantic or Mediterranean influences predominate during the vintage. I find something of a split, with some vintages tending more towards the savory, which I see as Atlantic influence, while others are softer and less obviously structured, which is more what you might expect of the Mediterranean.

The differences for me really amplify with age, and are typified by the 1982 and 1983 vintages, the former tending more towards classic savory characteristics of Bordeaux, the latter more towards the soft, perfumed quality of the south. Cabernet is more obvious in the Atlantic vintages; it can be more difficult to perceive in some Mediterranean vintages. Today's wines may be more elegant, with notes of the garrigue cutting the black fruits of the palate, but they may not be so long lived as those from the eighties.

At Daumas Gassac they tried the traditional local varieties of Carignan, Grenache, and Syrah for a while, but eventually pulled them out because they seemed to over-produce and lack finesse in this terroir. Almost adjacent, however, is the Domaine de la Grange des Pères, where the philosophy is almost the antithesis, but the wines are equally interesting. Laurent Vaillé established Grange des Pères soon after Daumas Gassac; his first vintage was 1982.

Vineyards at Mas de Daumas Gassac are individual parcels surrounded by woods and trees. Courtesy Mas de Daumas Gassac.

It's not especially easy to make an appointment with Laurent who is nothing if not reticent, but the rendezvous, if successful, takes place in the working cave, where samples can be tasted from barriques. The wine is a blend of roughly equal proportions of Syrah and Mourvèdre with a minor component of 20% Cabernet Sauvignon. Minor, but essential. "Grange des Pères should have a southern character, but with freshness, and that's what the Cabernet Sauvignon brings," Laurent says.

The Cabernet is planted in the coolest spots, and is always the last variety to harvest. Syrah is planted quite close by, and ripens reliably to make a rich, deep component of the wine. The Mourvèdre is planted a few kilometers away on a hot, south-facing terroir. Tasting barrel samples, you can see what each variety brings to the blend. All are rich and powerful with a good level of tannins, the Syrah full of rich, deep black fruits, the Mourvèdre distinctly spicy, and the Cabernet herbal and fresh. It's not so much the acidity of the Cabernet as such, but the tightness of its structure that freshens the blend. Without it, the wine would have more of that jammy fruit character of warm climates.

So here the Cabernet in effect is playing a moderating role on the forceful fruit character of the other varieties: almost exactly the opposite of the role it plays elsewhere as a "cépage ameliorateur" in strengthening weak varieties. The wines can be quite aromatic when young, but have long aging potential; 20 years is about the midpoint of development for a good vintage, and the wine should be good for at least another decade.

Because Cabernet Sauvignon was not permitted under local AOP rules, the first vintages at Mas de Daumas Gassac were labeled as Vin de Table. Subsequently the wines were labeled as IGP Pays d'Hérault, as are those of Grange des Pères, which also is excluded from the AOP because of its content of Cabernet Sauvignon. It's difficult to over-estimate the revolutionary extent of the concept of planting Cabernet Sauvignon at the time, as there was virtually none in the south of France prior to the 1980s. Domaine de Trévallon in Provence had been the first in 1973, when Eloi Dürrbach produced his 50:50 blend of Cabernet Sauvignon with Syrah.

These three domains produce some of the best known "grand vins" in the south, but they are typical neither of the AOPs nor of the IGPs. Did they lead the way for the subsequent wave of plantings that brought Cabernet Sauvignon and Syrah to prominence in the IGPs of the Languedoc? Not really. Most of the IGP wines originated from an impetus to compete in the market for wines that represent varieties rather than place; this is a completely different level. Varieties and styles were chosen more with an eye on New World competitors than by looking at existing wines and styles; indeed, the most planted black grape in the Hérault is now Merlot (followed by Syrah, Carignan, and Cabernet Sauvignon), and the most planted white grape is Chardonnay (followed by Sauvignon Blanc). The best wines of the south essentially represent themselves; but as they are sui generis, they have set few precedents and created little in the way of a halo for others in the region.

Roussillon

Moving from Languedoc to Roussillon, the scene changes. Here the region is divided essentially into two large AOPs, Côtes de Roussillon, and Côtes de Roussillon Villages (with 32 villages in the northern part now distinguished by the right to add their name to the label). A single IGP, Côtes Catalanes, covers the entire area, and accounts for 71% of all IGP production, which is 38% of all Roussillon, making it the largest source for dry wines. The AOPs account for another 34% of dry wines and 22% of sweet wines.

The construction of the railway to Paris in the mid nineteenth century gave a great boost to the region: production increased ten fold in two decades. Phylloxera crushed the region at the end of the century, but after replanting, production was even greater (largely because grafted vines gave double the yields). Roussillon is still making the painful transition from providing the bulk wines of the Midi towards the higher quality required today, compounded by a switch from sweet to dry wines.

Total production was around 27 million cases in the 1960s, roughly half being Vin de Table. Production today is under half this level, with table wine reduced to about 10%. Even in the past decade, the area of vineyards for table wine has dropped from 40,000 ha to 27,000 ha. A major part of the decline is due to Carignan being pulled out, leaving Grenache as the most important black variety. Relatively new to the area, Syrah is now in second place.

Côtes du Roussillon has a mixed reputation, and many producers declassify some of their top wines to IGP to avoid arguments with the authorities about typicity. Loïc Roure, who puts his wines at Domaine du Possible into the AOP, says this is changing. " We are lucky enough here, because there has been a large wave of newly formed estates in our region over the last ten years. This has brought a fresh perspective and open-mindedness to the tasting committees [and] has created a broader discourse for wines that have been traditionally judged 'atypical'. This means wines that are not yeasted or heavily sulfured."

Production in Côtes du Roussillon is more than half (55%) rosé, with 40% red and only 5% white. Roussillon's reputation for dry red wines historically has been that they are the strongest in the south. The rules for dry reds require that all wines are blended from at least two varieties, with two of the principal varieties comprising at least 80%, but no single variety being more than 70%. You can see why people might prefer to go to the IGP, where they can produce monovarietals or blends as they choose. If you want to make a cuvée from a single plot of very old vines, the IGP is your only option.

Roussillon Appellations	
AOP	*Grape Varieties*
	Dry Wines
Côtes de Roussillon	Red: at least two of GSM and Carignan >80% White: Macabeu & Grenache Blanc Rosé: Syrah + Mourvèdre >25%
Côtes de Roussillon Villages	Syrah & Mourvèdre (>30%), Carignan (<60%), Grenache, Lledoner
Maury Sec	60-80% Grenache
Collioure	GSM & Carignan, Grenache Blanc & Gris
	Sweet Fortified Wines
Rivesaltes	Grenache varieties, Macabeu, Muscat
Muscat de Rivesaltes	Muscat d'Alexandrie & Muscat à Petits Grains
Maury	>75% Grenache (Grenat & Tuilé)
Banyuls	>50% Grenache
Banyuls Grand Cru (Tuilé only)	>75% Grenache

Fortified Sweet Wines

Within the major AOPs are some smaller AOPs, with the best known, Maury, Banyuls, and Rivesaltes, producing sweet dessert wines. The climate makes this natural—Roussillon is the hottest and driest Département in France with the weather dominated by the Tramontane wind—and the classic sweet wine is the Vin Doux Naturel (VDN), lightly fortified by stopping fermentation by adding distilled spirits (the method is similar to the production of Port but uses less spirits). A third of production in Roussillon is devoted to this style, and the region provides the vast majority of fortified wine produced in France.

Until the eighteenth century, sweet wines were made by the technique of passerillage—allowing the berries to stay on the vine long enough to become desiccated. This produces such high sugar levels that there is still residual sugar when fermentation stops, usually around 14% alcohol. The development of distilleries in the eighteenth century allowed passerillage to be replaced by mutage, when fermentation is stopped by adding spirits.

Today the production of vin doux naturel in the AOPs is limited to growers of Muscat, Grenache, Macabeu, and Malvoisie. The grapes must have a natural richness with a sugar level of at least 252 g/l (equivalent to 14.5% alcohol), and 5-15% alcohol is added to block fermentation around two thirds of the way through, leaving a sweet wine. However, with the fashion for sweet wines in worldwide decline, the production of VDN has been falling for decades.

The distinctive features of the wines of Roussillon go back to Roman times, when Muscat was the main grape variety, and wines were made in an oxidized style (today known as rancio). The Muscat appears to have been the finest subvariety, Muscat à Petit Grains; the less refined Muscat of Alexandria (which is also grown as a table grape) was imported later from Spain. In black varieties, Mourvèdre and Grenache have been established since the Middle Ages, with Grenache being used for sweet dessert wines.

A distinction is made between Muscat and other varieties used for sweet wines, as indicated by the use of Muscat in certain appellation names. The Muscat grape is a natural for hot climates, and there are appellations devoted to it scattered all over Languedoc: Muscat de Lunel, Muscat de Mireval, Muscat de Frontignan, and Muscat de Saint Jean de Minervois, all make sweet fortified wines. In Roussillon, where fortified wines are more dominant, Muscat de Rivesaltes is distinguished from Rivesaltes and Maury, where the main varieties are Grenache and Macabeu.

The appellation system becomes complicated here, as there are different AOPs for dry wines and sweet wines. The Rivesaltes AOP for fortified wines overlaps the Côtes de Roussillon and Côtes de Roussillon Villages AOPs for dry wines, and the Banyuls AOP for sweet wines overlaps the Collioure AOP for dry wine. Maury is a rare AOP that now has both dry and sweet wines.

Sweet wines are now made in two types of style. The traditional oxidized styles are made in both vintage and nonvintage (the latter usually coming from a blend of two or three vintages). The key determinant of style is how long the wine ages before it is bottled. The wines can undergo aging for up to fifteen or twenty years in large wood casks. They can achieve a lovely concentration, but admittedly the oxidized style is an acquired taste. Today it is being partly replaced by wines made in a more modern idiom, using a nonoxidative approach. To avoid confusion, different names are used for the different styles. Grenat and Rimage are the new, nonoxidized, style; Ambré, Tuileé, and Hors d'Age arc oxidized, and Rancio is the fully oxidized traditional style.

The description of Rancio for highly oxidized wines can be used for both sweet and dry styles. If the label says simply Rancio, the wine is sweet; Rancio Sec means it is dry. Rancio Sec is a traditional style, but used to be consumed exclusively locally. It may go back to a wine style in the Roman era that Pliny the Elder described as exposed "to all the insults of the air." Rancio Sec is our 'Umami Catalan,' says Benoit Danjou, President of the growers' association.

Rancio Sec had become quite rare when the category was added to IGP Côtes Catalanes and IGP Côte Vermeille in 2004 after ten years of campaigning by producers. The rules require simply that the wine must come from local grape varieties (Grenache, Macabeu, and Carignan), must be aged

Fortified Sweet Wine Styles		
Ambré	oxidized	white varieties
Tuilé	oxidized	GSM & others
Hors d'Âge	oxidized >5 years aging	white or red
Rancio	highly oxidized	white or red
Grenat (Rivesaltes & Maury)	nonoxidized	Grenache
Rimage (Banyuls)	nonoxidized	>50% Grenache

The sweet fortified wines of Roussillon in traditional style are matured for a year in glass bonbons outside, before transfer to foudres for extended aging.

oxidatively for five years, and must be dry. As the result of oxidation, the color is usually amber. (Wine in a similar style is made across the Spanish border in Catalonia, where it is called Vi Ranci.)

Aging methods vary from using oak casks of various sizes (which are not topped up during aging), to using glass demijohns that are left in the sun, to a solera system in which wine from successive vintages is added to replace wine that is withdrawn. Styles are correspondingly variable, but the common feature is the development of strongly oxidized notes varying from nutty to curry to sickly. (The French rance, the origin of Rancio, translates as rancid, which gives an indication of style.) Production remains small, with only about thirty producers of the style.

Just north of Perpignan, Rivesaltes is divided into three colors: ambré (amber), tuilé (tawny), and grenat. The first two are oxidized styles: ambré is essentially white, coming from Grenache, Macabeu, Malvoisie, and Muscat, while tuilé is red and excludes Muscat. Hors d'âge indicates ambré or tuilé wines that have had at least five years of élevage under oxidative conditions. Rancio may be added to the label for wines made by traditional oxidative methods. Grenat comes only from Grenache and is made exclusively by reductive methods.

Collioure, Banyuls, and Maury

The history of Forte Sainte-Elme in Collioure shows how Roussillon has alternated between France and Spain.

<table>
<tr><td>Banyuls</td><td rowspan="2">9 cooperatives
83 producers</td><td>1,150 ha</td><td>28,000 cases
fortified red: >50% Grenache
fortified white: Grenache Blanc</td></tr>
<tr><td>Collioure</td><td>400 ha</td><td>21,000 cases
66% red: GSM >60%
30% rosé, white</td></tr>
<tr><td>Maury</td><td>2 cooperatives
56 producers</td><td>Sec 220 ha
VDN 310 ha</td><td>Sec 53,000 cases
VDN 52,000 cases
VDN >75% Grenache</td></tr>
</table>

The southernmost AOP in France, Banyuls is the flag carrier for sweet wines. It is divided into three types. The traditional Banyuls is an oxidized style; the Rimage style is a more recent introduction requiring aging for twelve months in an airtight environment. Banyuls Grand Cru is distinguished not by terroir, but by vintage (only the best) and aging (at least 30 months in oak for Tuilé style). All types of Grenache (black, gray, and white) are allowed, but Banyuls must have more than 50% Grenache Noir, and Banyuls Grand Cru must have more than 75%.

Banyuls has some of the most striking vineyards in the region. Small vineyards nestle into the steep hills, and access is difficult. There are amazingly convoluted folds of the hills, with channels for water run-off. The terroir is based on schist, which is evident everywhere. Differences between vineyards are due mostly to exposure and altitude (rising up to 400m from sea level).

The same vineyards can be used to make the sweet wines of Banyuls or the dry red or rosé wines of Collioure (and since 2002 white wines have also been allowed), but there are practical problems in making the transition from sweet to dry wines. The vineyards that are most suitable for achieving very high ripeness to provide berries for making sweet wines may not necessarily

Vineyards of Banyuls extend to the coast.

Inland the vineyards of Banyuls are on steep, convoluted hills.

be appropriate for harvesting earlier to make dry wines. "Plots are transitioned to dry wine because they have the right quality—they face north or east—and acquire the appropriate phenolic maturity," explains Jean-Marie Piqué at Mas Amiel.

"The tendency in reds is towards dry wine in Collioure. Oxidized styles (for Banyuls) are declining," says Jean-Emmanuel Parcé at Domaine de la Rectorie in Banyuls. Another sign of the times is that the focus here is as much on whites and rosé as on reds.

Reference Wines for Roussillon	
	Dry Red
IGP Côtes Catalanes	Domaine Gauby Olivier Pithon, Le Clot
Collioure	Domaine De La Rectorie, La Montagne
Côtes du Roussillon Villages	Domaine Gauby, Coume Gineste
	Sweet
Banyuls	Domaine de la Rectorie, Cuvée Thérèse Reig
Maury VDN (modern)	Mas Amiel, Vintage
Maury VDN (oxidized)	Mas Amiel, Classique
Muscat de Rivesaltes	Domaine Cazes

A revealing comparison at Domaine de la Rectorie is between two cuvées made from the same Grenache grapes, the dry Collioure l'Oriental and the Banyuls VDN Cuvée Thérèse Reig. The Collioure is an elegant dry wine, very much the style of the south in a modern take; but the Banyuls expresses sweet round black fruits that make you think that perhaps here is the real typicity of Grenache.

Maury is a small appellation that traditionally made fortified wine, but it's been possible to make dry as well as sweet wine since 2011, and the change at Mas Amiel is a sign of the times. Forty years ago, all production was sweet wines in an oxidized style. Today half of production is dry wine, and a third of that is white (there was no white as recently as ten years ago). The best selling wine in the sweet styles is modern (non oxidized) vintage. This is a sea change in the region.

The requirement for Grenache in the fortified wine has been steadily increased from a minimum of 50% to today's minimum of 75%, but in fact many wines are 100% Grenache. The dry reds are based on GSM blends with some Carignan. Before the AOP Maury Sec was created, they were labeled as Côtes du Roussillon Villages or IGP Côtes Catalanes, and many still are. A major part of production comes from the cooperative, Vignerons de Maury.

Southern Whites

White wine is very much a minor preoccupation in the Languedoc; overall it is less than 20% of production. It's allowed in only a few of the AOPs. The blended white wines of those AOPs are confined entirely to traditional varieties. In addition, there are two AOPs for varietal wines, Clairette du

Languedoc and Picpoul de Pinet. For whites made from traditional southern varieties, but coming from appellations that allow only red wine, Coteaux du Languedoc (now Languedoc) has become the AOP of choice.

The break between the AOPs and the IGPs is even more striking for white wine than for red, as the two major white varieties in Languedoc as a whole are Chardonnay and Sauvignon Blanc. Banned from all the AOPs, together they are 40% of all white plantings, and dominate the white IGP wines as varietal labels.

I'm not convinced that either Chardonnay or Sauvignon Blanc makes interesting wines in the south, but another import from the north, Chenin Blanc, makes some of the most interesting whites. "Chenin Blanc was introduced under the aegis of INAO about twenty years ago to get livelier white wines," explains Vincent Goumard at Mas Cal Demoura. "Because we are in France, there was a tasting after ten years. And the character was rejected as atypical. All the vignerons who took part decided to keep their Chenin, but were forced into the IGP." Vincent's white is IGP Pays d'Hérault, and he adds that, "Of course we have to find calcareous soil to magnify its character. I hope we'll have a white AOP in Larzac; it's a good terroir, and it's a pity but it probably won't happen for another twenty years." A little farther north, Rémy Pédréno at Roc d'Anglade achieves a steely minerality with an IGP de Gard that's a blend of Chenin Blanc with Chardonnay.

The dominant white varieties in the AOPs of the region are Grenache Blanc and Clairette, both somewhat nondescript. There's a tendency to apply more modern techniques to update the style. "Originally the white wines were like all the others of the Languedoc—heavy. Our objective was to have a dry wine with more minerality. It's done with vinification following Burgundy: fermentation in new barriques followed by élevage with battonage," explains Alain Asselin at Domaine du Puech Haut. But is this enough?

The problem with the whites of the south, to my mind, is a sort of amorphous aromatic quality, phenolics without flavor, that takes over the palate. One rare example of a white from a quality variety suited to the region is the monovarietal Roussanne from Domaine Les Aurelles. But yields are so low you can see why this might not generally be a viable option. Another example is Prieuré St. Jean de Bébian's white, a blend based on Roussanne, which has moved in recent years from a very ripe to a fresher style.

Indeed, freshness is the key. This makes it all the more remarkable that some of the most interesting whites come from Roussillon. Pushing up against the Spanish border, Roussillon is as hot and dry as it gets in France, but the trend is towards refinement. "In ten years there has been a revolution

Reference Wines for White Languedoc-Roussillon		
		Main Variety
IGP Pays d'Hérault	Mas Cal Demoura, Paroles de Pierres	Chenin Blanc
IGP de Gard	Roc D'Anglade	Chenin Blanc
IGP Côtes Catalanes	Domaine Gauby, Coume Gineste	Grenache Blanc
Coteaux du Languedoc	Domaine les Aurelles, Aurel	Roussanne
Pézenas	Prieuré St. Jean de Bébian	Roussanne

here. The cooperatives have advanced from the old wines of extraction and alcohol—there are many producers now who make whites based on freshness and balance. Gérard Gauby was the initiator of all this," says Olivier Pithon, whose winery is right in the center of the small town of Calce, a few miles northwest of Perpignan. Located in Calce, Gauby's wines are remarkable by any measure.

"The profundity of wine does not come from alcohol," Gérard believes. Gauby's wines are notable for their moderate alcohol: around 12.5-13%. Why and how are alcohol levels so much lower here than elsewhere? "I don't use herbicides or pesticides: it's all natural. Phenolic maturity arrives before alcoholic maturity. People say you need 14 or 15 degrees to get Grenache ripe; that's completely mad." Whether or not it's as simple as organic viticulture and early picking, the fact is that the wines, both red and white, are fully ripe yet always retain freshness. You leave Domaine Gauby wondering why other producers can't get the same level of flavor variety and interest without going to extremes.

Vintages

You might think that vintage variation would be less important in Languedoc-Roussillon as it is the driest and warmest region of France, but even if the summers produce a relatively reliable amount of heat, variations in rainfall from drought to floods, especially at the beginning or end of the season, make for significant variation. However, relatively few wines are made with aging in mind.

2019	*	The hot conditions of the year were not an advantage in Languedoc. Heavy rains in May, June, and August created pressure from mildew.

2018	*	Year started with record rainfall, then unusual frost reduced yields, hail in spring and summer created havoc, there was pressure from mildew in June, but harvest rescued by Indian summer, until severe floods stopped play in October.
2017	*	Unusual problems with frost at start of season reduced yields. After that, good conditions led to early harvest, but quantities are low although quality is good.
2016	**	Varying conditions across Languedoc, with August hail in Pic St. Loup reducing yields, but dry conditions elsewhere (driest season since 1944) gave good results. Tannins can be powerful.
2015	***	Very good year with warm, dry conditions except for some rain in August, and Indian summer leading to late harvest, giving a high quality vintage and well balanced wines.
2014	*	Hailstorms reduced yields in Languedoc, and rain in September created problems for harvesting Grenache and Mourvèdre, but the vintage was very good in Roussillon.
2013	*	Producers feel the vintage was better than elsewhere in France. After a wet Spring and late start to summer, poor flowering reduced yields (especially for Grenache); but summer continued into September, and a late harvest gave quality grapes, although with some difficulties for ripening Grenache and Mourvèdre.
2012		The vintage can best be described as problematic, with difficulties ranging from drought to mildew during the season, followed by uneven ripening at the end. Wines are less concentrated than usual.
2011	*	Rain restored quantities to normal after three drier years. Large harvest has decent quality.
2010	***	This was a standard year: dry conditions. Quality is high, but quantities are low.
2009	***	The vintage was as good here as virtually everywhere else in France, with wines achieving high concentration.
2008	*	A cooler vintage. Drought created problems in the summer, especially difficult for whites, but reds have good concentration.
2007	**	Summer was unusually cool, with more cloud cover than usual, but then there was good weather from August until harvest, and this is regarded as a very good year.
2006	*	This is a decent vintage without any special distinguishing characteristic that would make for interesting aging.

2005	**	This was a good year, and would have rivaled the classic regions elsewhere, but there was some rain at harvest.
2004	*	This is the most "typical" vintage of the decade, with reliable conditions everywhere in the region and no particular problems.
2003		The year of the heatwave was no easier in Languedoc than anywhere else, and many wines just went over the top.
2002		This was a cloudy summer and the disastrous floods in the Rhône extended into the eastern part of the region. Light wines at the time, not of interest now.
2001	*	A hot dry year with some storms. Results vary, with those who picked late making better wines than early pickers.
2000		Floods were a problem in November 1999, but after that conditions were good, and the wines are generally good quality.

Visiting the Region

This vast region is somewhat less tourist-oriented than other wine region of France, and it is more difficult to find hotels and restaurants for the evening, or casual places for lunch. In terms of organizing visits, a separate base is needed for each part of the region.

Montpellier is the obvious base for the eastern part. Some of the most interesting producers, such as Mas de Daumas Gassac or Grange des Pères, are within easy reach of the city, and the appellations to the north and immediate west are relatively accessible.

Moving farther along the coast, Béziers is a bit run-down but gives access to wineries in the immediate region. Pézenas looks like quite a nice little town, but actually the restaurants and hotels are best avoided. Farther down the coast, Narbonne is more of a tourist spot.

The Canal du Midi runs through Minervois.

The Center and South are more of a problem, with few obvious watering holes, although it's quite charming and lively in Homps where the Canal du Midi goes through Minervois. The Syndicat of Minervois producers is located there, and has a tasting room offering wines from many producers. The village of Minerve has been gentrified and offers restaurants and other tourist attractions. Corbières is a bit desolate, but Lagrasse is a nice little village.

To the far west of the region, Carcassonne is a major historical site in itself, and a good base for seeing the western appellations.

Perpignan is close to the only game in town (or more accurately, the only town) as a base for the northern part of Roussillon, but Banyuls-sur-Mer is a lively town well oriented for tourists at the southern end. Any farther south and you are in Spain.

Lagrasse is a medieval village in Corbières.

Banyuls-sur-Mer marks the southern border of Roussillon.

Some domains have an address that is only a zip code and a town name, sometimes with a lieu-dit added. Lieu-dits are mapped erratically, to say the least, in GPS devices in France, and the simplicity of the address does not necessarily mean the domain will be right in the center of town, however, as the zip code may extend well beyond into the countryside. Ask for directions and allow extra time.

In some regions, many of the Syndicats representing the producers in each appellation have opened boutiques, where wines can be tasted, and purchased at the same price as at the domain. The boutiques are often more accessible—usually in a town center—and have more extended opening hours than the producers themselves (often including weekends). They make it possible to directly compare many wines (although the top producers are not necessarily represented); usually tasting is free. The Languedoc is somewhat under-represented in this regard, but there is a Maison des Vins representing the entire region at:

- Maison des Vins du Languedoc
  Mas de Saporta, 34973 Lattes
  (+33 4 67 06 04 42) contact@languedoc-aoc.com
  www.maisondesvinsdulanguedoc.com

Tasting rooms for individual appellations are:

- La Maison des Vins de Saint-Chinian
  1 Avenue Charles Trenet, 34360 Saint-Chinian
  (+33 4 67 38 11 69) maisondesvins@saint-chinian.com
  www.saint-chinian.pro
- Maison des Vins du Minervois
  35 Quai des Tonneliers, 11200 Homps
  (+33 4 68 91 29 48) minervois@cru-minervois.com
  www.maisondesvinsduminervois.com

The etiquette of tasting assumes you will spit: tasting rooms are usually equipped with spittoons, and producers will be surprised if you drink, especially given the high alcohol levels in Languedoc. Tastings are usually free, although some of the more tourist-oriented producers have introduced small charges. Most producers expect to sell some wine to visitors.

Profiles of Producers

Ratings	
***	Excellent producers defining the very best of the appellation
**	Top producers whose wines typify the appellation
*	Very good producers making wines of character that rarely disappoint

Symbols for Producers	
Address	*Tasting room with especially warm welcome*
Phone	*Tastings/visits possible*
Owner/winemaker/contact	*By appointment only*
Email	*No visits*
Website	*Sales directly at producer*
Principal AOP or IGP	*No direct sales*
Red *White* *Sweet* *Reference wines*	*Winery with restaurant*
Grower-producer	*Winery with accommodation*
Negociant (or purchases grapes)	
Cooperative	
Conventional viticulture	
Sustainable viticulture	
Organic	
Biodynamic	
Natural Wine	
Wine with No Sulfur	
Vegan Wine	
ha=estate vineyards	
bottles=annual production	

The Languedoc Region

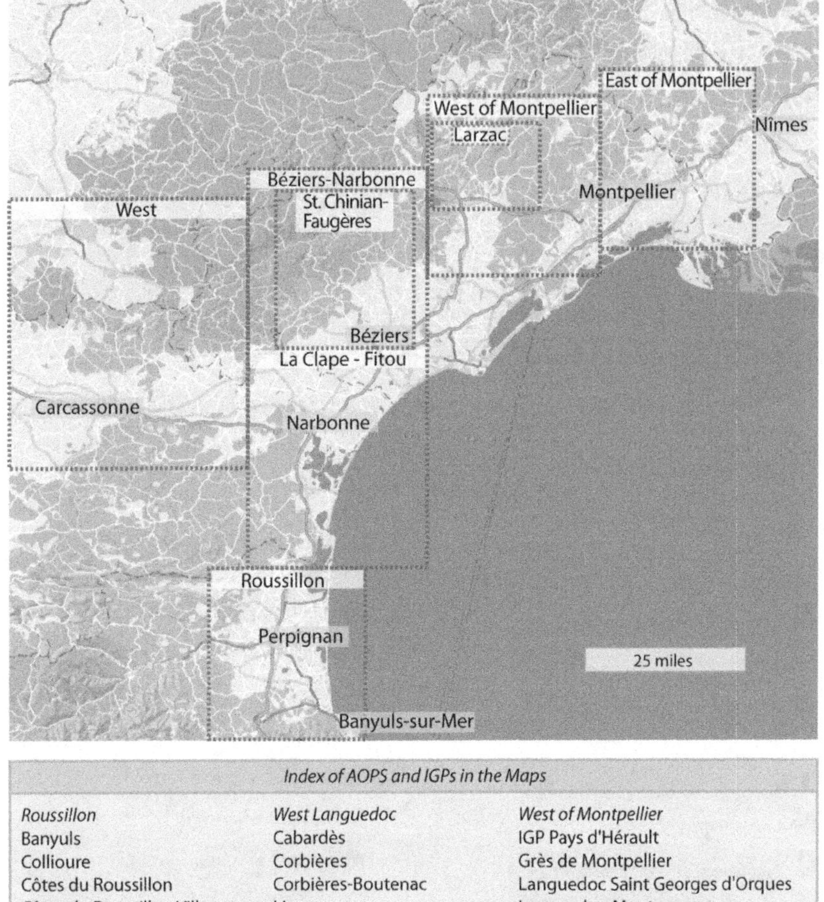

Index of AOPS and IGPs in the Maps

Roussillon	*West Languedoc*	*West of Montpellier*
Banyuls	Cabardès	IGP Pays d'Hérault
Collioure	Corbières	Grès de Montpellier
Côtes du Roussillon	Corbières-Boutenac	Languedoc Saint Georges d'Orques
Côtes du Roussillon Villages	Limoux	Languedoc-Montpeyroux
IGP Côtes Catalanes	Malepère	Languedoc-Pézenas
Maury	Minervois	Terrasses du Larzac
Rivesaltes	Minervois La Livinière	*East of Montpellier*
	Beziers-Narbonne	IGP de Gard
	Coteaux de Murveil	Grès de Montpellier
	Faugères	Languedoc Saint Drézéry
	Fitou	Languedoc Saint-Christol
	IGP des Coteaux d'Enserune	Languedoc Sommières
	La Clape	Muscat de Lunel
	St. Chinian	Pic St. Loup

East Of Montpellier

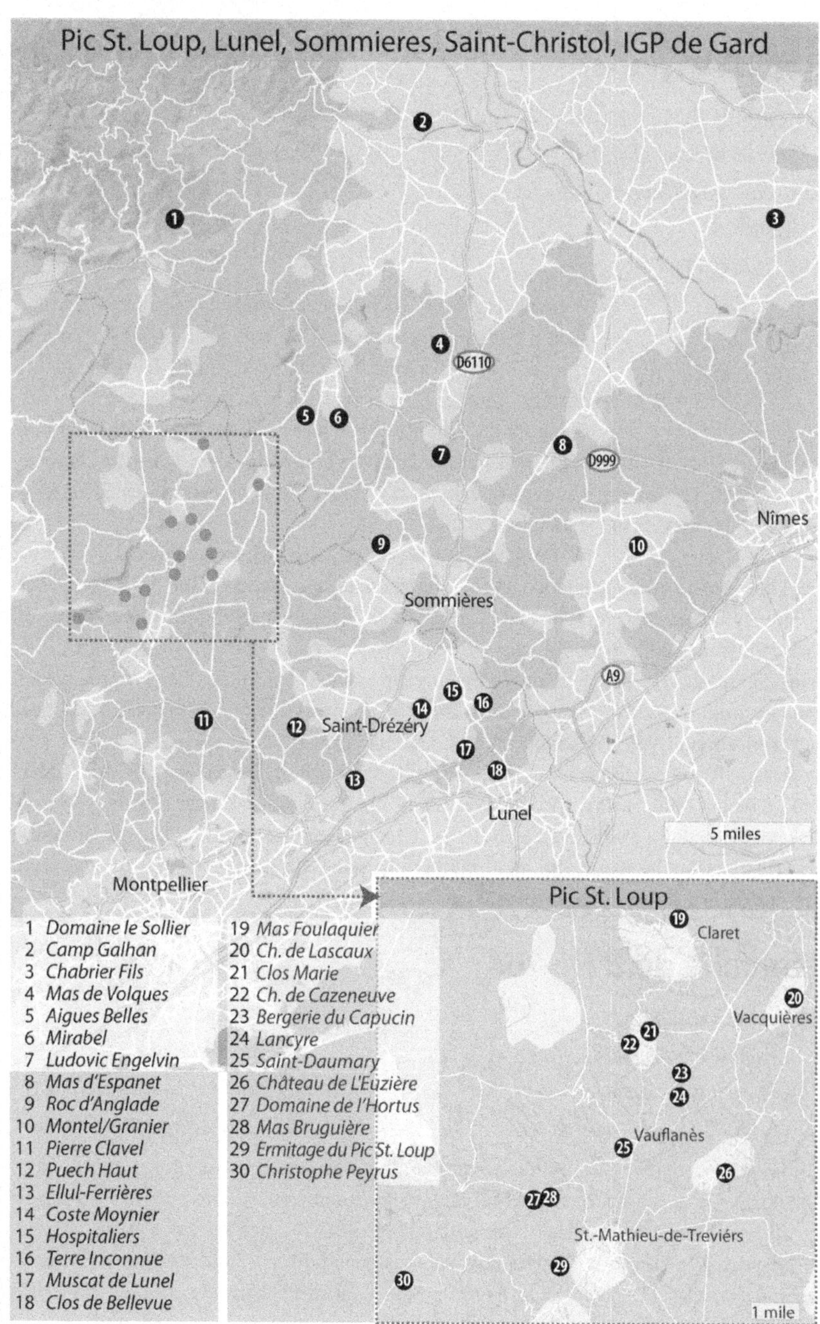

Profiles of Leading Estates

Roc d'Anglade *

700 Chemin de Vignecroze, 30980 Langlade	*+33 4 66 81 45 83*
contact@rocdanglade.fr	*Rémy Pédréno*
www.rocdanglade.fr	*IGP Gard [map p. 41]*
	IGP de Gard
8 ha; 32,000 btl	*IGP de Gard*

Winemaking is a second career for Rémy Pédréno. He had been a computer programmer for nine years when he discovered wine, and started by making a single barrique in his parents' garage. He became the winemaker when René Rostaing (from Côte Rôtie) wanted to make wine in the south in 1998, and then in 2002 he bought his own vines and became independent. The winery has two storeys, located under the family residence. Vineyards are in various parcels in the vicinity.

Rémy is an enthusiast for Carignan, to the point that his wines are labeled as IGP de Gard because he wants to include more Carignan than is permitted in the AOP. He makes his point with the concentration and elegance of an experimental Vieilles Vignes cuvée of Carignan from 2007. In the regular cuvée, the red is around half Carignan, with Grenache, Syrah and (in recent vintages) Mourvèdre. It's a wine that's very expressive of vintage, from a positively Burgundian 2002, to a savory 2004 with mineral overtones, and then a more typically southern 2011, but all vintages show a sense of reserve and elegance. "If you asked me to produce a wine to show why I chose this métier, this is the wine I would show today," Rémy says about his 2002 vintage. The rosé is based on Mourvèdre, and the white on Chenin Blanc, a good example of breaking out of the southern straightjacket by moving to more northern varieties. The white has lots of character, developing in a savory, mineral direction.

Domaine de L'Hortus *

D1E8, 34270 Valflaunès	*+33 4 67 55 31 20*
contact@domaine-hortus.fr	*Famille Orliac*
www.domaine-hortus.fr	*Pic Saint Loup [map p. 41]*
84 ha; 450,000 btl	*Pic St. Loup, Grand Cuvée*

The winery occupies a new, purpose-built building surrounded by carefully tended vines. The domain is in the center of Pic St. Loup, where its first vines were planted right under the cliffs of Mount Hortus. There was nothing here in 1979 when Jean and Marie-Thérèse Orliac started to construct the estate, which has been built up, little by little with many separate parcels. "The vineyards have reached their size: there are no new plantings planned. It's the story of the 2000s; we replanted some abandoned vineyards, but now we

have finished," says Jean Orliac. Now his sons Yves and Martin are involved. This is a very lively enterprise: the family gathers for lunch each day at the winery, and conversation to say the least is spirited.

There are three red cuvées, two whites, and a rosé. The entry-level wines are labeled as Bergerie de l'Hortus, and are intended for relatively rapid consumption. The Grande Cuvée label of Domaine de l'Hortus indicates wines that are intended to be more vin de garde. The Clos du Prieur red comes from the most recent acquisition, ten years ago, of a vineyard in Terraces de Larzac, about 20 miles to the west (where the climate is distinctly more Continental.) The style is modern. "We look for wines that aren't too powerful but have some finesse," says Martin Orliac. The Bergerie wines are very approachable, but I find the Grand Cuvée more mainstream, while the restraint of Clos du Prieur is attractive and ageworthy.

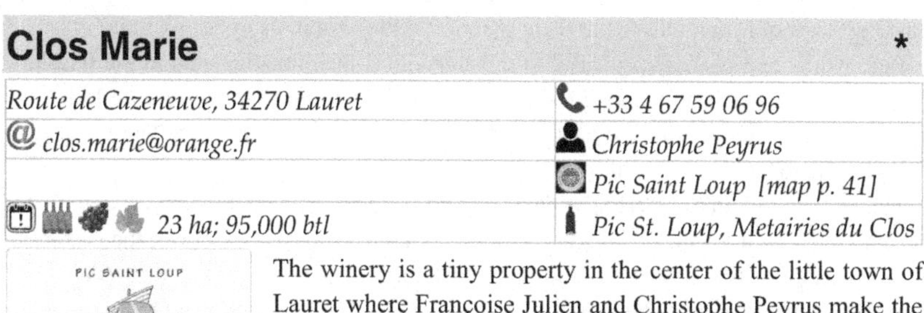

Clos Marie *

Route de Cazeneuve, 34270 Lauret	*+33 4 67 59 06 96*
clos.marie@orange.fr	*Christophe Peyrus*
	Pic Saint Loup [map p. 41]
23 ha; 95,000 btl	*Pic St. Loup, Metairies du Clos*

The winery is a tiny property in the center of the little town of Lauret where Françoise Julien and Christophe Peyrus make the wine. The estate was worked by Christophe's grandfather (who made wine) and father (who sent grapes to the coop), but Françoise and Christophe created Clos Marie as a domain when they decided to produce wine in 1992. They began with 8 ha, and today there are various parcels scattered around Lauret in the Pic St. Loup AOP. There are four red cuvées, two whites, and one rosé.

Terroir is the main criterion for distinguishing the cuvées—"even in Pic St. Loup there are variations of terroir," says Françoise—but there are also differences in assemblage and age of vines (with one cuvée coming from young vines). The objective is for Clos Marie to be mineral with freshness and precision. "It's very important to keep alcohol low to maintain freshness; we do vendange vert and pick relatively early," explains Françoise.

Viticulture is organic with some biodynamic treatments. Each parcel is vinified separately. "Originally each variety was vinified separately, but then we found we got better results with cofermentation." Wines are matured in oak, but there is no new wood. The style here is a long way from the old stereotype of the region: both reds and whites are light and fresh, in particular the red Metairies du Clos, which comes from old vines. Alcohol levels are moderate for the region. This is a standard bearer for the new style of the Languedoc. Christopher also started another project in 2013, Domaine Christopher Peyrus (see profile), where he makes wine just a mile away.

Château Puech Haut *

2250 Route de Teyran, 34160 Saint Drézéry	+33 4 99 62 27 27
contact@puech-haut.com	Alain Asselin
www.puech-haut.fr	Languedoc Saint Drézéry [map p. 41]
250 ha; 2,500,000 btl	Languedoc St. Drézéry, Tête de Bélier

This is quite a grand estate, surrounded by vineyards, with a long drive flanked by olive trees. There's a spacious tasting room in a nineteenth century house, with a large barrel room on display just behind. But when Gérard Bru purchased the property in 1985, the land was mostly bare garrigue. There were 80 ha in the estate at the start, and then twenty years later this was increased to 200 ha, which makes it one of the larger properties in Languedoc. Most (100 ha) of vineyards are in Saint Drézéry (just northeast of Montpellier), but there are some additional plots in Pic St. Loup.

Red, white, and rosé are produced in the entry-level line, Prestige, and in the flagship line, Tête de Belier. The Prestige red is more than half Grenache; the Tête de Belier is three quarters Syrah, with smaller amounts of Grenache and Mourvèdre. There's also a Loup St. Pic red and occasional production of special cuvées.

The style is full and powerful, with Châteauneuf-du-Pape as the model, to judge from the employment of Rhône oenologue Philippe Cambier as consultant. "Over the past four or five years the style has changed to be more Languedocian—warmer," says Alain Asselin in the tasting room. The whites have gone in a different direction. "Originally they were like all the others of the Languedoc—heavy," Alain says. The objective of a more mineral style for whites has been pursued by a Burgundian style of vinification, but they still show southern aromatics.

Profiles of Important Estates

Domaine d'Aigues Belles

Aiguebelle, 30260 Brouzet-lès-Quissac	+33 6 07 48 74 65
aigues.belles@orange.fr	Gilles Palatan
www.aigues-belles.com	Languedoc Sommières [map p. 41]
	21 ha; 60,000 btl

Located at the eastern end of the Languedoc, between Montpellier and Nîmes, this is an unusually old domain for the region, as it was already producing wine at the end of the nineteenth century. After the second world war, estate production stopped and grapes were sold to the cooperative. Gilles Palatan, together with his nephews Patrice and Thierry Lombard, replanted the vineyards and resumed production in 2000, with about two thirds estate-bottled, the rest still going to the cooperative. Two cuvées are labeled as AOP: Cuvée Classique is a blend with proportions of Grenache, Mourvèdre, and Syrah that change each year; Cuvée de Poirier is a rosé from local varieties that is well regarded. The focus is on IGP Pays d'Oc as the other cuvées all include international varieties that are not allowed in the AOP. Cuvée Lombarde varies widely from year to year, but may include Grenache, Syrah, Merlot, or Cabernet Sauvignon. Cuvée Nicole is Syrah, Cabernet Sauvignon, and Merlot. All the reds age in barriques, including a third new oak. Le Blanc is varietal Chardonnay, while L'Autre Blanc is a blend of Roussanne, Sauvignon Blanc, and Chardonnay; both age in new barriques.

Domaine Le Clos de Bellevue

Mas de Bellevue, route de Sommières, 34400 Lunel	*+33 4 67 83 24 83*
leclosdebellevue@gmail.com	*Nicolas Charrière*
www.domaine-le-clos-de-bellevue.com	*Lunel [map p. 41]*
	15 ha; 30,000 btl

Nicolas Charrière, formerly the director of a cooperative in the Ardèche, bought the domain in 2010 after the death of the former owner, Francis Lacoste. Located at a high point with panoramic views of the sea to the south and the mountains to the north, the domain is known for its Muscat de Lunel. The major cuvée is the Lacoste Cuvée Tradition, a nonvintage blend. A notch up, Clos Bellevue comes from vieilles vignes. Vendanges d'Octobre comes from a late harvest of *passerillé* grapes, and is one of the richest wines of the appellation. A dry Muscat is produced as a Vin de France. In addition, since 2004 there have been red wine, the Clos des Estivancs, from 4 ha in the AOP Saint Christol. The domain is readily accessible as it is right by exit 27 from the A9 autoroute.

Bergerie du Capucin

80 Impasse Puech Camp, 34270 Lauret	*+33 4 67 59 01 00*
contact@bergerieducapucin.fr	*Guilhem Viau*
bergerieducapucin.fr	*Pic Saint Loup [map p. 41]*
	15 ha; 90,000 btl

As its name indicates, the Bergerie du Capucin was a sheep farm (in fact, the original Bergerie still exists) where Guilhem Viau's grandmother tended sheep. Guilhem created the domain with the family vineyards in 2008, and was President of the AOP. The entry-level line, Les 100 Pas de Berger, has IGP whites of varietal Chardonnay and Viognier, and a red Syrah-Grenache blend in AOP Languedoc. The intermediate range is named Dame Jeanne for Guilhem's grandmother. The white is an IGP blend of Chardonnay and Viognier, and the rosé and red are GSM Pic St. Loup. The top red is Larmanela, a blend dominated by Syrah with Grenache making up the rest, aged in 400-liter barrels for 18 months. The Larmanela white is 100% Chardonnay, aged in barrels (or possibly just one barrel since production is very small).

Mas Bruguière

La Plaine, 34270 Valflaunès	*+33 4 67 55 20 97*
xavier.bruguiere@wanadoo.fr	*Xavier Bruguière*
www.mas-bruguiere.com	*Pic Saint Loup [map p. 41]*
	20 ha; 96,000 btl

Under the peak of Pic St. Loup, the domain was one of the pioneers in the move to quality. It was founded after the French Revolution, destroyed by phylloxera, and replanted at the end of the nineteenth century, destroyed again in the freeze of winter 1956, replanted with table grapes, and then in 1974 Guilhem Bruguière started the move to quality plantings for wine. His son Xavier runs the domain today. Plantings are mostly black, but there are 3 ha of whites. Les Mûriers Blanc is a blend of 80% Roussanne with 20% Marsanne. The red Calcadiz comes from the youngest vines, and is declassified to Languedoc. L'Arbouse is a blend of Syrah and Grenache aged in cuve. The flagship La Grenadière comes from the oldest vineyards and is 80% Syrah with some Grenache and Mourvèdre, aged in demi-muids and others casks. Le Septième is mostly Mourvèdre and ages in demi-muids.

Domaine Camp Galhan

305 Chemin du Camp Galhan, 30720 Ribaute-les-Tavernes	*+33 4 66 83 48 47*
contact@campgalhan.fr	*Orceline Martel & Lionel Pourquier*
campgalhan.com	*Duché d'Uzès* *[map p. 41]*
	30 ha; 45,000 btl

Located in the north of the Duché d'Uzès, about 25 miles north of Montpellier, the domain sent grapes to the cooperative until Lionel Pourquier took over from his father in 2001 and started estate-bottling. The winery is built into the hillside to allow gravity feed winemaking. Wines are divided between Duché d'Uzès (in the Southern Rhône) and IGP Cévennes and IGP Pays d'Oc (in Languedoc). Reds are mostly blends of Grenache and Syrah; whites may have local varieties (Viognier and Grenache Blanc) or international (Chardonnay). The range runs from bag-in-box to Ripa Alta, 100% Syrah fermented by carbonic maceration but aged in barriques.

Château de Cazeneuve

D17E7, 34270 Lauret	*+33 4 67 59 07 49*
contact@chateaucazeneuve.com	*Andre & Quentin Leenhardt*
www.chateaucazeneuve.com	*Pic Saint Loup* *[map p. 41]*
	38 ha; 110,000 btl

The château itself is an old building, with parts dating from the eleventh century, surrounded by vineyards located under the massive limestone cliff of the Falaise d'Hortus. When André Leenhardt purchased the estate in 1987, he replanted all the vineyards with varieties to match soil and exposure. Soils are calcareous clay. Whites are planting on the hills at the north, and reds on the warmer south-facing vineyards. The winery building itself is old, but full of modern equipment to allow gravity-feed winemaking. All the wines are under Pic St. Loup AOP. Everything is fermented, and whites and rosés age in stainless steel, while reds age mostly in barriques. Les Calcaires is a blend of Syrah, Grenache, Cinsault, and Carignan, Le Carignan is made by semi-carbonic maceration (like Beaujolais), Le Roc des Mates comes from the oldest, La Causse is a single vineyard wine from a plot of hard calcareous terroir (there is also a white from the same plot), and Le Sang du Calvaire is Mourvèdre. The Cynarah range is made by André's son, Quentin, from vineyards nearby.

Domaine Chabrier Fils

Chemin du Gres, 30190 Bourdic	*+33 4 66 81 28 54*
contact@chabrier.fr	*Christophe & Patrick Chabrier*
www.chabrier.fr	*Duché d'Uzès [map p. 41]*
	65 ha

Louis Chabrier founded the domain in 1925. His grandsons, brothers Christophe and Patrick Chabrier, took over in 1988, continued sending grapes to the cooperative for ten years, and then in 1998 built cellars and started estate-bottling. The domain is located at the eastern end of the Duché d'Uzès, so is closer to the Rhône than Languedoc, but cuvées are divided between the AOP Duché d'Uzès and IGPs Cévennes and Coteaux du Pont du Gard in Languedoc. AOP reds are blends of Grenache and Syrah; IGPs include Carignan and also a Merlot. Whites are Rhône varieties in AOP, but include Sauvignon Blanc, Chardonnay, and Muscat in IGP.

Domaine Clavel

Mas de Perié, Route de Sainte Croix de Quintillargues, 34820 Assas	*+33 4 99 62 06 13*
info@vins-clavel.fr	*Estelle & Pierre Clavel*
www.vins-clavel.fr	*Pic Saint Loup [map p. 41]*
	31 ha; 120,000 btl

The Clavel family is deeply imbedded in the Languedoc, as Jean Clavel was a historian of wine who was instrumental in creating the AOP Coteaux du Languedoc. His son Pierre, self-taught as a winemaker, created the domain in 1986, soon joined by his wife Estelle, who has made the wines since 2014. Their sons Antoine and Martin are now taking over. The domain started with vineyards in Méjanelle and Saint Christol, and then added Pic St. Loup and Terrasses de Larzac. Plantings are 90% black varieties. The 20 ha around the winery include olive trees and other crops as well as vines, and part is leased out for growing vegetables. Le Mas is the entry-level wine, a blend of Syrah, Grenache, and Carignan from Montpeyroux, aged in concrete. Les Garrigues is another blend of the three varieties, aged longer, also in concrete. Pierre's first release was the Copa Santa Languedoc red in 1992; he attributes the reputation of the domain to its immediate success. The source was Méjanelle until 2017, when it became Montpeyroux. Dominated by Syrah and Grenache, it ages for 20 months in foudre. Bonne Pioche is a GSM from Pic St. Loup, aged for 14 months in a mix of foudres and concrete eggs.

Domaine de la Coste Moynier

Chemin du Mas de La Coste, 34400 Saint Christol	*+33 4 67 86 02 10*
luc.moynier@wanadoo.fr,	*Luc Moynier*
www.domaine-coste-moynier.fr	*Languedoc Saint-Christol [map p. 41]*
	75 ha

Luc and Elisabeth Moynier, both from winemaking families in the Languedoc, created this domain with 9 ha of the old Mas de la Coste in 1975, at the eastern edge of the Languedoc between Montpellier and Nîmes. Today it has 30 ha in the Saint Christol AOP and another 45 ha in IGP Pays d'Oc. Many of the vineyards are planted in locations that had previously been abandoned. The soils are largely covered with round pebbles. There are red, white, and rosé from both the AOP and IGP. Wines vary from IGP bag-in-box to the GSM red of Saint Christol. The top wines are Cuvée Prestige and Cuvée Merlette, both mostly Mourvèdre, and Selection Fûts, 80% Syrah and 20% Grenache, which is the only wine aged in oak.

Domaine Ludovic Engelvin

Chemin du Gour du Cuisinier, 30260 Vic-le-Fesq	*+33 6 29 18 23 86*
domaineludovicengelvin@gmail.com	*Ludovic Engelvin*
www.ludovicengelvin.com	*IGP Gard [map p. 41]*
	10 ha; 17,000 btl

Ludovic Engelvin was a sommelier who opened a wine shop when he returned to the Languedoc after working in the Loire with Didier Dagueneau. He purchased a hectare of old vines Grenache and started making wine, and a few years later sold the shop and made wine full time. He now has three separate vineyards, 3 ha surrounding the winery Grenache with 1 ha of Mourvèdre in the middle, and two other plots planted only with Grenache. Vineyards are in Languedoc AOP, but the wines are labeled as IGP du Gard because there is no Syrah. Viticulture is extreme organic, with the soils essentially maintained by a flock of sheep. Aside from the red Cru Elles, which is 80% Grenache and 20% Mourvèdre, aged in cuve, and The Radiant rosé, which is 70% Mourvèdre and 30% Grenache, the wines are all monovarietal Grenache. They vary by vinification, using cuve plus barriques (Même Si), or only barriques (Aphrodite and El Charco de la Pava). Le Vieux Ronsard is a single parcel wine from the original plot of vines planted in 1955. Espontaneo is a Blanc de Noirs from Grenache.

Ermitage du Pic Saint-Loup

Cami Lou Castella, 34270 Saint Mathieu de Tréviers	*+33 4 67 54 24 68*
secretariat@ermitagepic.fr	*Jean-Marc, Pierre & Xavier Ravaille*
www.ermitagepic.fr	*Pic Saint Loup [map p. 41]*
	43 ha; 110,000 btl

From its foundation in 1951, the domain was a driving force in the formation of the local cooperative. In the 1970s they began to modernize the plantings, and in 1992 the three brothers, Jean-Marc, Pierre, and Xavier, took over and moved to estate bottling. Plantings now are 40% each of Grenache and Syrah, and 10% each of Mourvèdre and Carignan in blacks; whites are half Roussanne. Wines are aged in a mix of foudres and barriques. St. Agnès red and Tour de Pierres have a blend reflecting the plantings, St. Agnès coming from calcareous terroir in the middle of the slope, and Tour de Pierres from the stony terroir known locally as La Gravette. The top red is Guilhem de Gaucelm, an equal blend of Syrah and Grenache from 85-year-old vines. In the St. Agnès line there are also white and rosé.

Mas d'Espanet

Chemin de Robiac, 30730 Saint Mamert Du Gard	*+33 4 66 81 10 27*

masespanet@wanadoo.fr	Agnès & Denys Armand
www.masdespanet.com	IGP Cévennes [map p. 41]
	21 ha; 80,000 btl

The domain is close to the northeast border of the Languedoc with the new Rhone appellation of Duché d'Uzès. Agnès and Denys Armand established the domain in 1980 when they resurrected an abandoned vineyard and added new plantings; in 1999 the old buildings were restored to create a new cellar. Cuvées are divided between AOP Languedoc and the IGP Cévennes. The Languedoc red, Eolienne, is 50% Carignan, 40% Grenache, and 10% Syrah; the white is 80% Grenache Blanc with 10% each of Picpoul and Viognier. Both age in foudre for 12 months. The Camille white is half Grenache Blanc and half Picpoul, aged for 24 months in demi-muids. The Freesia range is IGP Cévennes, in all three colors, aged in cuve; the red is 90% Cinsault with 10% Grenache, and the white is half each of Sauvignon Blanc and Viognier. Chacun son Chenin is 100% Chenin Blanc. There is also a Pinot Noir.

Château des Hospitaliers

923 Avenue Boutonnet, 34400 Saint Christol	+33 4 67 86 03 50
martin-pierrat@wanadoo.fr	Serge Martin-Pierrat
www.chateaudeshospitaliers.fr	Languedoc Saint-Christol [map p. 41]
	46 ha

The domain dates from 1980, and is the reconstitution of an old domain that had been broken up. The main part is 32 ha, assembled parcel by parcel over time, with another 14 ha on the other side of the village. Serge Martin-Pierrat produces both AOP Saint Christol and Vin de France: there is little distinction between them in terms of quality or price, the difference being solely that wines from traditional varieties are AOP, while wines from international varieties are Vin de France. The specialty in fact seems to be producing some unusual combinations of varieties for the Vin de France. There's a large tasting room all set for oenotourism, and various types of tours and tastings are available.

Château de Lancyre

34270 Valflaunès	+33 4 67 55 32 74
contact@chateaudelancyre.com	Régis Valentin
www.chateaudelancyre.com	Pic Saint Loup [map p. 41]
	80 ha; 340,000 btl

Purchased in 1970 by the Durand and Valentin families, this is the largest domain in Pic St. Loup, with 50 ha in the appellation. It was converted from polyculture to viticulture by Bernard Durand, whose nephew Régis Valentin is now in charge. The estate had 15 ha planted with Carignan and Cinsault when it was purchased, and the families owned another 20 ha; since then they have planted Syrah and Grenache. The cuvées from Pic St. Loup are dominated by Syrah: Coste d'Aleyrac is 50% Syrah and 40% Grenache and 10% Carignan, Clos des Combes is 50:50 Syrah and Grenache from calcareous terroir, and the Vieilles Vignes is 65% Syrah, 35% Grenache. All age in cuve. Grande Cuvée is a GSM with 75% Syrah and ages in new barriques. In 2016 most of the crop was destroyed by hail, so a cuvée Lancyre-en-Liberté was made from purchased grapes.

Château de Lascaux

34270 Vacquières	*+33 4 67 59 00 08*
info@chateau-lascaux.com	*Jean-Benoît Cavalier*
www.chateau-lascaux.com	*Pic Saint Loup [map p. 41]*
	85 ha; 200,000 btl

The estate has been in the Cavalier family for fourteen generations, and took its modern form when Jean-Benoît took over in 1984 and reconstructed the vineyards and renovated the cellars. Since then, the estate has expanded considerably from its initial 25 ha, and the stony soils of the vineyards are surrounded by the 300 ha of garrigue. Jean-Benoît is involved in the organization of the AOC in his capacity as President of the Syndicate of the AOC Languedoc. Syrah is the driving force here, 60% in the Pic St. Loup Carra (with 40% Grenache), which is aged in cuve, and 80% in Les Nobles Pierres (with 20% Grenache), which comes from calcareous terroir, and ages in barriques including some new oak. Les Secrets is a range of three single-parcel wines, all aged in barrique. The whites have varying proportions of Vermentino, Roussanne, Marsanne, and other varieties.

Château de L'Euzière

Ancien Chemin Anduze, 34270 Fontanès	*+33 6 27 17 90 77*
leuziere@chateauleuziere.fr	*Marcelle & Michel Causse*
www.chateauleuziere.fr	*Pic Saint Loup [map p. 41]*
	25 ha; 60,000 btl

The family was involved in wine in the nineteenth century and moved to Fontanès, a few miles north of Montpellier, at the start of the twentieth century. Paul Causse started the move to higher quality by planting better varieties in the 1970s. His children Marcelle and Michel took over in the 1990s. The reds from Pic St. Loup are GSM blends; the entry-level L'Almandin is 70% Syrah, 25% Grenache, and 5 % Mourvèdre; the more structured Les Escarboucles has 10% more Syrah and 10% less Grenache. The white AOP Languedoc Grains de Lune is a blend of 50% Roussanne, 30% Vermentino, and 20% Grenache Blanc, aged in vat; L'Or des Fous is the same blend, but fermented and aged in barriques.

Mas Foulaquier

Route des Embruscalles, 34270 Claret	*+33 4 67 59 96 94*
contact@masfoulaquier.com	*Blandine & Pierre Jéquier*
boutique.masfoulaquier.fr	*Pic Saint Loup [map p. 41]*
	14 ha; 65,000 btl

Pierre Jéquier changed careers from architect in Switzerland to winemaker when he bought 8 ha of vineyards in 1998. Located in the northern part of Pic St. Loup, on a slope of calcareous terroir facing southwest, the vineyards were 8 years old at the time. The domain grew by another 3 ha in 2003 when his wife, Blandine Chauchet, who had worked at the parliament in Paris, added 3 ha of 50-year old Grenache and Carignan. The range of a dozen cuvées is red except for a white blend under IGP Saint-Guilhem-le-Désert. Also in the IGP, Gran' Tonillières comes from old Carignan aged in a mix of amphorae and barriques or demi-muids, and two varietal wines, Les Amours Vendangeurs en Grenache and Les Amours Vendangeurs en Syrah, both aged in amphorae. The reds under Pic St. Loup include the entry-level l'Orphée (a blend of Syrah and Grenache), and Les Calades (Syrah) and Le Petit Duc (Grenache), aged in a mixture of barrels and foudres.

Domaine Mirabel

30260 Brouzet-lès-Quissac	*+33 6 22 78 17 47*
domainemirabel@neuf.fr	*Samuel & Vincent Feuillade*
14 ha; 22,000 btl	*Languedoc Sommières* *[map p. 41]*

Brothers Samuel and Vincent Feuillade founded this domain at the northeast corner of Pic St. Loup when they withdrew from the cooperative in 2002. The vineyards are on the stony calcareous terroir known locally as La Gravette. Plantings are mostly black, with all five local varieties; there are 2 ha of white. There are two red cuvées from Pic St. Loup: Le Chant du Sorbier comes from younger vines, and Les Eclats is the top wine, with half Syrah and a quarter each of Mourvèdre and Grenache. Les Bancels is Languedoc AOP from vineyards outside the Pic St. Loup AOP. The white Languedoc AOP, Loriot, is 60% Viognier and 40% Roussanne. The reds age in old barriques; the white is fermented in barrique but ages in cuve.

Mas Montel - Mas Granier

2 chemin du Mas-Montel, 30250 Aspères	*+33 4 66 80 01 21*
dgranier@masmontel.fr	*Dominique Granier*
www.masmontel.fr	*Languedoc Sommières* *[map p. 41]*
	40 ha; 120,000 btl

Marcel Granier bought the Mas Montel in 1945. The domain took its present form when Jean-Philippe and Dominique Granier took over in 1992. A new winery was built in 2012. There are two names here, because Mas Granier is used for AOP wines (both Languedoc AOP and Sommières) and Mas Montel for IGP Pays d'Oc. Vineyards lower down, close to the winery, are used for Mas Montel, those higher up for Mas Granier. Plantings are three quarters black, focused on GSM: Languedoc AOP ages in cuve, Sommières in oak. The AOP white and rosé are AOP Languedoc. In IGP, the reds stay with GSM: Psalmodi ferments conventionally, while Jericho uses carbonic maceration for a light fruity wine. The white IGP has Chardonnay blended with local varieties.

Les Vignerons du Muscat de Lunel

route de Lunel-Viel, Vérargues, 34400 Entre-Vignes	*+33 4 67 86 00 09*
info@muscat-lunel.com	*Virginie Yonnet*
www.muscat-lunel.eu	*Lunel* *[map p. 41]*
	214 ha; 200,000 btl

The cooperative was founded in 1956 and has 45 members, including some estates that are bottled under their individual names (Château de la Devèze, Château de Vérarguess, Château de la Tour de Farges, and Domaine Saint-Pierre de Paradis). The cooperative accounts for the vast majority of production from the appellation of Muscat de Lunel. In addition to Muscat de Lunel, the coop produces IGP Pays d'Oc dry and sweet still wines, and sparkling wines, mostly also from Muscat, and white except for one rosé.

Le Clos des Reboussiers

11 Rue du Pic Saint-Loup, 34270 Cazevieille	*+33 4 67 91 20 12*
contact@closdesreboussiers.fr	*Jean-Pierre Girard*
8 ha; 30,000 btl	*Pic Saint Loup [map p. 41]*

Christopher Peyrus is well known for his wine at Clos Marie (see profile), and now also makes wine at this new domain, just a mile away, which he started with three friends in 2013. Vineyards are on calcareous terroir at 300m elevation, the idea being to keep freshness by altitude. Plantings are dominated by Syrah, supplemented by Grenache. The red cuvées are the Pic St. Loup and the Spoutnik, both 80% Syrah and 20% Grenache, and aged in concrete vats for 18 months. The white, which is labeled as Vin de France, is a quarter each of Carignan Blanc, Clairette, Grenache Gris, and Malvoisie.

Domaine Saint-Daumary

106 Rue des Micocouliers, 34270 Valflaunès	*+33 6 09 23 81 76*
julien.chapel@orange.fr	*Julien Chapel*
15 ha; 35,000 btl	*Pic Saint Loup [map p. 41]*

Julien Chapel is the third generation of vignerons in his family, but the first to have a domain, which he created by taking the family vineyards out of the cooperative in 1999 when he was only 19, making him the youngest winemaker in the Languedoc. Vineyards are on the plateau of Hortus at 150m elevation on calcareous terroir. Plantings are predominantly Syrah, Grenache, Mourvèdre, and Carignan. The cuvée Troisième Mi-Temps comes from Syrah (aged for 12 months in new barriques) and Grenache and Carignan (aged in cuve). L'Asphodèle is 70% Syrah with Grenache, Mourvèdre, and Carignan, aged in used barriques.

Domaine le Sollier

Mas du Saulier, 30170 Monoblet	*+33 6 29 99 81 96*
domainelesollier@gmail.com	*Laurent, Nicolas & Thomas Olivier*
www.domainelesollier.fr	*Duché d'Uzès [map p. 41]*
	15 ha; 60,000 btl

Laurent Olivier runs this family domain with his sons Thomas and Nicolas. Estate-bottling started when the winery was built in 2006. Most of the wines (four red cuvées, with various blends from Grenache, Syrah, Cinsault, and Alicante, two whites, and a rose) are IGP Cévennes, but Les Linthes is AOP Duché d'Uzès (80% Syrah and 20% Grenache). Whites are blends of Viognier, Roussanne, and Chardonnay.

Mas des Volques

Le Colombier, 30350 Aigremont	*+33 6 87 28 98 95*
contact@masdesvolques.fr	*Nicolas Souchon*
12 ha; 24,000 btl	*Duché d'Uzès [map p. 41]*

Nicolas Souchon founded the domain in 2010 with the oldest parcels of the family vineyards, where grapes had always been sent to the cooperative. Nicolas had worked in Châteauneuf-du-Pape, where he met oenologist Philippe Cambie, who advised him on establishing the domain. Located at the foothills of the Cévennes, vines are planted in clay-limestone slopes, with dry, shallow soils. Plantings are two thirds black and one third white. Les Portes de Dieu is an IGP Cévennes 100% Chardonnay, with 25% aged inn barriques. Duché d'Uzès Esus is 45% Syrah, 30% Grenache, 15% Carignan and 10% Cinsault. Alba Dolia is AOP Duché d'Uzès, with 50% Viognier, 30% Grenache Blanc, 15% Roussanne, and 5% Clairette fermented and aged in barriques. Volcae is 40% Syrah, 35% Grenache, and 25% Syrah from north-facing vineyards, with Syrah and Carignan aged in used barriques, and Grenache aged in concrete.

West Of Montpellier

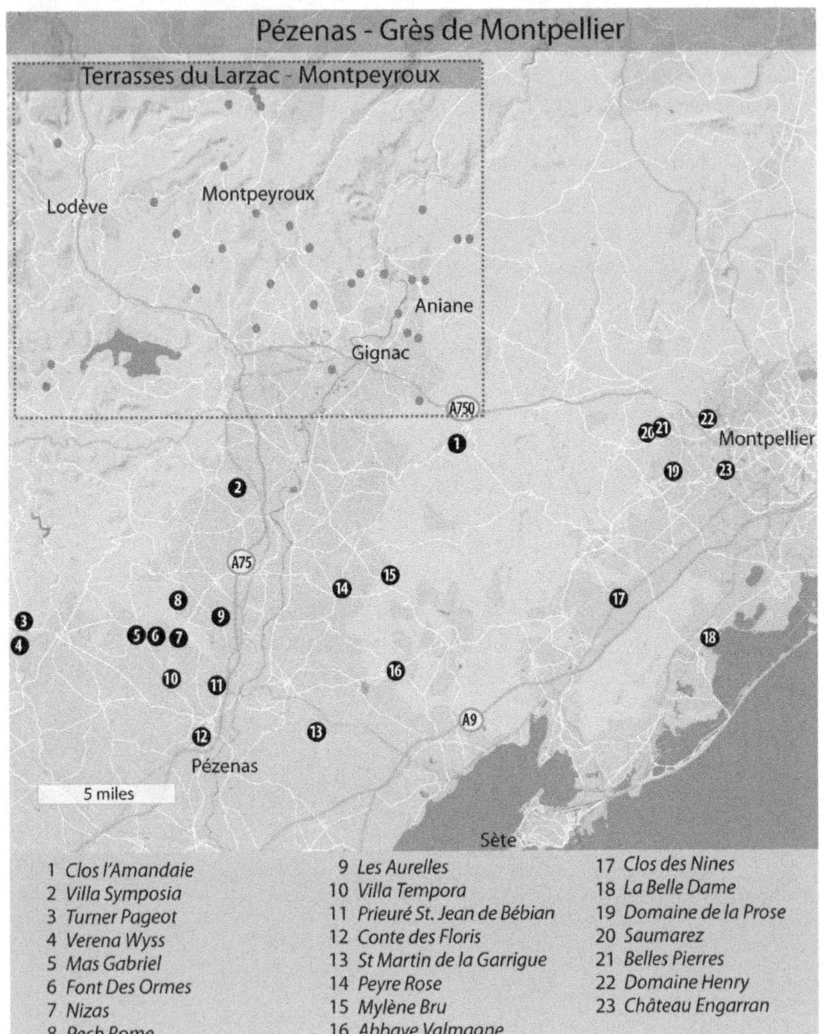

1 *Domaine Caujolle-Gazet*
2 *Mas Haut-Buis*
3 *Clos Maïa*
4 *Pas de l'Escalette*
5 *La Traversée*
6 *Ch. La Sauvageonne*
7 *Les Vignes Oubliées*
8 *Romain Portier*
9 *d'Aupilhac*
10 *Mas de Quernes*
11 *L'Aiguelière*
12 *Mas Combarèla*
13 *Mas Conscience*
14 *Mas Cal Demoura*
15 *Mas Jullien*
16 *Mas de l'Ecriture*
17 *La Pèira*
18 *Alain Chabanon*
19 *Saint Sylvestre*
20 *Montcalmès*
21 *Mas des Brousses*
22 *Domaine Vaïsse*
23 *Mas de la Séranne*
24 *Grange des Pères*
25 *Clos de la Barthassade*
26 *La Terrasse d'Élise*
27 *Daumas Gassac*
28 *St Jean d'Aumières*
29 *Domaine l'Hermas*
30 *Mas des Chimères*
31 *Malavieille*

Domaine d'Aupilhac *

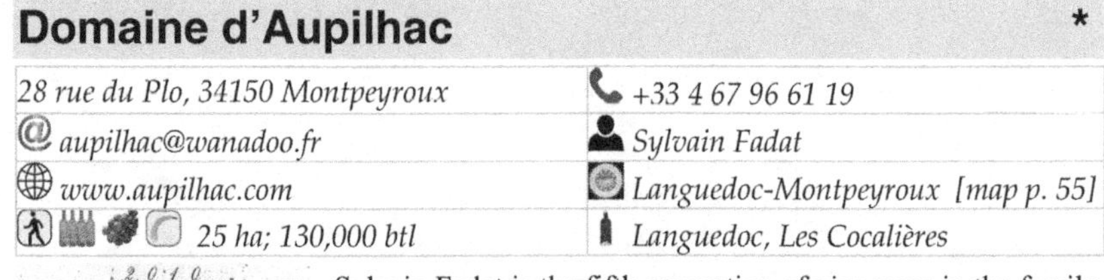

28 rue du Plo, 34150 Montpeyroux	+33 4 67 96 61 19
aupilhac@wanadoo.fr	Sylvain Fadat
www.aupilhac.com	Languedoc-Montpeyroux [map p. 55]
25 ha; 130,000 btl	Languedoc, Les Cocalières

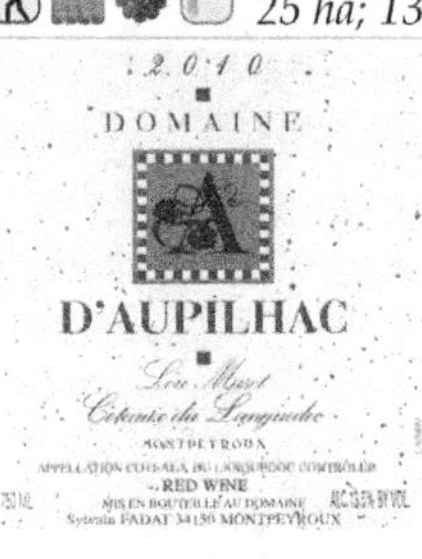

Sylvain Fadat is the fifth generation of vignerons in the family, but was the first to bottle his own wine in 1989. At that time the domain was still involved in polyculture, but since 1992 it has been concerned exclusively with viticulture. Its headquarters are in an unassuming house along what used to be the route for the stagecoach through Montpeyroux. But behind the house is a winery full of modern equipment. The main vineyards are at Aupilhac (close to Montpeyroux), including some extending directly behind the property, but there is another vineyard at Cocalières with an elevation of 350m, where Sylvain planted vines on a steeply terraced hillside in 1998.

The focus is on traditional Southern varieties: Carignan, Grenache, Cinsault, Mourvèdre, and Syrah for the reds, with Roussanne, Marsanne, Grenache Blanc, and Vermentino for the whites. It was the reds that established the reputation of the Domaine, all made by traditional methods of vinification. The wines are mostly labeled as Languedoc (formerly Coteaux du Languedoc), with the best cuvées in the category of Languedoc-Montpeyroux. Sylvain is known as somewhat of a specialist in Carignan, and Le Carignan, a monovarietal cuvée from 60-year-old vines, is one of the domain's best-known wines. (It's an IGP Mont Baudile, as is the monovarietal Cinsault.) It's a sign of progress in the area that Sylvain was a trendsetter in 1990 but is now one of several good producers in Montpeyroux.

Domaine Les Aurelles *

8 Chemin des Champs Blancs, 34320 Nizas	+33 4 67 25 08 34
contact@les-aurelles.com	Basile Saint Germain
www.les-aurelles.com	Languedoc-Pézenas [map p. 54]
9 ha; 25,000 btl	Languedoc-Pézenas, Aurel

Wine is in the family background as Caroline Saint Germain comes from Cognac, but the creation of Les Aurelles in 1995 was a new career for Basil Saint Germain. He was influenced by two years spent at Château Latour. "I chose this particular area because the first wine of the Languedoc I tasted came from here, and because the terroir seemed to resemble Château Latour, with an area of gravel," he says. Vineyards are located where alluvial deposits created a deep layer of gravel; plantings are Carignan, Mourvèdre, Syrah, and Grenache, with some Roussanne for white wine. The winery is a modern concrete bunker constructed on a high point in Nizas in 2001.

The domain is committed to organic viticulture to the point of including a statement on the back label certifying the absence of pesticides. Yields are low, under 25 hl/ha for reds and under 18 hl/ha for white. Basil is a devotée of Carignan, and has planted new vines as well as buying all the old vines he can find. There are three cuvées of red and one white. After the entry-level Déelle (a blend that changes with vintage), come Solen (Grenache, Carignan, and Syrah) and Aurel (Mourvèdre, Syrah, and Grenache). These express vintage: Solen shows its best qualities in cooler years, while Aurel really requires warmer years for the Mourvèdre's character to emerge. The white Aurel is Roussanne. The style is moderate, in line with Basil's purpose: "I want above all to make a wine to have with food not to win competitions."

Mas Cal Demoura *

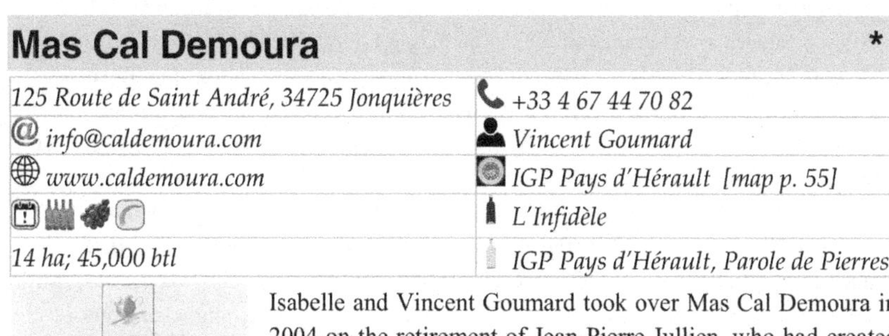

125 Route de Saint André, 34725 Jonquières	*+33 4 67 44 70 82*
info@caldemoura.com	*Vincent Goumard*
www.caldemoura.com	*IGP Pays d'Hérault [map p. 55]*
	L'Infidèle
14 ha; 45,000 btl	*IGP Pays d'Hérault, Parole de Pierres*

Isabelle and Vincent Goumard took over Mas Cal Demoura in 2004 on the retirement of Jean-Pierre Jullien, who had created the estate in 1993. Vincent was a consultant in Paris before he took up wine as a second career. The winery is a small practical facility packed with equipment. Vineyards are in two main groups on either side of Jonquières. The majority have clay-calcareous soils, and are planted with black grapevines, including all five varieties of the appellation; the rest have calcareous pebbles and are where the white varieties are planted, mostly Chenin Blanc (going back to an experiment of the 1990s), with smaller quantities of the usual southern varieties. Wines are matured in a mixture of demi-muids and barriques (except for the more aromatic white varieties, which are vinified in cuve).

There are three red cuvées, two whites, and a rosé. L'Infidèle is the principal red cuvée, a blend of all five varieties. Coming from a selection of parcels with calcareous pebbles, Les Combariolles is 35% each Syrah and Mourvèdre with 15% Carignan, and is the most structured wine of the house. Grapes are partially destemmed and it ages in a mix of demi-muids and foudres. At the other extreme is Feu Sacré, based on old vines Grenache. In the whites, L'Etincelle is half Chenin Blanc, but the top white wine, Paroles de Pierres, is three quarters Chenin with Roussanne making up most of the rest of the blend. The style varies quite a bit through the reds, but tends to be smooth and harmonious. The whites have a fresh character far removed from the old amorphous phenolics of the south.

Domaine Alain Chabanon *

Chemin de St Etienne, 34150 Lagamas	*+33 4 67 57 84 64*
domainechabanon@gmail.com	*Alain Chabanon*
www.alainchabanon.com	*Languedoc-Montpeyroux [map p. 55]*
18 ha; 55,000 btl	*Languedoc, Campredon*

After qualifying in oenology at Bordeaux and Montpellier, and apprenticing with Alain Brumont in Madiran, Alain Chabanon returned to his roots in the Languedoc where he purchased vineyards between Jonquières and Montpeyroux. His first vintage was 1992 (only 2,500 bottles). A new winery was built in 2001. Originally the domain was called Font Caude (named for a nearby warm spring), but now the wines are labeled as Domaine Chabanon.

Alain produces a wide range of wines, including Languedoc, IGP Pays d'Oc, and Vin de France, from vineyards spread over several communes just below the Terrasses de Larzac. Under IGP and Vin de France are wines from varieties that aren't common in the region, including Chenin Blanc and Vermentino (Trélans is a blend of two thirds Vermentino to one third Chenin Blanc), and Merlot (this is the well-regarded Merle aux Alouettes cuvée); the Languedoc AOP wines are GSM (Grenache-Syrah-Mourvèdre) or Syrah plus Mourvèdre. In fact, the first wine of the domain was the l'Esprit de Font Caude blend of equal proportions of Syrah and Mourvèdre.

There are nine cuvées altogether, the idea being to demonstrate the characters of the very different plots. "This is not a range from petit vin to a grand vin, it's several different choices to suit different tastes, sometimes at the same price so that consumers aren't tempted to choose by cost. Of course, some are ready to drink today and others need three years," Alain explains.

Mas de Daumas Gassac **

Mas Daumas, 34150 Aniane	*+33 4 67 57 71 28*
contact@daumas-gassac.com	*Samuel Guibert*
www.daumas-gassac.com	*IGP Pays d'Hérault [map p. 55]*
40 ha; 205,000 btl	*IGP Pays d'Hérault*

Aimé Guibert was looking for a country house when he purchased the estate in 1970. The geographer Henri Enjalbert, a family friend, suggested that the Gassac valley, with red glacial soils and a microclimate of cool nights, was suitable for wine production. Emile Peynaud from Bordeaux became a consultant, and the creation of the domain pioneered the production of high quality wine in Languedoc. Today the domain has about 50 small individual vineyards separated by the original garrigue.

Based on Cabernet Sauvignon, but with many subsidiary varieties, the red wine is by no means a typical Cabernet. "We are not looking for the modern jammy fruity style. We belong more to the Bordeaux 1961 attitude—wine with 12.5% alcohol and good acidity," says Samuel Guibert, who now runs the domain. Older vintages seem to alternate between Atlantic austerity and the spices and herbs of the Mediterranean garrigue, with long aging potential: the 1982 and 1983 vintages were still vibrant in 2013. Current vintages are more forward but less complex. The white is based on a blend of Chardonnay, Viognier, and Petit Manseng, with the balance from many other varieties. It is rendered fairly soft by a just perceptible level of residual sugar (6-8 g/l).

In addition to the regular cuvées, there is now a cuvée Emile Peynaud in some vintages; made from the oldest Cabernet Sauvignon vines in one of the original vineyards, it is powerful in the modern idiom. (I usually prefer the regular red cuvée.) In addition to the regular cuvées, there is now a cuvée Emile Peynaud in some vintages; made from the oldest Cabernet Sauvignon vines in one of the original vineyards, it is powerful in the modern idiom. (I usually prefer the regular red cuvée.) Moulin de Gassac is an entry-level line. Success is indicated by the constant stream of visitors to the tasting room. Success is indicated by the constant stream of visitors to the tasting room.

Château de L'Engarran *

Route de Lavérune D5E, 34880 Lavérune	*+33 4 67 47 00 02*
caveau.lengarran@orange.fr	*Diane Losfelt*
www.chateau-engarran.com	*Grès de Montpellier [map p. 54]*
	Grès de Montpellier
55 ha; 220,000 btl	*IGP Pays d'Oc Sauvignon Blanc, La Lionne*

Housed in a grand building, a historic monument dating from the eighteenth century on the outskirts of Montpellier, Château de l'Engarran has been owned by the same family since 1923, and for successive generations the women of the family have been the winemakers. Sisters Dianne Losfelt and Constance Rerolle are the present generation; Diane has been the winemaker for thirty years.

There are both whites and reds in the IGP Pays d'Oc for wines from international varieties (the whites based on Sauvignon Blanc are more successful than the Cabernet Franc, and I prefer the unoaked La Lionne to the oaked Adélys), but most of the wines are in the general AOP Languedoc at the introductory level, or in the Grès de Montpellier or St. Georges d'Orques AOPs, moving up.

The whites show varietal character; the reds range from elegant to rich, usually with some freshness on the finish, and the best convey a silky impression. The wine I like best is the eponymous Château de l'Engarran from Grès de Montpellier, which is a classic GSM blend (Grenache-Syrah-Mourvèdre) where the Syrah comes to the front and the impression is more restrained than the more overtly southern Grenat Majeur or Quetton Saint Georges.

Domaine de La Grange des Pères ***

34150 Aniane	*+33 4 67 57 70 55*
+33 4 67 57 32 04	
15 ha; 30,000 btl	*IGP Pays d'Hérault [map p. 55]*

Laurent Vaillé established his domain in 1989 on ungiving terroir of hard limestone by dynamiting and bulldozing to clear land for planting. The winery is actually in the middle of uncultivated fields with not a vine in sight, but the Syrah and Cabernet vineyards are fairly close by, the main difference being that Cabernet is planted in the cooler exposures. Mourvèdre is 4-5 km away, on a rather hot south-facing plot covered in galets. There are only two wines here, one red and one white. Laurent is a perfectionist: "Any lot that isn't satisfactory is discarded, I don't want to make a second wine."

The red wine for which the domain is famous is a blend of 40% Syrah, 40% Mourvèdre, and 20% Cabernet Sauvignon. "The Cabernet Sauvignon is like salt in food. I do not want Cabernet Sauvignon to dominate my assemblage," says Laurent. Vines are grown low to the ground. Yields are always very low, often below 25 hl/ha. Laurent refuses to draw any distinction between vins de garde and wines to drink now, but in my view the red wine needs considerable age to show its best. The 1994 showed a seamless elegance in 2012, with a subtlety comparable to a top northern Rhône. The 2000 vintage was still dense and rich at this point; and it was vinicide to drink the 2008 or 2009, because sheer power and aromatics hid much of their potential. Only 10% of production, the white is based on Roussanne with smaller amounts of Marsanne and Chardonnay.

After he died in 2021, with the future of the domain uncertain, prices for prior vintages exploded on the auction market.

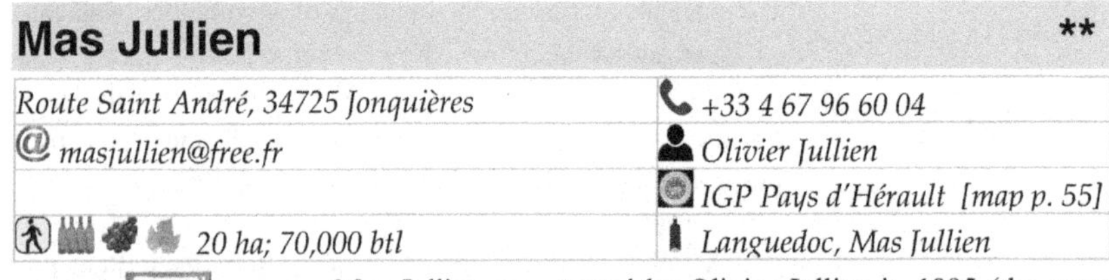

Mas Jullien **

Route Saint André, 34725 Jonquières	*+33 4 67 96 60 04*
masjullien@free.fr	*Olivier Jullien*
	IGP Pays d'Hérault [map p. 55]
20 ha; 70,000 btl	*Languedoc, Mas Jullien*

Mas Jullien was started by Olivier Jullien in 1985 (the same year the AOC of Coteaux du Languedoc was created), when he was twenty. (His father, Jean-Pierre, was a grower who sent his grapes to the coop. He started Mas Cal Demoura next door after Olivier's success, and later sold it.) The winery has grown into a collection of buildings, with a tasting room to accommodate the constant trek of visitors. From a small start with 3 ha of rented vines, the domain has expanded into many separate holdings with various soil types, with many changes in the vineyard holdings over the years. Olivier is still buying and selling vineyards to balance the terroirs: there is a sense of restless movement here, with Olivier often giving the impression he wants to be off to the next thing.

Based on the traditional Southern varieties of Carignan, Grenache, Cinsault, Syrah, and Mourvèdre, there are three red cuvées (all Terrasses de Larzac AOP). The principal cuvée is called simply Mas Jullien. The introductory wine is Les Derniers Etats de l'Ame (a reference to an earlier cuvée, L'Etat de l'Ame, which Olivier had proposed to stop producing, but resumed after protests). Its constitution changes from year to year. The top wine, Carlan, is a parcel selection from terroir of schist (in some years there are also other parcel selections). The single white cuvée, a blend of Carignan Blanc and Chenin Blanc, is IGP Pays d'Hérault. There are also a rosé (with the varieties changing each year), and a dessert wine, Cartagène.

Domaine de Montcalmès *

Chemin du Cimetière, 34150 Puéchabon	*+33 4 67 57 74 16*
gaecbh@wanadoo.fr	*Frédéric Pourtalié*
www.domainedemontcalmes.fr	*Terrasses du Larzac [map p. 55]*
23 ha; 60,000 btl	*Terrasses du Larzac*

His grandfather produced wine, but his father sold grapes to the coop, until Frédéric Pourtalié took over the domain in 1998, after working elsewhere in the south, with internships at Grange des Pères and Alain Graillot. His first vintage was in 1999, just 5,000 bottles for the domain. The entrance to the winery is quite unassuming, just an ordinary building off the main street in Puéchabon, but behind are extensive caves packed with stainless steel tanks for fermentation and barriques for maturation. Vineyards are planted in many parcels on a variety of terroirs in Terrasses de Larzac. [The size of the domain was reduced when Frédéric's partner, Victor Guizard, left in 2010 to form Domaine Saint Sylvestre (see profile) with his wife Sophie.]

Blending is the focus here. "We vinify each cépage from each terrace in order to understand the terroir, but it takes 15 years, so as yet there aren't any single-vineyard wines," Frédéric says. Montcalmès is planted with 60% Syrah, 20% Grenache, and 20% Mourvèdre; there is also a white (from a hectare divided between Roussanne and Marsanne). Wines are matured in 1- to 3-year-old barriques for two years, and bottled by the waning moon without filtration. The variety of terroirs provides Grenache varying from broad fleshiness to steely structure, and the house style is for a precise, harmonious elegance, very much a representation of the modern style of Languedoc. The red is labeled as Terrasses du Larzac, the white as Languedoc.

Domaine Peyre Rose *

Route Villeveyrac, 34230 Saint Pargoire	*+33 4 67 98 75 50*
peyrerose@orange.fr	*Marlène Soria*
	Grès de Montpellier [map p. 54]
23 ha; 32,000 btl	*Coteaux du Languedoc, Clos des Cistes*

To say that Peyre Rose is a bit tricky to find is an understatement. It's not easy to spot the entrance to the narrow unpaved track in Saint Pargoire that winds for several kilometers until it reaches the domain. "Follow the telegraph poles," the instructions say, but the faint of heart might well lose confidence along the way. It's entirely understandable that Marlène Soria used to come here on vacation for the savage quality of the countryside. She purchased 60 ha of garrigue, and then in 1970 planted some vines to make wine for personal consumption. The domain started later, with some plantings of Syrah in the 1980s, followed in 1985 by Mourvèdre and Grenache. Almost all of the plantings today are black varieties, with Syrah dominant, and just 3 ha of Rolle and Roussanne.

This remains an intensely personal operation, with Marlène making the wines single-handed in the cave. Until 2002, everything was vinified in cuve, but since then about a quarter has been matured in foudres. Aging is quite extended here, with at least 7-8 years of élevage. A tasting at Peyre Rose in 2013 focused on current releases: 2003 and 2004. This is not your usual economic model. The wines move from the fleshy sex appeal of Marlène #3, to the more classic balance of Clos des Cistes (80% Syrah and 20% Grenache, the only wine really to show any restraint), and Clos Léone (80% Syrah and 20% Mourvèdre), but the general style is for intense, very ripe, exuberant fruits.

Prieuré Saint Jean de Bébian *

Route de Nizas, 34120 Pézenas	*+33 4 67 98 13 60*
info@bebian.com	*Karen Turner*
www.bebian.com	*Languedoc-Pézenas [map p. 54]*
33 ha; 120,000 btl	*Languedoc, Le Prieuré*

The winery sits on the site of a Roman villa, where perhaps vines were grown long ago, but the modern story starts with M. Roux, who sourced Syrah from Chave, Grenache from Château Rayas, Mourvèdre from Domaine Tempier, and Roussanne from Château Beaucastel. The estate was bought in 1994 by Chantal Lecouty and Jean-Claude Lebrun (formerly of the Revue du Vin). Karen Turner came as winemaker in 2004, and stayed on when the estate was sold to Russian owners in 2008. She also makes wine at her own domain, Turner-Pageot (see profile).

The top wine is labeled Grand Vin du Languedoc; the red has a high proportion of Syrah and Mourvèdre, and the white is more than half Roussanne. A second wine, La Chapelle de Bébian, is made in all three colors; the red is half Grenache, and the white is half Grenache Blanc. With more of an eye on the market, a new entry-level line has been introduced under the name La Croix de Bébian. In addition, there is a Cabernet Sauvignon under the label L'Autre Versant.

Even after some softening, the reds remain somewhat counter to the trend for instant gratification. "I have the impression that no one in Languedoc wants tannins any more, but I want them. One of the most important things about Bébian is that it's one of the few wines in Languedoc that ages well. It's probably best at 10-20 years after the vintage,"

Karen says. In my view, even La Chapelle isn't really ready after five years, and Prieuré does not open out until after ten years, making it one of the region's more ageworthy wines.

Profiles of Important Estates

Abbaye de Valmagne

34560 Villeveyrac	*+33 4 67 78 06 09*
rdallaines@valmagne.com	*Roland d'Allaines*
www.valmagne.com	*Grès de Montpellier* *[map p. 54]*
	35 ha; 73,000 btl

The abbey was founded in 1138, became part of the Cistercian order in 1159, and from then until the fourteenth century was one of the richest Cistercian abbeys in France. It was sacked in the French Revolution and the church was turned into a winery. In 1820, foudres were installed in the nave, and it became known as the 'cathedral of wines.' The Abbey is a historic monument, open to visits, and it has a large vineyard. The southern part of the vineyard has clay-limestone terroir and is AOP; the northern part has red sandstone and marl and makes IGP wines. The entry-level range, called Vitrail sur l'Abbaye, comes in all three colors and is IGP Pays d'Oc. The Portalis range is named for Jean-Baptiste Portalis, who introduced gravity-feed cellars in 1920. Labeled as AOP Languedoc, the red is GSM and the white is a blend of Roussanne and Grenache Blanc. There is also a small production of rosé. Under Grès de Montpellier, Turenne is more ambitious: the red is Syrah and Mourvèdre, aged in barriques for 12 months; there is a small production of a white blend from Roussanne, Marsanne, and Viognier. Cardinal de Bonzi is the top red, produced by a selection of the best lots in the best years.

Domaine de L'Aiguelière

2, Place du Square, 34150 Montpeyroux	*+33 4 67 96 61 43*
auguste@aigueliere.com	*Auguste Commeyras*
19 ha; 50,000 btl	*Languedoc-Montpeyroux* *[map p. 55]*

Aimé Commeyras was president of the local cooperative before he established the domain in 1984 with the intention of producing high quality wines in Montpeyroux. L'Aiguelière was a pioneer; with developments in the region over the past few years, it is now one of many good producers, and is run by Aimé's daughter, Christine. Montpeyroux lies between the plain of Hérault and the hills of Larzac, where the vineyards are located. Aside from the entry-level Sourire de Lise (Coteaux du Languedoc), the wines divide into the traditional varieties under AOP Montpeyroux and international cuvées under IGP Mont Baudile. L'Esprit and Velours are conventional blends of Grenache, Syrah, and Mourvèdre, but the two top Montpeyroux wines that established the reputation of the domain are La Côte Dorée and the Vieilles Vignes La Côte Rousse. Earlier vintages had some Grenache, but both are now varietal Syrah, coming from the oldest vines. La Côte Rousse comes from clay-calcareous soils, whereas La Côte Dorée comes from gravel-based soils. The wines rest for a year in new oak barriques (from Nevers for Rousse, from Alliers for Dorée). Pégase, a blend based on Cabernet Sauvignon, is made in top vintages, and Peyre Brune is a varietal Cabernet Sauvignon. The style is rich, sometimes overwhelming, with lots of new oak.

Clos de la Barthassade

Chemin du Mas de Cambon, 34150 Aniane	*+33 6 34 23 03 09*
info@closdelabarthassade.fr	*Hélène & Guillaume Baron*
www.closdelabarthassade.fr	*Terrasses du Larzac [map p. 55]*
	13 ha; 60,000 btl

After qualifying in oenology, Hélène and Guillaume Baron worked in Burgundy and Provence before buying their first 10 ha in the Terrasses du Larzac. The first vintage was 2014. They describe themselves as performing 'natural vinification with traditional aging.' One unusual feature is the use of whole clusters for the reds, often around 50%. Wines may age in concrete eggs or old barriques. Wines are mostly red, split between blends and varietals. Blends are GSM (Cuvée H), Syrah, Mourvèdre, and Grenache (Les Ouvrées) or Grenache, Cinsault, and Syrah (Les Gravettes). Varietals are Carignan (K Libre), Billes de Grenache (100% Grenache), and Pur C (Cinsault). Blanc de Cinsault is an orange wine from Cinsault. Les Cargadous is a blend of Roussanne with Chenin Blanc, aged in barriques and 500-liter barrels.

Domaine de la Belle Dame

Route de Mireval, 34110 Vic-la-Gardiole	*+33 6 62 24 10 10*
contact@belledame.fr	*Jean-Luc Mazas*
belledame.fr	*Muscat de Mireval [map p. 54]*
	19 ha

Just along the coast to the south of Montpellier, 9the domain is in the small Muscat de Mireval location, in an area classified as a Natura 2000 zone (a protected area covering threatened birds and habitats), close to the inland water of Étang de Vic, which is separated from the Mediterranean by a long sand bar. There are fewer than 10 producers in Muscat de Mireval. Jean-Luc Mazas created the domain in 1996 and started to bottle and sell his own wines in 2007. Muscat à Petit Grains for the sweet fortified wine of Mireval is the major planting, overlooking the ocean. There are also dry and pétillant (lightly sparkling) Muscats, and a series of other products, including olive oil, apple juice, lavender, etc. The domain welcomes oenotourism.

Domaine Belles Pierres

Route Bel-Air D102, 34570 Murviel-lès-Montpellier	*+33 4 67 47 30 43*
bellespierres@wanadoo.fr	*Damien Coste*
www.domaine-bellespierres.com	*Grès de Montpellier [map p. 54]*
	17 ha; 70,000 btl

Joseph Coste was a member of the cooperative in Murviel, northwest of Montpellier, until he left to form the Domaine des Clauzes in 1989. His son Damien created Domaine des Belles Pierres in 1992, making the wines in Joseph's cave until 1998. Damien is known for his focus on white wines, coming from a wide range of varieties, and amounting to 40% of production. Cuvée Mosaique is a blend of Sauvignon Blanc with Viognier, Muscat, and Grenache Blanc. Les Clauzes de Jo is a blend of Roussanne and Viognier; Chante des Ames also includes some Grenache Blanc. Latino d'Oc is a pure Viognier.

Labels vary from IGP Pays d'Oc, to St. Georges d'Orques (the local appellation), and Coteaux du Languedoc. There is also a Vin de France, Ineptie, based on Petit and Gros Manseng and Viognier; off-dry, it was initially made by accident, when fermentation failed to complete, and was denied the agrément for the AOP. Passidore Exception is a sweet wine from Petit and Gros Manseng. The reds are more conventional, based on the usual black varieties of the region.

Mas des Brousses

2, Chemin du Bois, 34150 Puéchabon	*+33 4 67 57 33 75*
geraldine.combes@wanadoo.fr	*Géraldine Combes & Xavier Peyraud*
www.masdesbrousses.fr	*Terrasses du Larzac [map p. 55]*
	10 ha; 32,000 btl

Mourvèdre is in the blood, because Xavier Peyraud is the grandson of Lucien Peyraud at Domaine Tempier in Bandol. So when Xavier married Geraldine Combes and they started to produce wines from her family's vineyards in 1997 (previously grapes had been sent to the coop), they planted Mourvèdre taken from cuttings at Domaine Tempier. It is now about a third of plantings, just a little more than Syrah; the other black varieties are Grenache, Cinsault, and Merlot. All the plots are Terrasses de Larzac, except for the Merlot, which is IGP. There's also a hectare of white varieties. The red Terrasses de Larzac (aged in 400-liter barrels) and the rosé Languedoc are both 50% Mourvèdre, with the rest split between Grenache and Syrah. The Mataro cuvée is 70% Mourvèdre and ages in almost new barriques. IGP Saint-Guilhem-Le Désert red is an unusual blend of young Mourvèdre with old Merlot. The white IGP is a blend of 11 different varieties, coplanted and cofermented.

Domaine Caujolle-Gazet

51 Grand Rue, 34520 La Vacquerie-et-Saint-Martin-de-Castries	*+33 6 13 79 63 50*
domainecaujollegazet@gmail.com	*Alain Caujolle-Gazet & Benoît Huet*
www.domainecaujollegazet.fr	*Terrasses du Larzac [map p. 55]*
	11 ha; 35,000 btl

Alain Caujolle started making wine at Domaine des Grécaux in Montpeyroux in 1998. He sold the domain in 2010 and started a new venture in Terrasses de Larzac, setting up his cellar in the village of La Vacquerie. Called the Chai en Paille (cellar of straw), the cellar won an ecological award for its construction from wood, using straw for insulation, and finished with limestone. The eight cuvées are split between AOP Terrasses du Larzac and IGP Hérault. The AOP reds are based on Grenache, Syrah, Carignan, and Cinsault. The IGP reds vary from a blend of Merlot, Grenache and Syrah, to Pinot Noir. The white IGPs are blends of Grenache Blanc and Chardonnay or varietal Carignan Blanc. The wines age in concrete vats.

Mas des Chimères

26 Rue de la Vialle, 34800 Octon	*+33 4 67 96 22 70*
mas.des.chimeres@wanadoo.fr	*Guilhem Dardé*
masdeschimeres.com	*Terrasses du Larzac [map p. 55]*
	23 ha; 50,000 btl

The Dardé family were engaged in polyculture until the 1960s when they turned to viticulture, but sent the grapes to the cooperative. In 1993, Guilhem left the cooperative and started to produce his own wine. His wife, Palma, and daughter, Maguelone, are also at the domain. The domain is located on the edge of the Larzac plateau, with two types of terroir, red soils which are sandy-clay rich in iron oxide, and basaltic rocks. Plantings are almost all black varieties, with just 2 ha of whites. Cuvées are split between the IGP d'Hérault (mostly from the red soils) and the Terrasses du Larzac AOP (from basaltic terroir). Until 2005 there was a single AOP red, Nuit Grave, which has 45% Syrah, 38% Grenache, and 17% Mourvèdre. When the Terrasses du Larzac AOP was introduced, another cuvée was added, Caminarèm, which has equal proportions of Cinsault, Carignan, Mourvèdre, Grenache, and Syrah. They age in a mix of 400- and 600-liter barrels for 12 months. Two varietal cuvées are IGP: l'Oeillade is 100% Cinsault, and Marie et Joseph is 95% Carignan (plus 5% Syrah). L'Hérétique is a nod to modernity, 85% Merlot and 15% Cabernet Sauvignon, aged in used barriques. Whites are all IGP: Le Blanc is a blend of more than six varieties, and there are both dry and sweet Muscats.

Clos de l'Amandaie

34230 Aumelas	*+33 6 86 68 08 62*
closdelamandaie@free.fr	*Philippe Peytavy*
www.closdelamandaie.com	*Grès de Montpellier [map p. 54]*
	20 ha

The Petavy family has been making wine for six generations, and in 2002 Philippe and Stéphanie founded the domain with 12 ha in Aumelas, about 15 miles west of Montpellier. In 2008 they built a new, environmentally-friendly, winery, half underground. The name of the domain reflects the history of the area, which was an almond basis, between the Massif Central and the Mediterranean. Soils are stony limestone and red clay. Chat Pitre is an entry-level line in all three colors under IGP Pays d'Oc. The AOP reds are Grès de Montpellier, and the whites are AOP Languedoc. The estate red is a blend of Grenache, Syrah, Carignan, and Cinsault, aged in cuve except for aging a third of the Syrah in barriques. The white is 80% Grenache Blanc and 20% Roussanne, aged in cuve. Huis Clos comes from the best plots, harvested manually. The red is an equal blend of Syrah and Grenache, aged in 500-liter barrels for 12 months. The white is the same blend as the estate wine, but ages in the 500-liter barrels, with battonage, for 12 months. There is also a dessert wine, Les Ménades, harvested late from Petit Manseng (more usually found in the Pyrenees), and aged in acacia for 12 months.

Clos Maïa

1, Grand-Rue, 34520 La Vacquerie	*+33 6 12 83 42 89*
closmaia@hotmail.fr	*Géraldine Laval*
www.closmaia.fr	*Terrasses du Larzac [map p. 55]*
	6 ha; 26,000 btl

Géraldine Laval comes from the Charente and studied in Bordeaux. She worked at Olivier Leflaive in Burgundy, Jean-Louis Chave in the Rhône, and Olivier Julien and Pas de L'Escalette in the Languedoc, before establishing her own domain not far from her mentors in the Terrasses du Larzac. She shares the cellars at Mas Haut Buis, just along the street in the village, with her partner Olivier Jeantet. Plantings are mostly black varieties at 400-500m altitude on soils with limestone bedrock. Her first vintage was 2009. The red Terrasses du Larzac is 80% Grenache with 20% of several old grape varieties of the area; average vine age is 65 years. The wine ages for 12 months in 500-liter barrels. Le Petit Clos is a similar blend under IGP d'Hérault, aged in concrete, and is about half of production. The white IGP started as a blend of local varieties, but Chenin Blanc was added in 2014, and since then Chenin, Grenache Gris, and Roussanne have been 30% each, with 10% Terret Bourret. aged for 12 months in 400-liter barrels.

Domaine de Clovallon

Route de Béziers, 34600 Bédarieux	*+33 4 67 95 19 72*
mas@alezon.fr	*Alix Roque*
www.clovallon.fr	*IGP Pays d'Hérault [map p. 83]*
	10 ha; 40,000 btl

Originally an architect, Catherine Roque created this domain just north of Faugères in 1989. She then acquired the Mas d'Alezon (see profile) in Faugères in 1997, and her daughter Alix took over at Clovallon in 2014. It's located in the IGP of the Haute Vallée de L'Orb, a river valley that runs east to west between high dolomite cliffs. Vineyards are planted up to 500m on red sandstone soils. It's considered too cold for the usual regional varieties, and the domain made its name for Pinot Noir. The estate wine comes from younger vines, aged for six months in 3-year barrels. The cuvée Pomarèdes comes from a 1 ha parcel on calcareous soils. Joli Cantel is a white from 80% Chardonnay and 20% Roussanne, aged in old foudres. Alix has introduced cuvées from more conventional varieties. Les Indigènes is a red from a 1 ha clos of very old vines, some pre-phylloxera, with many varieties intermingled, and Les Aires is Viognier. Les Aurièges is an orange wine from a blend of mostly local varieties but also including Chardonnay and Riesling.

Domaine Le Conte des Floris

19 avenue Emile Combes, 34120 Pézenas	*+33 7 68 51 29 49*
domaine.floris@gmail.com	*Daniel Le Conte des Floris*
www.domainelecontedesfloris.com	*Languedoc-Pézenas [map p. 54]*
	8 ha; 25,000 btl

Formerly at *La Revue du Vin de France* , Daniel Le Conte des Floris created this domain in Pézenas in 2000. Vineyards are spread over the communes of Pézenas, Caux, and Gabian. Daniel's focus is on matching grape varieties to terroirs: Grenache from sedimentary soils dominates the cuvée Villafranchien, Syrah grown on schist dominates the cuvées Carbonifère and Six Rats Noir, and Carignan comes from volcanic soils. Homo Habilis is a GSM. Daniel is best known for his white cuvées, to the extent that noted critic Michel Bettane said his Lune Blanche from Carignan Blanc demonstrates that the general uprooting of Carignan Blanc from Languedoc. was a mistake. Pierre Lune is a blend of Marsanne with Carignan, and Lune Rousse is a blend of Roussanne with Carignan. All wines age for a year in barriques, usually followed by further aging in cuve before release. There are also orange and sweet wines.

Le Mas de l'Écriture

232 Rue de la Font du Loup, 34725 Jonquières	*+33 6 80 15 57 72*
contact@masdelecriture.fr	*Pascal Fulla*
www.masdelecriture.com	*IGP Pays d'Hérault [map p. 55]*
	10 ha; 30,000 btl

Pascal Fulla changed careers from the law to winemaking when he bought this estate in 1999. He has now been joined by his daughter Ida. Just outside the village of Jonquières, at the foot of the Larzac plateau, vineyards are on calcareous terroir, but with heterogeneity ranging from quartz to clay. Plantings are all black varieties. Yields are only 25-30 hl/ha, and there are just three cuvées. L'Ecriture is a GSM blend dominated by Syrah, varying from 50-80% with the vintage, Les Pensées is usually about half Grenache, together with Syrah, Cinsault, and Carignan, and Emotion Occitane is a blend of Carignan, Grenache, Cinsault, and Syrah, with proportions varying widely between vintages. Wines age in demi-muids.

Domaine Ellul-Ferrières

RN110 Fontmagne, 34160 Castries	*+33 6 15 38 45 01*
contact@chateau-ellul.com	*Sylvie Ellul*
www.chateau-ellul.com	*Grès de Montpellier [map p. 41]*
	5 ha

Sylvie (who is an oenologue) and Gilles Ellul created the domain 1997. There are several cuvées from Grès de Montpellier. Les Romarins is 70% Grenache and 30% Syrah, with long aging in cuve. Grande Cuvée is also mostly Syrah with a minority of Grenache, and ages in barrique. Carnavalo is 95% Grenache from 50-year old vines, supplemented by a little Syrah, aged partly in cuve and partly in 500-liter barrels for 36 months. Gourmandise is an unusual cuvée, a sweet wine from Grenache harvested very late (in November), with some botrytis, and medium-sweet with 70 g/l residual sugar.

Domaine De La Font Des Ormes

Route De Nizas, 34720 Caux	*+33 4 67 11 09 48*
contact@fontdesormes.fr	*Guy Cazalis de Fondouce*
www.fontdesormes.fr	*Languedoc-Pézenas [map p. 54]*
	23 ha; 20,000 btl

Guy Cazalis de Fondouce changed career from psychiatrist on Reunion Island to winemaking after he bought the property in 2002. (He comes originally from the Languedoc.) He renovated the eighteenth century stone buildings, and after a meeting with Claude Bourguignon in 2004, decided to start making wine. Vineyards are mostly on basalt terroir (the remnants of an extinct volcano in the vicinity), although the winery itself stands on a calcareous hill. There are old plantings of Carignan and Terret Bourret (an indigenous white variety), and Guy expanded the vineyards by planting the GSM trio. There's also production of olive oil from trees on the estate. The white IGP Pays de Caux comes from 60-year-old vines of Terret Bourret. The red IGP is a blend of Merlot, Syrah, and Marselan, aged in concrete. Under Pézenas AOP, Terres Mélées is 50% Syrah, 40%

Grenache, and 10% Carignan, while Basalte is 50% Grenache with 30% each of Syrah and Carignan; they age in demi-muids.

Mas Haut-Buis

52 Grand Rue, 34520 La Vacquerie-et-Saint-Martin-de-Castries	*+33 6 13 16 35 47*
mashautbuis@hotmail.fr	*Olivier Jeantet*
mashautbuis.com	*Terrasses du Larzac [map p. 55]*
	14 ha; 50,000 btl

Olivier Jeantet founded the estate in 1999. The cellar is in the village of La Vacquerie, but vineyards are on the other side of the valley (five miles away, across the autoroute near Lauroux), and at up to 650m altitude, are cool for Languedoc. There are 12 parcels, based on Grenache, Carignan, and Syrah for reds, and Roussanne and Chardonnay for whites. Grenache and Carignan are up to 80-years old; Syrah is 40-years old. A self-taught winemaker, Olivier favors lighter extraction and aging in barrels. He introduced tronconique concrete vats to get lighter extraction, and has moved away from barrels towards demi-muids and foudres. 1ha30 Clos is IGP Hérault from a recent planting of Merlot, aged in concrete. Other red cuvées are Terrasses de Larzac AOP. Carlines is an entry-level cuvée from Grenache, Carignan, and Syrah, aged in concrete. Costa Caoude is old vines Grenache and Carignan, aged since 2010 in foudres from Stockinger in Austria (previously it was aged in concrete). The white, Les Agrunelles, is a blend of Roussanne and Chardonnay, now aged in foudre (previously in demi-muids), labeled as IGP Hérault. Plume Coq is a collaborative venture with others to produce light rosé and red from a newly planted parcel.

Domaine Henry

6 Avenue d'Occitanie, 34680 Saint Georges d'Orques	*+33 4 67 45 57 74*
contact@domainehenry.fr	*François Henry*
www.domainehenry.fr	*Languedoc Saint Georges d'Orques [map p. 54]*
	11 ha; 30,000 btl

The Henry family been in wine for several generations. The family estate was at Domaine St. Martin de la Garrigue (between Beziers and Montpellier) but François and Laurence Henry established a new estate at St. Georges d'Orques (immediately west of Montpellier) in 1992. They divide their wines into four groups: Vins de Copains are entry-level red and white ("simple but authentic"). The Terroir group includes St. Georges D'Orques (GSM plus old Cinsault), Les Paradines (a second wine from younger vines), and a rosé. and white. The top wines, Sélection Terroir, come from specific plots: Les Chailles is a GSM from calcareous terroir; and Villafranchien is very old Grenache with some Cinsault from sedimentary terroir. All age in cuve. The final group has a sweet red wine, Passerillé, and the most unusual, Le Maihol, which is an attempt to recreate the style of St. Georges d'Orques before phylloxera, based on the ancient varieties l'Oeillade and l'Aspiran.

Domaine l'Hermas

Lieu dit Mas de Ratte, 34150 Gignac	*+33 6 64 89 20 29*
mt@lhermas.com	*Matthieu Torquebiau*
www.lhermas.com	*Terrasses du Larzac [map p. 55]*
	10 ha; 20,000 btl

"Oenologue by training, but above all not a 'winemaker'," is how Matthieu Torquebiau describes himself. His idiosyncratic approach is indicated by the fact that he produces only two cuvées, one red and one white, from the domain that he created in 2004. He inherited some parcels on the plain at Gignac, "but I wanted garrigues, facing north, with some altitude," he says. He bought parcels in the surrounding area, cleared the land, and planted vines. His first vintage was not until 2009. The red comes from a calcareous plateau at 250m elevation. It is 55% Syrah, 40% Mourvèdre, and 5% Grenache, and ages for 24 months in 700-liter barrels. The white is 70% Vermentino, 20% Roussanne, and 10% Chenin Blanc, coming from clay soil with grès (compacted sand). It also ages in 700-liter barrels, for 12 months.

Domaine de Malavieille-Mas de Bertrand

Hameau de Malavieille, 34800 Mérifons	*+33 6 72 11 72 19*
domainemalavieille.merifons@wanadoo.fr	*Benoit Bertrand*
www.domainemalavieille.com	*Terrasses du Larzac [map p. 55]*
	65 ha; 150,000 btl

The double name indicates that there are two estates in the Hérault. Malavieille is located on the basalt terroir typical of the Terrasses de Larzac. Mas de Bertrand is at Saint Saturnin de Lucian, farther east towards Montpeyroux, with sandstone and marl. The domains are roughly equal in size. Malavieille is a bit off the beaten track, just southwest of Lac du Salagou. It's been in the Bertrand family for six generations. Vineyards are planted with 17 grape varieties. The mainstay of the reds is Permien, a GSM from Terrasses du Larzac. Alliance is also GSM, but produced in smaller amounts. Louise is a Carignan made by carbonic maceration, and is a Vin de France. Charmille is an IGP from Merlot, Cabernet Franc, Syrah, and Portan. Whites have traditional varieties in AOP and move into international varieties for IGP and Vin de France.

Mas Combarèla

1833 Route de Montpeyroux, 34150 Saint-Jean-de-Fos	*+33 6 19 42 07 00*
contact@mas-combarela.com	*Olivier Faucon*
www.mas-combarela.com	*IGP Pays d'Hérault [map p. 55]*
	12 ha; 40,000 btl

After a career in marketing, Olivier Faucon decided to become a winemaker. He qualified in oenology in Beaune, worked at A. F. Gros in Pommard, then at Mas Cal Demoura in the Languedoc, and purchased vineyards in the Terrasses du Larzac, founding the domain in 2016. Des Si Et Des Mi is an entry-level range in all three colors. Under IGP St.-Guilhem-le-Dèsert there are varietal Cinsault and Carignan, and also the white blend of Carignan Blanc and Chenin Blanc. Terrasses du Larzac offers Ode Aux Ignorants, a blend of 50% Syrah with Carignan and Grenache, and Lueurs d'Espar (introduced in 2021 as a blend of 70% Mourvèdre with Carignan and Syrah and small amounts of Grenache and Cinsault, aged for 30 months in new 500-liter barrels).

Mas Conscience

Route de Montpeyroux, 34150 Saint Jean de Fos	*+33 6 76 78 56 14*
hello@mas-conscience.com	*Audrey Bonnet-Koenig*
mas-conscience.com	*IGP Pays d'Hérault* *[map p. 55]*
	15 ha; 50,000 btl

The name of the domain refers to a legend that monks used to travel between villages, asking villagers to donate what their conscience allowed. They received wine and olive oil in clay pots, which became known as the 'conscience.' Éric Ajorque had worked in furniture in France, met his wife Nathalie in India, and returned to France to buy the domain in 2013. Roman Kocholl and Birger Veit, formerly entrepreneurs in Germany, came to France to make wine, and bought Mas Conscience, where they work with consulting oenologist Claude Gros and winemaker Audrey Bonnet-Koenig, formerly of La Pèira (see profile). Cuvées are now a mix of those developed by the Ajorque's, and new cuvées introduced by Audrey Bonnet-Koenig. Terrasses de Larzac reds are blends of Syrah, Grenache and Cinsault (L'Eveil) and Mourvèdre, Syrah, and Grenache (Mahatma), aged for 24 months in tronconique wood vats. Varietal wines are IGP Saint Guilhem le Désert, 100% Cinsault (Cieux) or Carignan (Le Cas). Whites are Languedoc (L'In is Roussanne, Grenache Blanc, and Viognier aged for 6 months in barriques), IGP (Tapade is Vermentino and Grenache Blanc, aged in vat), and Vin de France (Pure is Petit Manseng, aged in vat).

Mas Gabriel

9 avenue de Mougères, 34720 Caux	*+33 7 88 22 94 40*
info@mas-gabriel.com	*Deborah & Peter Core*
www.mas-gabriel.co.uk	*Languedoc-Pézenas* *[map p. 54]*
	7 ha

Deborah and Peter Core were in business in London when they decided to change careers in 2002. After working in New Zealand and Bordeaux, they bought a small vineyard near Pézenas in 2006. The estate has 4.7 ha of volcanic basalt and gravel at Caux, and 1.4 ha in St-Jean de Bébian with galets roulants (rounded pebbles). They've expanded the estate with new plantings by crowdfunding, effectively selling the wine ahead. The AOP Languedoc white, Champ des Bleuets, is 80% Vermentino with 10% each of Grenache Blanc and Grenache Gris, from Caux, made by whole-cluster pressing, aged 70% in cuve and 30% in barrels of acacia. The rosé, Les Fleurs Sauvages, comes from Carignan at St. Jean de Bébian. The red Languedoc-Pézenas, Clos des Lièvres, comes from basalt terroir at Caux, has 75% Syrah and 25% Grenache, and ages in 500-liter barrels with 15% new oak. Les Trois Terrasses has 75% Carignan from 50-65-year-old vines, with Grenache and Syrah, aged in concrete. Because of the proportion of Carignan, it has to be classified as IGP d'Hérault instead of AOP Languedoc.

Domaine Mylène Bru

Lieu-dit La Fon de Lacan, 34230 Saint-Pargoire	*+33 6 83 08 97 30*
mb@domainemylenebru.fr	*Mylène Bru*
www.domainemylenebru.fr	*Grès de Montpellier [map p. 54]*
	7 ha

Mylène Bru, who comes from Corbières, started by buying 4 ha of vines in an isolated spot in 2008. She had to install water and electricity before she could make wine. Now she has 15 parcels, surrounded by garrigue, ten miles north of Sète. Winemaking tends towards 'natural,' with no fining or filtration, and minimal use of sulfur. A sense of the style is given by Mylène's description of her wines as 'Vins de Garrigue' (scrubland). There is a very large range for such a small domain. Most of the wines are Vin de France and include some unusual varietals. Lady Chasselas is 100% varietal (distinctly unusual for the area), Zingara is Marsanne from a small plot surrounded by wild fennel, and Serve the Servant comes from an almost extinct variety (Servant). In reds, Franquette is 100% Syrah, Rita is 100% Carignan, Senzo is 100% Pinot Noir, and Karm is 100% Tempranillo. More conventionally, blends include Cartouche (80% Grenache and 20% Cinsault), and Soleil de Nuit, from a single parcel of 70% Carignan and 30% Cinsault. Zulu is 90% Grenache with 10% Hamburg Muscat, and Night Moves is a Blanc de Noir from a similar blend. In AOP Languedoc, Far-Ouest is the original cuvée of the estate, a blend of all black varieties, and Les Moulins de Mon Coeur has equal Syrah, Carignan, and Cinsault. Wines age in vat.

Clos des Nines

Route de Cournonsec - D5E7, 34690 Fabrègues	*+33 4 67 68 95 36*
isabelle@closdesnines.com	*Isabelle Mangeart*
www.closdesnines.com	*Grès de Montpellier [map p. 54]*
	10 ha

The domain has an unlikely location, in the area of scrub between Montpelier and the inland lake at Sète. Isabelle Mangeart, who comes from the Champagne region, bought the property in 2002 with her husband Christian Marbler as a change of career from marketing. The name of the domain refers to their three daughters, Nines in Occitan dialect. Vineyards are in a single block on clay-limestone slopes, with just enough elevation to see over to Sète; plantings range from 80-year old Carignan and Alicante to Mourvèdre that was planted in 2008. The domain produces two ranges of wines and olive oil. The entry-level is called PULP and is IGP in all three colors. From the appellation, Obladie is a white blend of Grenache Blanc, Roussanne, Vermentino, and Viognier from a hectare that Isabelle planted. In reds, l'Orée is Grenache supplemented by Syrah and Cinsault, while O du Clos is 80% Syrah and ages in barriques. There are two olive oils from different varieties of olive, Lucques and Picholine.

Domaine de Nizas

Hameau de Sallèles, 34720 Caux	*+33 4 67 90 17 92*
contact@domaine-de-nizas.com	*François Lurton*
www.domaine-de-nizas.com	*Languedoc-Pézenas [map p. 54]*
	40 ha

John Goelet and Bernard Portet were involved in creating Clos du Val in Napa Valley in the 1970s, followed by Taltani Vineyards in Victoria, Australia, and Clover Hill in Tasmania. They established Clos de Nizas near Pézenas in 1998, but leased it in 2018 to François Lurton, who owns vineyards in Languedoc (including Mas Janeil: see profile) and elsewhere in France, as well as Spain, Chile, and Argentina. The vineyards at Nizas have soils varying from basalt, to calcareous clay, to Villafranchien (a mix of galets roulants [rounded pebbles] and red clay. The entry-level range is called Mazet de Sallèles, and is blended from all three terroirs. Les Clos red and rosé come from basaltic terroir, predominantly Syrah with some Grenache and Mourvèdre, aged in cuve. The top wines are the red Languedoc-Pézenas, with Syrah from basaltic terroir, and Grenache and Carignan from calcareous terroir, and the AOP Languedoc Blanc, from Viognier and Vermentino aged in stainless steel, and Roussanne aged in new barriques.

Domaine du Pas de l'Escalette

Le Champ-de-Peyrottes, 34700 Poujols	*+33 4 67 96 13 42*
contact@pasdelescalette.com	*Delphine Rousseau*
www.pasdelescalette.com	*Terrasses du Larzac [map p. 55]*
	20 ha; 80,000 btl

Julien Zernott and Delphine Rousseau worked for several years at Henry Pellé in the Loire before buying 8 ha in the Terrasses du Larzac in 2002, off the beaten track just outside the village of Poujols. They built a new cellar in 2009. The objective is to go for finesse, and the vineyards face east or west at elevations of 350-400m, planted on calcareous terroir at the base of the plateau of Larzac, in about 50 separate terraces with the dry stone walls known locally as clapas. The size of the vineyards has more or less doubled since the start. Vines average 45-years old. Plantings are exclusively local varieties. The cuvée Clapas Blanc is 40% each of Grenache Blanc and Carignan Blanc, with10% each of Grenache Gris and Terret Bourret. Clapas Rouge is 50% Syrah with 30% Carignan and 20% Grenache. Le Grand Pas is dominated by 70% Grenache, with 20% Cinsault and 10% Carignan. There are also some parcel selections: Mas Rousseau is Carignan Blanc, Ze Cinsault is an old vines monovarietal, and Les Frieys stands out in blended wines.

Domaine Pech Rome

17 rue Montée des Remparts, 34320 Neffiès	*+33 6 08 89 58 11*
contact@domainepechrome.com	*Mary & Pascal Blondel*
www.domainepechrome.com	*Languedoc-Pézenas [map p. 54]*
	12 ha; 30,000 btl

Pascal and Mary Blondel were not winemakers, but came from outside when they created the domain in 2001. Most of the vineyards are in the AOP of Pézenas, with 1.5 ha in IGP. 10 ha are black varieties. Syrah is planted on the stoniest soils, Mourvèdre on volcanic, and Grenache on clay-limestone. Under AOP Languedoc, there is one red and one white, both blends from several varieties, aged in cuve. From Pézenas there are two reds: Clemens is more than half Grenache, with Mourvèdre, Carignan, and Syrah, aged in cuve; Opulens is a GSM with two thirds Syrah, aged partly in barrique and partly in cuve. Under IGP there is the unusual varietal of Tempranillo.

La Pèira

Route de Sainte-Brigitte, 34750 Hameau de Sainte-Brigitte	*+33 6 12 27 94 13*
contact@la-peira.com	*Karine Ahton*
www.la-peira.com	*Terrasses du Larzac [map p. 55]*
	15 ha; 35,000 btl

Rob Dougan, an Australian musician who lives in London, purchased La Pèira together with his French wife, Karine Ahton, in 2004. The vineyards are planted on limestone terraces. Consulting oenologist Claude Gros, well known in the region. has been involved from the start, and Audrey Bonnet-Koenig came as winemaker in 2015. Les Obriers de la Pèira is the entry-level wine, a blend of Cinsault and Carignan, the second wine La Flors de la Pèira is GSM with a little Cinsault, and the flagship La Pèira is Grenache and Syrah. Deusyls was the sole white at first, a blend of Viognier and Roussanne; since 2013 there has also been La Pèira Blanc, a broader blend based on selection of the best lots, intended to be a white counterpart to the red La Pèira. The reds are AOP Terrasses du Larzac and the whites are IGP Hérault. Syrah and Mourvèdre are aged in barrels of 500 l or 600 l, with only a little new oak, while Carignan and Cinsault are aged in large casks or vats. Yields are low, so quantities are small, and the wines have attracted something of a cult following in the Anglo-Saxon world.

Château de Perdiguier

34370 Maraussan	*+33 4 67 90 37 44*
info@domaineperdiguier.fr	*Pauline Feracci*
www.domaineperdiguier.com	*IGP Pays d'Hérault [map p. 83]*
	26 ha; 20,000 btl

Thirty hectares of vineyards (including 8 ha of Cabernet Sauvignon and 6 ha of Merlot) partly surround the eighteenth century château, although the property also contains 200 ha of cereals; indeed, some of the vineyards immediately behind the château were replaced by cereal because the land proved too sandy for vines. Production started out with a monovarietal Merlot, but then the Ferracis, who have owned the property for three generations, decided that a blend made better wine. The Cabernet-Merlot blends have a distinct resemblance to Bordeaux. Indeed, in Bordeaux-like fashion, Cabernet Sauvignon is planted on the plain near the Orb river where soil is very pebbly, and Merlot is planted on soils with more clay. The entry-level wine is an equal blend of Cabernet Sauvignon and Merlot, which spends 18 months in old oak; the higher level cuvée, the Cuvée d'en Auger, is 85% Cabernet to 15% Merlot, and spends 12 months in new oak. All the wines are IGP des Coteaux d'Enserune.

Romain Portier

7, route de Jonquières, 34725 Saint Saturnin-de-Lucian	*+33 6 20 65 21 75*
romainportier@free.fr	*Romain Portier*
5 ha; 10,000 btl	*Terrasses du Larzac [map p. 55]*

Romain Portier produced his first vintage in 2012 from a small parcel of old Mourvèdre, less than a hectare of vines that had been abandoned, while he was working at a wine shop in Montpellier. The original parcel is at Saint-Jean-de-Fos (on red and yellow calcareous clay), another small parcel was added at Montpeyroux, and his main holding now is 4 ha in Jonquières (calcareous and rocky). He has worked full time at the domain since 2019. Referring to the small size of the domain (it's one of the smallest in the area), his cuvées are labeled as La Petite Parcelle. The white is a blend of Marsanne and 30-year-old Grenache Blanc; the red cuvées are varietal Cinsault and Grenache. These age in concrete or stainless steel for 9 months. A Mourvèdre from an 0.7 ha plot ages in for 18 months in a mix of stainless steel and 5-10-year demi-muids. These are all Vin de France. The AOP Terrasses du Larzac is a blend of GSM plus Cinsault, aged in concrete and 1-2-year demi-muids.

Domaine de la Prose

Route de Saint-Georges-d'Orques, 34570 Pignan	*+33 4 67 03 08 30*
domainedelaprose@wanadoo.fr	*Bertrand De Mortillet*
28 ha	*Languedoc Saint Georges d'Orques [map p. 54]*

Alexandre and Patricia De Mortillet founded Domaine de la Prose in 1989 with their son Bernard, who qualified in oenology in Bordeaux. They built a gravity-flow cellar and the first vintage was 1995. The domain is located on a hill in an isolated spot a few miles west of Montpellier, at 100m altitude facing south towards the sea. Vineyards include 17 ha in the small AOP of Languedoc Saint Georges d'Orques (which only has about ten growers). There are also plots in Grès de Montpellier. One unusual feature is a concentration on Vermentino in whites, as Alexandre believed soils and climate were similar to Patrimonio in Corsica. Languedoc Cadières is 100% Vermentino, aged in vat. Embruns is 40% each of Roussanne and Grenache Blanc with 20% Vermentino, fermented and aged in barrique. Cadières red is St. Georges d'Orques, 70% Grenache with Cinsault, Mourvèdre, and Syrah, aged in vat. Embruns red is Grès de Montpellier, 70% Syrah, 20% Grenache, and 10% Cinsault, aged mostly in vat but with 10% in barrique.

Mas des Quernes

1 bis, impasse du Pressoir, 34150 Montpeyroux	*+33 3 36 61 08 22*
pierre@mas-des-quernes.com	*Pierre Natoli*
mas-des-quernes.com	*Languedoc-Montpeyroux [map p. 55]*
	16 ha; 175,000 btl

The domain is a collaboration between oenologue Jean Natoli, who advises many domains in the Languedoc, and German negociant Peter Riegel. They started in 2009 by purchasing a 12 ha block of vines, olive trees, and garrigue. It has grown a bit, and there is also a negociant activity, Gens et Pierres. Jean's son Pierre joined the domain in 2012. The AOP Languedoc red, Les Petit Travers, is the flagship, with a typical blend of Cinsault, Syrah, Grenache and Mourvèdre. Other traditional cuvées include Les Ruches, a blend of Grenache, Carignan, and Mourvèdre, under Terrasses de Larzac, and Le Blaireau, an IGP Hérault from 50-year old Carignan, made with carbonic maceration. Mourvèdre Armand is 90% varietal under IGP St Guilhem de Désert. Villa Romaine is a single-vineyard wine, 40% each of Carignan and Mourvèdre and 20% Grenache, from Terrasses du Larzac.

Domaine de Ravanès

Lieu-dit Aspiran, 34490 Thézan lès Béziers	*+33 4 67 36 00 02*
ravanes@wanadoo.fr	*Marc Benin*
www.ravanes.com	*Coteaux de Murveil [map p. 83]*
	34 ha; 80,000 btl

Marc Bernin's father started the domain and didn't believe in following conventional wisdom. He planted Merlot in 1970-1972, followed by Cabernet Sauvignon, and subsequently Petit Verdot. Some subterfuge was needed to establish the Bordeaux varieties. "When the first Merlot was planted here it was actually forbidden. This is just protectionism by the Bordelais," says Marc, who studied at Montpellier and Beaune and has a Ph. D. in oenology. "Why plant Cabernet Sauvignon? It's a vin de passion. So we dared. The terroir is very close to the Médoc, it's well-drained gravel coming off the Orb river, which is 800m or so away." All the wines are IGP Coteaux de Murveil. Originally there was a 100% Merlot and a 100% Cabernet Sauvignon. Today the main wine is a 50:50 blend. "Cabernet Sauvignon is not regular and does not give top results every year, but the Merlot is more regular. The blend has more complexity than a monocepage." The entry-level wines use no oak, but the Grand Reserve wines age in 1-3-year oak. Cuvée Diogene is made in lighter years and is a blend of 60% Petit Verdot, 30% Merlot, and 10% Cabernet Sauvignon. There is also a 100% Petit Verdot. Higher up the scale is the 50:50 Merlot/Petit Verdot of Les Gravières de Taurau.

Château Saint Jean d'Aumières

Gignac, 34150 Languedoc Roussillon	*+33 4 67 57 23 49*
severine.b@josephcastan.com	*Vianney Castan*
saintjeandaumieres.com	*Terrasses du Larzac [map p. 55]*
	35 ha; 200,000 btl

Just to the west of Montpellier, this domain has had a chequered history, with changes of ownership in recent years, until it was purchased by negociant Joseph Castan in 2013. A new winemaking team has been engaged, and it's a work in progress. The present range includes varietal wines under IGP Pays d'Oc, with Les Collines (Merlot), Les Marnes (Cabernet Sauvignon), L'Autodictate (Viognier). Under AOP Languedoc there are blends from local varieties. The top wines is L'Alchemiste from the Terrasses du Larzac, which has Syrah and Grenache fermented conventionally, and Carignan by carbonic maceration, with the assemblage aged in barriques.

Château Saint Martin de la Garrigue

34530 Montagnac	*+33 9 71 05 68 67*
contact@stmartingarrigue.com	*Jean-Luc Parret*
www.stmartingarrigue.com	*Grès de Montpellier [map p. 54]*
	65 ha; 300,000 btl

The estate has a very long history. There are signs people were living here in Iron Age, the Romans may have built a villa and planted vineyards, it was given to the Church by the Kings of France in the Middle Ages, there is a ninth-century chapel, and the eighteenth century château (which now offers accommodation) was constructed in

Renaissance style. Near Pézenas, overlooking the Hérault river, vineyards are surrounded by 110 ha of century-old pine trees and garrigue. Jean-Claude Zabalia made the wine for twenty years, and established the reputation of the property before he left to start his own domain (Château des Deux Rocs in Cabrières). Jean-Luc Paret took over in 2011, with Gilles Habit as winemaker. Seventeen different grape varieties are planted on the soils of red sandstone and brown limestone. The domain is known for producing a rich style of Picpoul de Pinet (there is also a sparkling wine). Languedoc cuvées are divided into the Bronzinelle red (the largest production cuvée) and white (blends of several varieties each) and Tradition (56% Carignan fermented by carbonic maceration with 30% Syrah and 14% Grenache for the red). The Grès de Montpellier is 30% Syrah, 50% Mourvèdre, and 20% Grenache, aged in foudre.

Domaine Saint Sylvestre

Rue de la Grotte, 34150 Puéchabon	*+33 9 60 50 30 15*
contact@domaine-saint-sylvestre.com	*Sophie & Victor Guizard*
www.domaine-saint-sylvestre.com	*Terrasses du Larzac [map p. 55]*
	8 ha; 15,000 btl

Victor Guisard was a partner in Domaine de Montcalmès (see profile) but left in 2010 to start his own domain with his share of the vineyards. Vincent and his wife Sophie then built a small winery on the edge of the village. They have four separate vineyards in the hills above Puéchabon. Plantings are the traditional varieties for the AOP: GSM for the red Terrasses du Larzac, and Marsanne, Roussanne, and Viognier for the white AOP Languedoc. There's also a monovarietal Carignan, Les Vignes des Garrigues, which is IGP Pays d'Oc. The wines are aged in old barriques. The motto of the domain is Finesse et Elégance.

Domaine Saumarez

Chemin de Cathala, 34570 Murviel-lès-Montpellier	*+33 6 24 41 56 20*
desaumarez@yahoo.fr	*Liz & Robin Williamson*
www.domainedesaumarez.com	*Grès de Montpellier [map p. 54]*
	13 ha

Liz and Robin Williamson came from working in finance in Britain to found the domain in 2004. Vineyards are a few miles west of Montpellier, dispersed around three villages, at altitudes of 80-150m, on iron-rich calcareous terroir that is typical for the Languedoc. Reds come from the GSM trio, all aged in concrete vats. Trinitas has a third of each variety, S' Rouge is 60% Grenache and 40% Syrah, and Aalenien (this is the name of the terroir) is 90% Syrah and 10% Grenache. The rosé is 70% Grenache and 30% Syrah, and the S' Blanc is 50% Grenache, 40% Marsanne, and 10% Roussanne.

Château la Sauvageonne

34700 Saint Jean de La Blaquière	*+33 4 67 44 71 74*
la-sauvageonne@wanadoo.fr	*Cédric Lecareux*
www.gerard-bertrand.com/en/domains/chateaux-la-sauvageonne	*Terrasses du Larzac [map p. 55]*
	57 ha

Gérard Bertrand is one of the largest producers in south, with a concentration of properties around his flagship Château l'Hospitalet (see profile) at La Clape near Narbonne, and he added Château la Sauvageonne to the portfolio in 2011. Vineyards here are at 150-300m altitude with volcanic terroir of red ruffes (iron-rich rocks) and sandstone. The red Grand Vin comes from Grenache planted on schist together with Syrah, Mourvèdre and Carignan planted on ruffes. Pica Broca is a blend of Grenache and Syrah. The white Grand Vin is a blend of Grenache Blanc, Vermentino, and Viognier, from schist. The domain is well known for its rosés. Volcanic Rosé is a blend of Grenache, Cinsault, and Syrah. La Villa is an unusual blend of two thirds Grenache together with cofermented Vermentino, Viognier, and Mourvèdre; part spends six months aging in old oak barriques.

Le Mas de la Séranne

Route de Puechabon, 34150 Aniane	*+33 4 67 57 37 99*
mas.seranne@wanadoo.fr	*Jean-Pierre Venture*
mas-seranne.com	*Terrasses du Larzac [map p. 55]*
	16 ha; 65,000 btl

Jean-Pierre and Isabelle Venture come from the Languedoc, but had been away for twenty years when they changed careers from the food industry and returned to create the domain in 1998. They started by purchasing 5 ha at Aniane, and then expanding the estate. (The name refers to the hills on the slopes facing the village.) Vineyards cover three types of terroir, yellow sandy-clay, round pebbles on red clay, and calcareous pebbles on red clay. Most plantings are the usual; black and white varieties of the region, but 2 ha are planted with some old varieties and some Greek and Italian varieties. The range includes three cuvées in Terrasses de Larzac, three on Languedoc, and IGP. The Terrasses de Larzac are all blends based on the GSM trio plus Carignan and Morrastel (the Spanish Graciano) and age in 1-3-year barriques for just over a year. Two red Languedoc cuvées are based on Grenache, Syrah, and Cinsault, and age in cuve. There are also white Languedoc and rosé IGP.

Domaine La Terrasse d'Élise

1320, Chemin de Capion, 34150 Aniane	*+33 6 22 91 81 39*
terrassedelise@gmail.com	*Xavier Braujou*
14 ha; 40,000 btl	*IGP Pays d'Hérault [map p. 55]*

Xavier Braujou comes from a family of vignerons, but start off in forestry, until after working at Daumas Gassac and elsewhere, he decided to make wine. He bought his first vineyards at St.-Jean-de-Fos, later expanding to plots at the next village, Aniane. He focuses on blending single varieties from different locations, so the wines do not fit the requirements of the AOP and are labeled as IGP Pays d'Hérault. Many of the vines are old, and yields are correspondingly low, around 20 hl/ha. There are monovarietal cuvées from Syrah (XB), Cinsault (Les Hauts de Carol's and Le Pradel), Carignan (Le Pigeonnier), and Mourvèdre (L'Enclos). The exception is the Elise blend, 70% Syrah and 30% Mourvèdre, under Languedoc AOP. There is a white blend, Siclène, from 40% Roussanne, 40% Marsanne, and 20% Chardonnay.

Domaine Terre Inconnue

62 rue Albizzias, 34400 Saint Sériès	*+33 4 90 99 08 11*
	Robert Creus
4 ha; 8,000 btl	*Grès de Montpellier [map p. 41]*

Robert Creus is a research chemist (currently working for the Chamber of Commerce) with a passion, who started in 1996 to buy small vineyards of very old vines. All of his wines are Vin de France as AOP regulations are somewhat of an irrelevance from this perspective. He has 2.2 ha of Carignan, 0.9 ha of Grenache, 0.7 he of Syrah, and 0.2 ha of Tempranillo. Yields naturally a very low, from 10-25 hl/ha. Winemaking is natural: minimal sulfur and very little interference during aging in old barriques. Léonie was his first cuvée, very old Carignan coming from terroir of *galet roulants* at Lunel. Bruyère also comes from old Carignan, Abuelos comes from Grenache, and Sylvie is a mix of Syrah and the old cultivar of Syrah known as Sérine. Guilhem seems to be a blend of all the grapes that don't go into the individual varietal wines.

La Traversée

6 Rue des Deux Ponts, Hameau Les Salces, 34700 St. Privat	*+33 6 11 23 72 73*
info@latraversee.fr	*Gavin Crisfield*
www.latraversee.fr	*Terrasses du Larzac [map p. 55]*
	4 ha; 10,000 btl

Gavin Crisfield is an oenologist and sommelier who came from Ireland before settling in the Terrasses de Larzac and founding this domain in 2009. The four vineyard plots are on different terroirs of schist, stone, volcanic, and limestone. The Terrasses du Larzac is a blend of 50% Syrah, 30% Carignan, 15% Cinsault, and 5% Grenache, aged in concrete eggs. There is a 100% Cinsault in Vin de France.

Turner Pageot

3 Avenue de la Gare, 34320 Gabian	*+33 4 67 00 14 33*
contact@turnerpageot.com	*Emmanuel Pageot*
www.turnerpageot.com	*Languedoc-Pézenas [map p. 54]*
	9 ha; 35,000 btl

Australian Karen Turner has been the winemaker at Prieuré St. Jean de Bébian (see profile) for many years, and in 2008 started an additional project with her husband, former sommelier Emmanuel Pageot. Their vineyard is in the same area as Bébian, with two thirds black and one third white plantings. The reds are conventional blends: Le Rouge is Grenache and Syrah, and Carmina Major is Syrah and Mourvèdre. The particularity of the whites is the use of skin contact, ranging from just slight enough to add structure to full orange wines. Le Rupture is a Sauvignon Blanc where about 20% of the skins are included. Le Blanc is about half Roussanne with Marsanne and Picpoul, and has about two weeks skin contact to add richness. Les Choix is a Marsanne orange wine, made like a red wine in macerating and fermenting whole bunches. The funky labels give an idea of the style, which is subject to continued experimentation.

Domaine Vaïsse

271 Chemin Bas d'Aniane, 34150 Aniane	*+33 4 67 57 28 86*
domaine.vaisse@orange.fr	*Pierre Vaïsse*
16 ha	*Terrasses du Larzac [map p. 55]*

Pierre Vaïsse founded the domain in 2007 with 2 ha in Puéchabon inherited from his parents, helped by Frédéric Pourtalié at Domaine Montcalmès and Laurent Vaillé at Grange des Pères. The terroir is red clay and *galet roulants*. He's expanded the vineyards, but makes wine from only half, sending the rest of the grapes to the cooperative. Plantings are black varieties except for 1.5 ha of Viognier. He ages the wines for an unusually long time for the Languedoc, typically 24 months. The AOP La Galibaou de Russe (previously called Les Capitelles) is an equal blend of Mourvèdre and Syrah. The IGP cuvée Pur is Carignan. The IGP L'Aphyllante is a blend dominated by Mourvèdre, with Syrah and Grenache. The wines age in 1-year barriques.

Les Vignes Oubliées

3 rue de la Fontaine, 34700 Saint Jean de La Blaquière	*+33 6 72 77 38 88*
lesvignesoubliees@gmail.com	*Jean-Baptiste Granier*
www.lesvignesoubliees.com	*Terrasses du Larzac [map p. 55]*
	9 ha; 35,000 btl

This is a collaborative venture to rescue parcels of old wines with various owners at St. Privat at the Terrasses du Larzac, mostly at an altitude of 300-400m. Previously the grapes just went into the general blend at the cooperative. Jean-Baptiste Granier became interested in the old vines when he was working at Mas Jullien in 2007, and together with Olivier Jullien set out to find sources. The first vintage was 2009. The Terrasses du Larzac comes from Grenache, Syrah, and Carignan, the AOP Languedoc is based on Cinsault—"Cinsault is too often relegated to rosé"—with some Grenache, Syrah, and Carignan, and the white comes from Clairette, Roussanne, and Grenache Blanc.

Villa Symposia

Chemin Saint-Georges, 34800 Aspiran	*+33 5 57 40 07 31*
villa.symposia@orange.fr	*Éric Prissette*
www.villasymposia.com	*IGP Pays d'Hérault [map p. 54]*
	18 ha; 60,000 btl

Former soccer star Éric Prissette must have a good eye for terroir. In 1994 he founded Château Rol Valentin in Bordeaux, which became a successful boutique winery, and then in 2003 he founded Villa Symposia. (He sold Rol Valentin in 2009 but kept an interest in Bordeaux by buying Château Roc in Côtes de Castillon.) Plantings are almost all black varieties, but there is a hectare of white, used to make a Vin de France from 45% Terret Bourret, 40% Carignan Blanc, and 15% Grenache Blanc. It ages in a mix of stainless steel and demi-muids. The reds at the outset were aged in barriques, but oak-aging has mostly switched to foudres to get softer tannins. The vineyards are in AOP Pézenas, but the red cuvées are labeled AOP Languedoc as Éric feels that Pézenas is not widely recognized. Entry-level Amphora is half Syrah (using the youngest vines) and half Cinsault, and ages in stainless steel. Equilibre is 60% Syrah (aged in oak) with 20% each of Carignan and Grenache (aged in cuve). Origine is 95% Syrah from the oldest vines; the other 5% has been Mourvèdre, Grenache, or Carignan.

Villa Tempora

Ancien Chemin de Caux, 34120 Pézenas	*+33 6 61 29 39 63*
contact@villatempora.com	*Agathe Dalisson & Amaury Coste*
www.villatempora.com	*Languedoc-Pézenas [map p. 54]*
	8 ha; 25,000 btl

Agathe Dalisson comes from Bordeaux and Amaury Coste from Burgundy, but they met in Kabul. They bought Villa Tempora in 2017 from Serge Schwartz and Jean-Pierre Sanson, who had founded it ten years earlier. For a small domain, there's a sizeable range, with 2 whites and a rosé in AOP Languedoc, and four reds in Languedoc-Pézenas. Production was much reduced in 2019 by the dry conditions of the year. In whites, Un Temps Pour I is Clairette, aged in cuve, and Un Temps Pour Elle is mostly Bourboulenc, aged in 400-liter barrels. The rosé comes from saignée of 80% Syrah and 20% Grenache. Les Copains D'Abord is the entry-level red (AOP Languedoc). In Languedoc-Pézenas, Villa Tempora is 40% Carignan, 30% Syrah, and 30% Grenache, aged 85% in cuve and 15% in barrique, Le Démon du Midi is 70% Syrah and 15% each of Grenache and Carignan, aged 30% in cuve and 70% in barriques, and L'Ange Vin is mostly Grenache, aged in 2-year-old barriques.

Verena Wyss

Chemin du Pétrole, 34320 Gabian	*+33 4 67 24 77 63*
contact@domaineverenawyss.com	*Patrick Goma*
domaineverenawyss.com	*Languedoc-Pézenas [map p. 54]*
	14 ha; 40,000 btl

Verena Wyss and her husband, both formerly architects in Switzerland, bought the domain in 1999. Today there are 38 ha of grounds with 14 ha of vineyards in production, all reconstructed since the original purchase, and a new winery. Planted varieties include Viognier and Roussanne in the whites, Cabernet Sauvignon, Merlot, Petit Verdot, and Lledonner-Pelut in the blacks. The vineyards surround the winery, enabling them to be maintained and harvested without much extra help. Terroirs are limestone but rather heterogeneous. Merlot is planted on the areas richer in clay; Cabernet Sauvignon and Petit Verdot are essentially planted on the same south-facing slope, more or less according to the proportions needed for the wine. By contrast with Bordeaux, the Petit Verdot matures reliably, giving nice small berries. The microclimate in these vineyards is a bit advanced relative to Gabian (the local town). Half of production is white and half red. Verena retired in 2018, and Patrick Goma, who has worked at the domain for more than 20 years, runs it under a lease.

Beziers-Narbonne

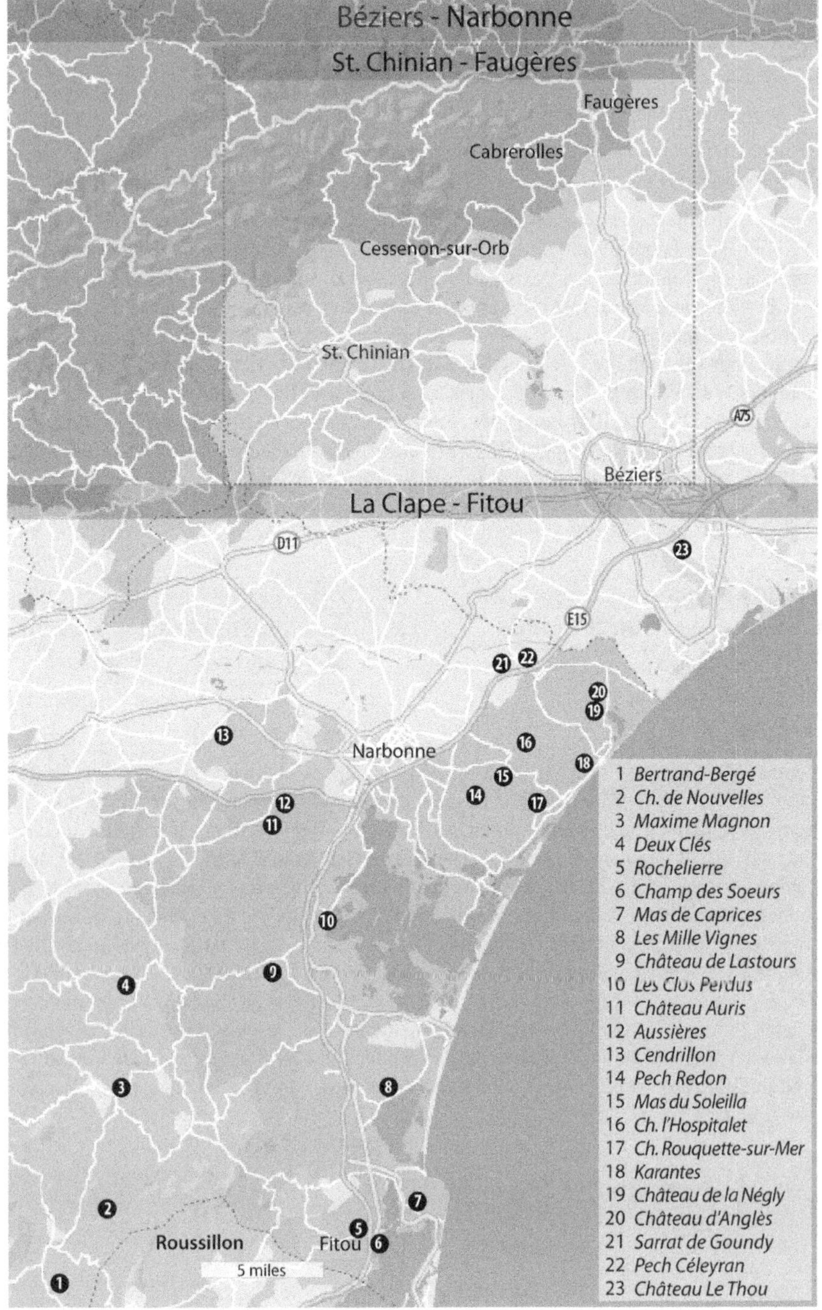

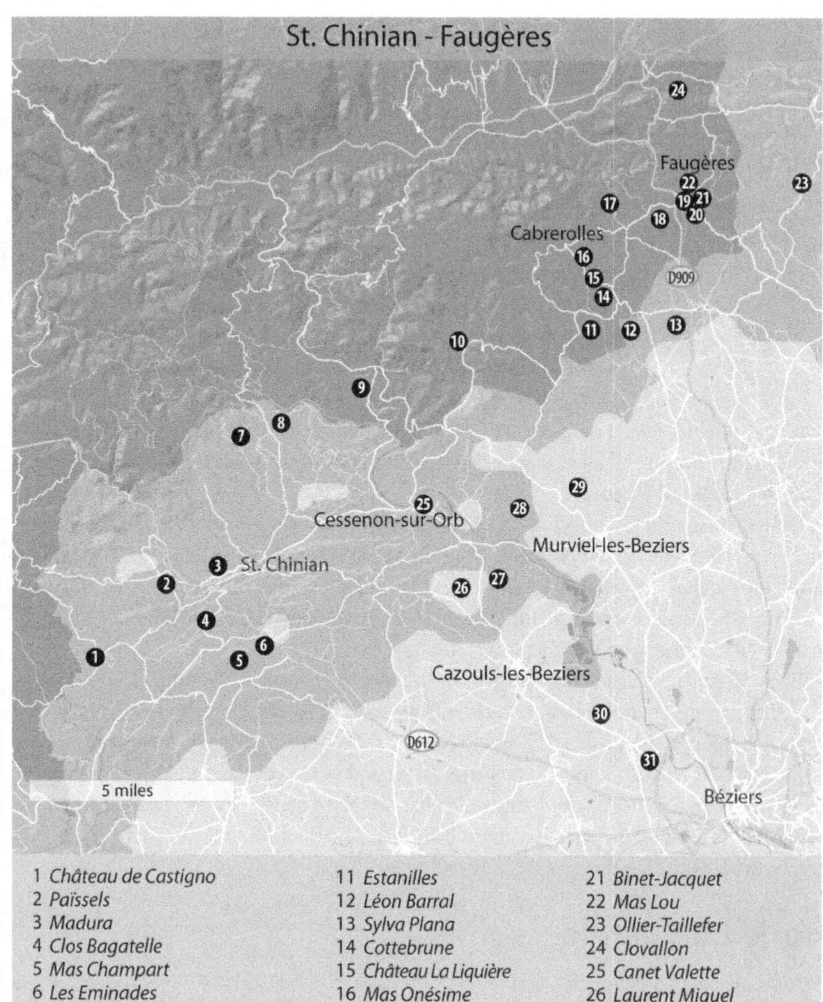

1 *Château de Castigno*	11 *Estanilles*	21 *Binet-Jacquet*
2 *Païssels*	12 *Léon Barral*	22 *Mas Lou*
3 *Madura*	13 *Sylva Plana*	23 *Ollier-Taillefer*
4 *Clos Bagatelle*	14 *Cottebrune*	24 *Clovallon*
5 *Mas Champart*	15 *Château La Liquière*	25 *Canet Valette*
6 *Les Eminades*	16 *Mas Onésime*	26 *Laurent Miquel*
7 *Grange Léon*	17 *Graine Sauvage*	27 *Borie La Vitarèle*
8 *Rimbert*	18 *Cebène*	28 *Mas de la Gabinele*
9 *Thierry Navarre*	19 *Bardi d'Alquier*	29 *Terre des Dames*
10 *La Lauzeta*	20 *Mas d'Alezon*	30 *Ravanès*
		31 *Ch. Perdiguier*

Domaine Léon Barral *

Hameau de Lenthéric, 34480 Cabrerolles	*+33 4 67 90 29 13*
didier.barral@club-internet.fr	*Didier Barral*
www.domaineleonbarral.com	*Faugères [map p. 83]*
33 ha; 90,000 btl	*Faugères*

This committed biodynamic domain is well known for its natural wines, and when I arrived, Didier Barral was about to set out to move his cows to new pasture. He has a herd of around 40 cows, not to mention some horses and pigs; during summer they graze on pastures near the vineyards, then during winter they are allowed into the vines. "We do polyculture, to get balance you have to have polyculture," explains Didier, under the enquiring gaze of the cows, some of which are a recreated medieval breed.

Didier founded the domain in 1993 (it is named after his grandfather). It consists of many vineyard parcels, varying from 0.3 to 5 ha in size, with many old vines. The vineyards look quite old fashioned, with the vines pruned in gobelet style as free-standing bushes. "This makes a parasol for the sun, which is important. I don't think a trellis is well adapted to the climate," Didier maintains.

Back in the cave, a stone building in the hamlet of Lenthéric, a tasting of barrel samples runs through many varieties, each still separate in barrique. Each variety shows its character through the prism of a highly refined style—even Carignan. The single white cuvée is based on the old variety of Terret Blanc and is an IGP Pays d'Hérault. The three reds cuvées are Faugères, the Faugères Jadis, and the Faugères Valinière, the first two being half Grenache, but the last more than three quarters Mourvèdre. Fine, tight, and precise would be a fair description of house style.

Borie La Vitarèle *

34490 Causses-et-Veyran	*+33 4 67 89 50 43*
contact@borielavitarele.fr	*Cathy Izarn*
www.borielavitarele.fr	*Saint Chinian [map p. 83]*
18 ha; 60,000 btl	*St. Chinian, Les Schistes*

Cathy and Jean-François Izarn bought this 100 ha estate, located up a dirt track a few miles from the village of Causses-et-Veyran in 1986. It was mostly virgin land, and has been gradually built up to its present size, with vineyards in several separate parcels. Plantings are 40% Syrah and 40% Grenache, with smaller amounts of Merlot, Mourvèdre, Carignan, and white varieties. "We look for concentration but we don't want anything massive. We want refinement more than power," is how Jean-François explained his objectives. "We use very little new oak, we want to respect the terroir. I like to represent the unique character, the particularité of each terroir. It's more interesting to make cuvées from each terroir in a Burgundian way rather than to follow the Bordeaux model and make a grand vin and second wine."

In reds, there is an introductory cuvée (Les Cigales: "This is my equivalent to rosé, I don't like rosé but this is easy to drink"), three cuvées from specific terroirs (Terres Blanches from calcareous soils, Les Schistes from schist on the slopes, and Les Crès from galets): these become progressively richer. Midi Rouge is the grand wine of the domain, made in small amounts from a blend of varieties and terroirs. The style is rich, in the direction of the generosity of Châteauneuf-du-Pape, something of a modern take on the tradition of the Languedoc. Sadly, Jean-François died in an accident in 2014, but Cathy continues to run the domain.

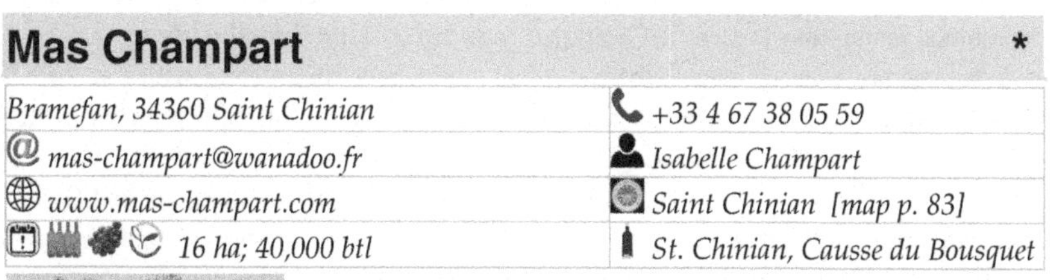

Mas Champart *

Bramefan, 34360 Saint Chinian	*+33 4 67 38 05 59*
mas-champart@wanadoo.fr	*Isabelle Champart*
www.mas-champart.com	*Saint Chinian [map p. 83]*
16 ha; 40,000 btl	*St. Chinian, Causse du Bousquet*

Isabelle and Mathieu Champart moved from Paris to take over an old farm in 1976; with no experience in winemaking, grapes were sold to the cooperative until 1988 when they began to bottle their own wine. A winery was constructed in 1995. Since taking over, they have expanded the estate from its original 8 ha, sometimes by buying abandoned vineyards of old vines. In addition to the vineyards, the property includes another 8 ha of other fruits and crops. The vineyards comprise around twenty small plots on limestone hills, at altitudes between 200 m and 300 m. Grenache is grown on the higher locations, Syrah on north-facing slopes, and Mourvèdre on the clay-limestone terraces.

The wines come in all three colors of St. Chinian, with three different red cuvées: going up the scale, Côte d'Arbo is a classic blend aged in vat (a lively introductory wine); Causse de Bousquet is two thirds Syrah with Mourvèdre and Grenache, aged partly in vat and partly in barrel (this is the major wine of the domain); and Clos de la Simonette is almost three quarters Mourvèdre (the rest is Grenache) aged in demi muids. The white St. Chinian is a conventional blend of local varieties. The Champarts' interests include some grapes that aren't allowed in the St. Chinian AOP, so there's an unusual IGP Pays d'Oc which is a blend of 70% Cabernet Franc to 30% Syrah, and a white IGP Pays d'Hérault made from 80% Terret and 20% Grenache Gris.

Château La Liquière *

La Liquière, 34480 Cabrerolles	*+33 4 67 90 29 20*

info@chateaulaliquiere.com	*Famille Vidal Dumoulin*
www.chateaulaliquiere.com	*Faugères [map p. 83]*
55 ha; 250,000 btl	*Faugères, Cistus*

The modern tasting room is located in an old castle in the center of the town of Cabrerolles. The vineyards are in many different parcels scattered throughout all four villages of Faugères. "The domain has increased since the 1960s but now we have decided not to grow any more," says François Villard, whose grandparents established the domain in the 1960s. Vinification by parcel produces 50 different lots, and it's only later that the decision is made on which to bottle as separate cuvées and which to blend together.

There are five red cuvées, three whites, and two rosés. The entry-level line goes under the name of Les Amandiers and is matured in concrete and steel. The white Cistus has a few months maturation in new oak barriques, new because the period is short; and then the barriques are used to mature the red wine. Amandiers comes from wines at lower altitudes, and Cistus from those higher up, so there's a correlation at Liquière between the top of the hill and the top of the scale.

A Vieilles Vignes red cuvée comes from a blend of old vines of Carignan and Grenache; and the Nos Racines cuvée comes from a 110-year-old plot of Carignan that's planted in a field blend with some other old varieties. It's a paradox that these are the oldest vines but the wine seems the most modern in the range. The house style is round and smooth and elegant (although of course there is some stylistic variation from the entry-level to the top wines).

Château Pech Redon *

Chemin de la Couleuvre, Route de Gruissan, 11000 Narbonne	*+33 4 68 90 41 22*
chateaupechredon@orange.fr	*Christophe Bousquet*
chateaupechredon.wordpress.com	*La Clape [map p. 82]*
30 ha; 50,000 btl	*La Clape, L'Epervier*

Pech Redon is a truly unique location, on the site of an old Roman villa, several miles along a dirt track at the end of a large rocky plateau surrounded by impressive calcareous cliffs. The environment could not be more different from the seaside town of Narbonne, which is the official postal address. Christophe Bousquet bought the domain in 1988 upon the death of the previous owner, Jean Demolomben, a negociant in Narbonne. It's very isolated, but that was part of the appeal for Christophe. Regarded as a young Turk at the time, he is now one of the most established producers in the La Clape AOP. Pech Redon is at the highest point in La Clape (Pech Redon means "rounded peak.") Its elevation (about 200m) makes it cooler and fresher than the rest of La Clape.

All the wines are AOP La Clape (Christophe was much involved in its creation: he is president of the local producers' association). There is a classic Languedocian mix of the five black grape varieties (and also some whites). The terroir is relatively homogeneous, so differences between cuvées are due more to assemblage and élevage. The L'Epervier white cuvée is fresh and lively, but the main focus here is on the red cuvées, which ascend from Les Cades (8 months in cuve, fresh and lively, based on Syrah, Grenache, Cinsault, and Carignan), to L'Epervier (the flagship wine, 18 months in cuve, from Syrah, Grenache, Mourvèdre, and Carignan), and the weightiest, Centaurée (classic GSM, 24 months in oak fûts).

Château Rouquette-sur-Mer *

Route Bleue, 11100 Narbonne-Plage	*+33 4 68 49 90 41*
bureau@chateaurouquette.com	*Jacques Boscary*
www.chateaurouquette.com	*La Clape [map p. 82]*
55 ha; 200,000 btl	*La Clape, Clos de la Tour*

Faithful to its name, Château Rouquette sur Mer is on the sea, overlooking Narbonne Plage. A family domain since the 1940s, this is a large estate; vineyards surround the property and run down towards the sea, but altogether around 50 separate parcels are scattered all over La Clape, making for significant heterogeneity in the soils. Château Rouquette is definitely on the oenotourism circuit, with a professional tasting room open almost every day, and a constant stream of visitors, many bringing their own containers to be filled with one of the three colors right out of the spigot in the tasting room.

There are wines at all levels from Vin de France to IGP to AOP, with the range extending all the way from the bulk wines to special cuvées. It would be easy to be put off by the touristic atmosphere in the tasting room, but the special cuvées are in fact the antithesis of the bulk wine, with something of a concentration on Mourvèdre, which is a minor component in Cuvée Henry Lapierre (matured in new barriques), but is three quarters of Clos de la Tour. The top wine is Cuvée Absolute, where only 2,000 bottles are produced from a selection of the best lots, with the parcels and varieties changing each year, but Mourvèdre was always dominant in my tastings. The wide range makes it hard to define house style here, but at the level of cuvées, the animal quality of Mourvèdre stands out. A dessert wine, Vendanges d'Automne, is made from late harvest Bourboulenc in some years.

Profiles of Important Estates

Mas d'Alezon

1 Route de Pézenas, 34600 Faugères	*+33 4 67 95 19 72*
mas@alezon.fr	*Catherine Roque*
12 ha; 20,000 btl	*Faugères [map p. 83]*

Catherine Roque created Domaine de Clovallon (see profile) in 1989, just north of Faugères, where she produced Pinot Noir. In 1997 she purchased 7 ha at Faugères from a vigneron who was retiring. The highest estate in the appellation at 350-400m, with soils of schist, it has now expanded to about the same size as her first estate. Initially the wine was labeled as Coteaux du Languedoc, but since 2003 has been Faugères AOP. There are two reds: Montfalette is 80% Mourvèdre with the rest Syrah and Grenache; Presbytère is 80% Grenache with the rest Mourvèdre and Syrah, from the oldest vines. The white Cabretta is Roussanne, Clairette, and Grenache Blanc.

Bardi d'Alquier

37 Route de Pézènes Les Mines, 34600 Faugères	*+33 4 67 23 07 89*
contact@bardi-alquier.fr	*Thibaud Bardi de Fourtou*
bardi-alquier.fr	*Faugères [map p. 83]*
11 ha; 40,000 btl	*Faugères, La Maison Jaune*

The winery is located in the center of town, with the cellar just opposite the family house. "I am the fifth generation on the property," says Jean-Michel. His grandfather left the area to become a negociant in Paris, but his father, Gilbert, returned, and began to renew the vineyards in the 1960s, with a focus on Syrah. "This was how the domain began to acquire its present reputation," Jean-Michel explains. The domain was split after Gilbert's death between Jean-Michel and Frédéric Alquier, and it's Jean-Michel's wines that are now considered to be a leading light of the appellation.

There's only one hectare for white grapes. For red wines, vineyards are divided according to position on the slope (all south-facing) to make three cuvées: La Première (half Syrah) comes from the base of the slope where the soils are deepest; Maison Jaune comes from the slope and is more structured, although it's 70% Grenache; and Les Bastides comes from the top of the hill and is always very ripe, although it's 70% old vines Syrah. All the wines are matured in barrique. The style here is modern, but the wines display it in different ways. La Première has a freshness you would not have seen in Faugères ten or twenty years ago, satisfying the objective of being ready to drink soonest. Maison Jaune has a smoothness and elegance that shows the progress of recent years. And Les Bastides has structure rather than simple expression of overt fruit, requiring at least a decade to begin to open up.

Château d'Anglès

Route des Cabanes de Fleury, 11560 Saint Pierre Sur Mer	*+33 4 68 33 61 33*
info@chateaudangles.com	*Éric Fabre*
www.chateaudangles.com	*La Clape [map p. 82]*
	45 ha; 180,000 btl

Éric Fabre was technical director at Château Lafite Rothschild for eight years before he decided that he really wanted to make wine from Mourvèdre. In 2001 he and his wife Christine bought the old Château La Rivière-Haute, which had been owned by Jean Ségura, a pioneer of white wine in the south, but which fell into disarray after his death. Éric also bought the adjacent property of Château La Rivière-Basse . He called his estate Anglès after the founder of the original estate in 1796. Éric's son Vianney joined him at the estate in 2010 after working for five years at Champagne Bollinger. Plantings at Anglès are two thirds black and one third white. The cellars at the old Rivière-Haute have been modernized for producing red wine; the whites are made at the cellars of Rivière-Basse. Wines are divided into the Classique series (all three colors) and the Grand Vin (red and white). The red Classique is 40% each of Syrah and Grenache with 20% Mourvèdre; the white has 50% Bourboulenc (the predominant white grape in La Clape), blended with 30% Grenache Blanc and 10% each of Marsanne and Roussanne. The rosé is 80% Mourvèdre with 10% each of Syrah and Grenache. They age in cuve. The Grand Vin Rouge is 55% Mourvèdre, 30% Syrah, 10% Grenache, and 5% Carignan; the Grenache ages in cuve, and the Syrah and Mourvèdre age in 3-4-year barriques. Grand Vin Blanc is a blend from 40% Bourboulenc, 20% old vines Grenache Blanc, and 20% each of Marsanne and Roussanne. It ages for 6 months in barriques with battonage.

Château d'Aussières

Hameaux d'Aussières Rd163, 11100 Narbonne	*+33 4 68 45 59 54*
tourisme.aussieres@lafite.com	*Fanny Brieau*
www.aussieres.com	*La Clape [map p. 82]*
	167 ha; 650,000 btl

Aussières has made wine since the Roman era. The Church took over the vineyard in the Middle Ages, and it was part of the Cistercian abbey of Fontfroide until it was confiscated at the French Revolution. It was then bought by one of Napoleon's ministers, and expanded at the end of the nineteenth century to fill the gap created by phylloxera: it became as large as 270 ha in the 1920s-1930s. It declined when the Languedoc got into difficulties after the second world war, and in 1999, Lafite Rothschild bought the 550 ha estate. Located just outside Narbonne, two thirds of the vineyard is in Corbières AOP; the rest makes wine for IGP Pays d'Oc. The estate was replanted with the traditional varieties (the GSM trio plus Carignan for the AOP), and international varieties including Cabernet Sauvignon, Merlot, and Chardonnay (which go into the IGP). A new winery was constructed in the old cellars. In AOP Corbières, the domain follows the precedent of Bordeaux in making a Grand Vin (48% Syrah, 37% Mourvèdre, 8% Grenache, and 7% Carignan, aged 60% in vat and 40% in barriques with half new oak for 12-16 months) and a second wine, Blason d'Aussières (20% aged in barriques for 12 months).

Clos Bagatelle

route de Saint Pons, 34360 Saint Chinian	*+33 4 67 93 61 63*
closbagatelle@wanadoo.fr	*Christine Deleuze*
www.closbagatelle.com	*Saint Chinian [map p. 83]*
	60 ha; 300,000 btl

The family has been in the region since 1623. The domain started in St. Chinian, and Marie-Françoise Simon, who took over in 1963, extended it by purchasing vineyards of Muscat in Saint Jean de Minervois. Her children, Christine Deleuze and Luc Simon now run the domain together, with the focus on St. Chinian, and another 8 ha of Muscat. There are three separate plots in St. Chinian, with terroirs varying from schist to sandstone, represented in a wide range of cuvées. The reds are traditional blends, with varying proportions of Syrah, Grenache, Mourvèdre, and Carignan. Aux 4 Vents is an IGP from the

Hérault with 50% Cabernet Franc. Whites vary from predominantly Cinsault to Roussanne.

Domaine Bertrand-Bergé

38, avenue du Roussillon, 11350 Paziols	*+33 4 68 45 41 73*
bertrand-berge@wanadoo.fr	*Jérôme Bertrand*
www.bertrand-berge.com	*Fitou [map p. 82]*
	36 ha; 110,000 btl

In the south of the Languedoc, Jérôme Bertrand is the sixth generation at this estate, which came out of the coop to bottle its own wine in 1993, and has now become one of the leaders in AOP Fitou. The winery is a large building in the village of Paziols. Plantings for the reds are the indigenous varieties Carignan, Syrah, Grenache, and Mourvèdre. Under AOP Fitou, there are various blends: Cuvée Ancestrale has all the varieties, variously aged in cuve and barriques, while Origines is a blend of Carignan and Grenache aged in cuve, and La Boulière has Carignan, Mourvèdre, and Grenache aged in demi-muids. The top cuvées are Jean Sirven, a blend of Carignan and Syrah with a little Grenache, aged in new barriques, and Les Mégalithes, mostly Carignan with some Grenache, from 90-year-old vines. In IGP Vallée du Torgan, Le Méconnu Rouge is a blend of Merlot and Carignan; there is also a rosé from Syrah, and a white from Muscat. There are also sweet wines from Rivesaltes.

Domaine Binet-Jacquet

11 rue du Ponget, 34600 Faugères	*+33 6 21 14 82 07*
domaine@binet-jacquet.com	*Pierre Jacquet & Olivier Binet*
www.binet-jacquet.com	*Faugères [map p. 83]*
	9 ha; 30,000 btl

The domain is a collaboration between Pierre Jacquet, who worked at wineries in the Languedoc for many years, and journalist Olivier Binet. They planted vineyards between 2002 and 2007, with their first harvest in 2005, and renovated a cellar in the village of Faugères in 2006. Production reached its current level in 2012. Vineyard soils are based on schist. All the wines are blends of Syrah, Carignan, Grenache, and Cinsault The Faugères ages in cuve. La Réserve comes from the best parcels, and is weighted towards Grenache. La Grande Réserve, made only in the years, has mostly Grenache and Mourvèdre, and ages in a mix of barriques, concrete eggs, and amphorae. La Grande Réserve du Schiste comes from a single parcel, principally Mourvèdre, and ages in amphorae and barriques.

Domaine Canet Valette

Route Causses-et-Veyran, 34460 Cessenon-sur-Orb	*+33 4 67 89 51 83*
canetvalette@gmail.com	*Marc Valette*
www.canetvalette.com	*Saint Chinian [map p. 83]*
	18 ha; 80,000 btl

Northwest of Beziers, the domain was created in 1992 when Marc Valette took back the family vines from the cooperative. He pulled out Carignan and replaced it with Syrah,

Grenache, and Mourvèdre. He built a new gravity-feed cellar in 1998 and expanded the vineyards, and is considered to be one of the pioneers in resurrecting St. Chinian. The entry-level cuvée, Antonyme, is an equal blend of Cinsault and Mourvèdre; Une et Mille Nuits has Syrah, Grenache, Carignan, and Mourvèdre; Ivresses is 90% Grenache and 10% Syrah; and the top cuvée, Maghani, is an equal blend of Syrah and Mourvèdre, selected from the best lots. The wines have long élevage, three years for Maghani, and are correspondingly powerful on release, although the style softened somewhat after 2015. The wines can create enthusiasm for their exuberance or criticism that they are not typical for St. Chinian.

Le Mas Des Caprices

8 Rue du Boulodrome, 11370 Leucate	*+33 6 76 99 80 24*
masdescaprices@free.fr	*Mireille & Pierre Mann*
mas-des-caprices.com	*Fitou [map p. 82]*
	12 ha

Mireille and Pierre Mann originally ran a restaurant near Colmar, but moved to winemaking, settling in Languedoc after a trial period in Provence. Their vineyards are partly in the maritime part of Fitou and partly in Corbières (for dry wines), with some in Rivesaltes (for VDN). The Fitou cuvées are typical for Languedoc, with rich fruits and a sense of southern warmth, although Retour aux Sources has more sense of structure to cut the fruits on the palate compared with Ze Fitou. Both are dominated by Carignan with a good dash of Mourvèdre, but Retour aux Sources has Lledoner Noir (a variant of Grenache) whereas Ze Fitou has Grenache. The Muscat de Rivesaltes is typically perfumed and grapey. From Rivesaltes, there are two 100% Grenache VDN cuvées: g grenat'in has greater fruit intensity to take the edge of the sweetness than the g grenat cuvée. The Rancio is not overblown, but veers more towards a savory oxidative character with good acidity.

Château de Castigno

34360 Villespassans	*+33 4 67 24 43 03*
oenotourisme@chateaucastigno.com	*Marc Verstraete*
villagecastigno.com	*Saint Chinian [map p. 83]*
	32 ha; 90,000 btl

This vast 150 ha estate in the garrigue near St. Chinian contains a complex with a hotel and Michelin-starred restaurant as well as vineyards. Dutch couple Tine Claeys and Marc Verstraete restored a ruined hamlet into an "organic wine village," with advice from Michel Tardieu (of negociant Tardieu-Laurent) and oenologue Philippe Cambie (of Châteauneuf-du-Pape) on vineyards and winemaking. The entry-level line, Grâces des Anges, comes in all three colors, and is IGP d'Hérault. Château Castigno red and white are St. Chinian AOP. The top dry wine, Nirwana, at a price 10x the entry-level, is 100% Grenache from 80-year-old vines, aged in wood vats for 18 months, but production is less than 1,000 bottles annually. There are also wines produced in the rancio oxidative style by aging for 5-8 years, Vin de Justin (white) and Vin de Mona (red), and Eau de Vie distilled from Grenache. In an area that has been somewhat lacking in facilities for oenotourism, Château de Castigno is a welcome development.

Domaine de Cébène

route de Caussiniojouls, 34600 Faugères	*+33 6 74 96 42 67*
bchevalier@cebene.com	*Brigitte Chevalier*
cebene.com	*Faugères [map p. 83]*
	11 ha; 35,000 btl

Coming from Bordeaux, where she was export manager at Jean-Luc Thunevin, Brigitte Chevalier came to Faugères to start her own domain in 2007. The domain is named for an ancient Celtic goddess of the region. The estate has several plots running around a hill with varying exposures at 320m elevation. There are three cuvées from Faugères. Les Bancèles (the terraces) comes from north-facing plots of Syrah and Grenache on schist, with a little Mourvèdre. Il y a Belle Lurette (meaning a long time ago) comes from old vines Carignan on a north-facing plot of schist, with a little Grenache and Syrah. Felgaria is based on Mourvèdre from full south-facing plots. This is the only wine that sees any oak, being fermented and aged in 500-liter barrels. In addition, there is Ex Arena, an IGP Pays d'Oc, which is based on Grenache from a quite separate vineyard of sandier terroir near the Mediterranean. Brigitte's aim is to make wines in a restrained style, which she calls "vin du Nord in the South." She also runs a negociant, Chevalier Vins.

Château Champ des Soeurs

19, Avenue des Corbières, 11510 Fitou	*+33 6 03 68 26 94*
laurent.maynadier@orange.fr	*Marie & Laurent Maynadier*
www.champdessoeurs.fr	*Fitou [map p. 82]*
	13 ha; 45,000 btl

The estate originated in the seventeenth century. Laurent Maynadier comes from a family that has been in Fitou for generations, but he left the family estate (Maynadier) in 1999 to take over Champ des Soeurs with his wife Marie, a qualified oenologue. Laurent manages the vineyards and Marie makes the wine. Vineyards face the sea. From Fitou, Bel Amant is 40% Grenache with 30% each of Carignan and Mourvèdre, aged in vat, and La Tina is 80% Carignan aged in wood vats with 10% each of Grenache and Mourvèdre aged in demi-muids. The La Tina white is a Corbières from Grenache Blanc and Roussanne. From IGP Aude, the Pépettes red is 100% Carignan and the white is Muscat. There is also a Muscat de Rivesaltes (fortified).

Château Le Thou

Domaine des Deux Ruisseaux, 10 Route de Béziers, 34410 Sauvian	*+33 6 32 92 39 83*
info@famillevalery.	*Laurent Salin-Valéry*
www.famillevalery.com	*Languedoc [map p. 82]*
	30 ha; 300,000 btl

This is one estate but two domains. The Valéry family has been producing wine here for three generations, and divides the production under two labels. Château le Thou is for AOP wines while Domaine des Deux Ruisseaux is used for IGP Pays d'Oc wines. Gilbert Valéry bought the first 30 ha in 1950, but it was not until 2001 that his children, Patricia and Michel, started to bottle the wines as Domaine des Deux Ruisseaux. In 2008 they took over the 15 ha of Château Le Thou, which produces AOP Languedoc. The third generation, Gilles (Michel's son) and Jérôme and Laurent (Patricia's children) are now at the domain.

Domaine Les Eminades

9 Rue Saint-Baulery, 34360 Cébazan	*+33 4 67 36 14 38*
contact@leseminades.fr	*Patricia & Luc Bettoni*
leseminades.fr	*Saint Chinian [map p. 83]*
	16 ha; 60,000 btl

Patricia and Luc Bettoni met while studying oenology at Toulouse, then worked in various French wine regions, before establishing their domain. Vineyards are in 18 separate parcels on a variety of terroirs around St. Chinian, including the two major soil types of schist and calcareous clay. at altitudes from 170-300m. Plantings include some old vines, including Carignan from 1902, and 30-60-year old Syrah and Cinsault. There's an IGP white, Silice, which is 100% Sauvignon Blanc from silex soils, and a St. Chinian white, Montmajou, from Marsanne and Grenache Blanc, aged in barriques, Four red cuvées come from St. Chinian. La Pierre Plantée is 40% 60-year old Cinsault together with 40% Syrah and 20% Grenache, and is aged in cuve to produce a light, fruity, entry-level wine. Cebenna is a GSM with a third of each variety and ages in 350-liter barrels. Sortilège is 70% 30-year-old Syrah and 70% 60-year-old Grenache, aged in 3-5-year barriques for 18 months. Vieilles Canailles from the old Carignan (and includes 1% Syrah) and ages in 350-liter barrels for 18 months.

Château des Estanilles

Hameau de Lenthéric, 34480 Cabrerolles	*+33 4 67 90 29 25*
contact@chateau-estanilles.com	*Julien Seydoux*
www.chateau-estanilles.com	*Faugères [map p. 83]*
	35 ha; 100,000 btl

Michel Louison bought the vineyards and created this domain in 1976; then in 2009 he moved to a 10 ha property in Limoux and sold Estanilles to Julian Seydoux, who is an offshoot of the Schlumberger oil company and was a trader on the Paris stock exchange before he bought Estanilles. Julien says he spent two years looking for a domain to fit his criteria: "I enjoy sunny, fruity wine with good minerality." He plans to make some technical improvements and to reduce the effects of oak to make the wines more accessible. The reds have included the l'Impertinent blend of five varieties (aged in cuve), the GSM Inverso in which Mourvèdre is the driving force, GSM Raison d'Être which is half Syrah, and the flagship Clos du Fou, which is mainly Syrah. The last three are aged in wood. There's also a rosé from Pic St. Loup and a white Languedoc, mostly from Roussanne.

Mas de la Gabinele

1750 chemin de Bédarieux, 34480 Laurens, France	*+33 4 67 89 71 72*
info@masgabinele.com	*Thierry Rodriguez*
www.masgabinele.com	*Faugères [map p. 83]*
	20 ha; 80,000 btl

Thierry Rodriguez, who is the grandson of a winemaker bought his first vineyard in Faugères in 1997, and slowly built the domain up to its present size. There are 26 parcels in three areas, on terroir of schist. Reds are Faugères; whites are IGP d'Hérault. Tradition is a typical red blend, of Grenache, Syrah, Carignan, and Mourvèdre, Rarissime is 70% Syrah, with 20% Grenache and 5% Mourvèdre, and Inaccessible is 60% Mourvèdre with 20% each of Syrah and Grenache. All age in barriques, the last two in exclusively new oak. Grenache Gris is a monovarietal white, aged partly in stainless steel and partly in barrique, Péchaligous is a blend of 12 Gris or Rosé grape varieties, and Rarissime comes from Grenache Gris planted in 1958. The whites age in a mix of stainless steel and barriques, with new oak for Rarissime.

La Graine Sauvage

Chemin des Combes d'Amaran, 34600 Caussiniojouls	*+33 6 52 58 39 29*
sybil.wine@gmail.com	*Sybil Baldassarre*
www.facebook.com/lagrainesauvage	*Faugères* *[map p. 83]*
	3 ha; 6,000 btl

Italian oenologue Sybil Baldassare came to Faugères in 2013 with her partner, Alexandre Durand, who runs Domaine Pèira Lavada in Bergerac. She qualified in Milan, performing research on grape varieties, and worked in Sicily before finding a small plot in Faugères. "It's made for organic viticulture," she says, "it's windy and dry, I found 3 ha of whites at 450 altitude, surrounded by woods with an astounding view." Sybil financed the purchase by crowd funding. "I have 123 associates, I pay them with a special cuvée." Cuvée Lutz is 50% each of Marsanne and Roussanne. Rocalhas is 70% Grenache Blanc with equal Roussanne and Marsanne. There are varietal cuvées from Grenache Blanc (Velvet Underschiste) and Vermentino. Production is white wine only, aged in stainless steel and made with no added sulfur; the wines are labeled as Vin de France.

Domaine La Grange Léon

3, rue du Paillos, 34360 Berlou	*+33 6 73 83 37 68*
lagrangeleon@orange.fr	*Joël Fernandez*
20 ha; 25,000 btl	*Saint Chinian* *[map p. 83]*

Joël Fernandez's father and grandfather sold their grapes to the cooperative, but in 2008 Joël created his own domain. He has not abandoned the cooperative completely, as half his grapes are used to produce estate wine, while the other half continue to go to the coop at Roquebrun. Yields are low. "Berlou is a very specific appellation in St. Chinian, because the schist soils are not productive and the only choice for vignerons is to follow a path of quality." There are 3 reds from St. Chinian, and 2 whites and a rosé under IGP Pays d'Oc. L'Insolent is a blend of all the local varieties, L'Audacieux is 60% Mourvèdre and 40% Grenache, and the top wine, D'Une-Main-à-l'Autre, is Syrah, Grenache, and Carignan, partly aged in demi-muids.

Château L'Hospitalet

Route de Narbonne Plage 11100 Narbonne	*+33 4 68 45 36 00*
caveau@gerard-bertrand.com	*Feargal Nolan*
www.gerard-bertrand.com/en/domains/chateau-lhospitalet	*La Clape* *[map p. 82]*
	85 ha; 300,000 btl

Formerly an international rugby player but coming from a winemaking family, Gérard Bertrand has become a major negociant, producing millions of bottles, and owning 15 estates with 750 ha of vineyards in the Languedoc. He purchased Château l'Hospitalet, which stands in a 1,000 ha estate in La Clape, in 2002. It has become his flagship, with a hotel and restaurant, intended to be a center for oenotourism. In 2014 he rented nearby Château des Karantes (see profile), and in 2018 he purchased neighboring Mas du Soleilla (see profile).Whites include a varietal Viognier, and a blend of Bourboulenc, Vermentino, Marsanne and Roussanne. In addition to the red blend from the estate, there is a single-vineyard wine from the 3 ha plot of L'Hospitalitas, which is planted with Syrah and Carignan. Wines from other Bertrand estates can also be tasted at the domain, which is committed to oenotourism, and has hotels and a restaurant, and a jazz festival each summer.

Château des Karantes

Karantes Le Haut, 11100 Narbonne	*+33 4 68 49 84 72*
+33 4 68 32 14 58	*Jean-Jacques Fertal*
www.facebook.com/ChateaudesKarantes	*La Clape [map p. 82]*
	44 ha; 120,000 btl

Located in a small valley just outside Narbonne, the domain is within the rocky appellation of La Clape, surrounded by massive calcareous cliffs. Walter Knysz, of the American family who own Eagle Eye Brands, bought the 200 ha estate in 2004. Since 2014 the domain has been rented to Gérard Bertrand of neighboring Château L'Hospitalet (see profile), and has effectively become one of his estates in the Languedoc. Under American ownership, the style was initially strongly influenced by the New World, with lots of extraction and new oak, but calmed down after Nicolas Laverny became the winemaker. The entry-level Bergerie line of red, white, and rosé is vinified in cuve; the red has more or less equal parts of Grenache, Syrah, and Mourvèdre, while the white is an equal blend of Grenache Blanc and Terret Blanc. The château red is 60% Syrah, 30% Mourvèdre, and 10% Grenache, aged in a mix of 300- and 500-liter barrels; the white is a mix of several varieties, vinified in cuve. The top wine is the Diamant, a monovarietal Syrah, aged in new oak.

Domaine Laurent Miquel

Hameau Cazal Viel, 34460 Cessenon-sur-Orb	*+33 4 67 89 74 93*
contact@laurent-miquel.com	*Laurent Miquel*
www.laurent-miquel.com	*Saint Chinian [map p. 83]*
	150 ha

The property was part of the Abbaye de Fontcaude, confiscated in the Revolution, and under then name of Domaine Cazal Viel was then acquired by the Miquel family. Henri Miquel started producing estate wines in 1980. His son Laurent was an engineer, before he returned to start making wine in 1996. This is now the largest family-owned domain in St. Chinian. Vineyards are at 150m elevation, with plantings predominantly of Syrah and Viognier. Overall white wine is about half of production. The entry-level range, called Père et Fils, are blends under the IGP, Solas and Nord-Sud are varietals, and there is a jump in quality to the Bardou St. Chinian and Larmes des Fées reds, and the Verité Viognier. In 2009, Laurent bought Les Auzines, a 143 ha estate in Corbières, where he produces AOP red and rosé, and Albariño.

Domaine La Lauzeta

6 place de l'Eglise, 34490 Saint Nazaire de Ladarez	*+33 4 67 38 18 84*
florian@domainelalauzeta.com	*Florian Bruneau*
www.domainelalauzeta.com	*Saint Chinian [map p. 83]*
	23 ha; 15,000 btl

Located at the border of St. Chinian with the Cru St. Chinian Roquebrun, the estate has grown wine since the Roman era, passed through a period of ownership by Benedictine monks, and was bought by Englishman Tom Hill in 2015. (Lauzeta is local dialect for skylark.) Vineyards are on clay and schist at up to 300m altitude, with vines up to 80-years old of Syrah, Grenache, Carignan, and Cinsault. Corteza is a blend of all the varieties, aged in stainless steel. Mezura is a blend of 60% Syrah, 25% Grenache, and 15% Carignan, aged 60% in vat and 40% in a mix of French and Austrian barrels of 400-600 liters. La Lauzeta is 75% Syrah and 25% Grenache, aged in new French and Austrian 400-600-liter barrels. A rosé is made by direct pressing of 45% Cinsault, 40% Grenache, and 15% Syrah. All the wines are AOP St. Chinian.

Domaine la Madura

Route de Salabert, 34360 Saint Chinian	*+33 4 67 38 17 85*
info@lamadura.com	*Cyril Bourgne*
www.lamadura.com	*Saint Chinian [map p. 83]*
	13 ha; 50,000 btl

Cyril Bourgne was winemaker at Château Fieuzal in Graves before establishing his own estate in St. Chinian in 1999. The cellars were originally in the town, but a new cave was constructed in 2015 just outside. Vineyards are fragmented into many plots, with a variety of terroirs. A modern approach focuses on quality varieties, with Grenache, Syrah, Mourvèdre, and a little Carignan for the reds, and mostly Sauvignon Blanc, with a little Picpoul, for the whites. The range follows the Bordeaux pattern of one simpler and one more complex wine. The "Classic" range ages in cuve; the "Grand Vins" age in barriques, with one red and one white in each range, based on similar blends.

Le Mas Lou

4,Rue du Portail d'Amont, 34600 Faugères	*+33 6 77 81 06 44*
lemaslou@gmail.com	*Adèle Arnaud & Olivier Gill*
mas-lou.com	*Faugères [map p. 83]*
	9 ha; 20,000 btl

Both qualified as oenologues, after traveling in Peru (as seen in the names of the cuvées), Adèle Arnaud and Olivier Gil established their domain in Faugères in 2013. Vineyards are at 200-400m altitude, mostly Grenache and Syrah, most around 30 years old. Aksou is 70% Syrah with 15% each of Grenache and Carignan. Angaco is 55% Carignan, 40% Grenache, and 5% Syrah. Tio comes from a single parcel of Syrah on schist, and ages in barrique. There is a white IGP Côtes de Thongue from Viognier and Vermentino.

Domaine les Mille Vignes

24 avenue San Brancat, 11480 La Palme	*+33 6 07 75 58 68*
les.mille.vignes@free.fr	*Valérie Guérin*
www.lesmillevignes.fr	*Fitou [map p. 82]*
	11 ha; 25,000 btl

Jacques Guérin founded the domain when he retired as Professor of Oenology in 1979; his daughter Valérie has run the estate since 2000. Vineyards are in 13 separate small parcels. The focus is on red wines from Fitou and sweet wines from Rivesaltes. Cadette is a blend of Mourvèdre, Grenache, and Carignan, and then there are cuvées each dominated by one of the varieties, Atsuko by old Grenache, Denis Royal by old Carignan, Vendangeurs da la Violette by Mourvèdre, and L'Idyllique (introduced in 2017) with Lledonner Pelut (a variant of Grenache). The reds age in cuve. In sweet wines there are Rivesaltes and the 'Noir de' series of monovarietal VDNs from Grenache, Mourvèdre, or Carignan.

Domaine Thierry Navarre

15 avenue de Balaussan, 34460 Roquebrun	*+33 4 67 89 53 58*
thierry.navarre@orange.fr	*Thierry Navarre*
www.thierrynavarre.com	*Saint Chinian [map p. 83]*
	14 ha; 35,000 btl

Thierry Navarre's grandfather founded the estate in the north of St. Chinian. The terroir is brown schist. The AOP wines are based on Grenache and Carignan, with some Syrah and Cinsault, but Thierry is an enthusiast for ancient varieties, in particular Ribeyrenc (also known as Aspiran Noir), which he resurrected from some old vines his father had. La Laouzil is the principal St. Chinian, a blend of all four varieties, and Cuvée Olivier comes from old vines of Carignan, Grenache, and Syrah, and is a classic representation of St. Chinian. The wines of the old varieties are Vin de France, including Vin d'Oeillades and Ribeyrenc. Lignières is a blend of old white varieties from plantings intermingled in the vineyard. At the other extreme, La Conque is a blend of Cabernet Sauvignon, Merlot, and Syrah from the highest altitude vineyards.

Château de la Négly

La Negly, 11560 Fleury d'Aude	*+33 4 68 33 87 17*
lanegly@wanadoo.fr	*Jean*
www.lanegly.fr	*La Clape [map p. 82]*
	65 ha; 500,000 btl

They can be rather reserved at Château la Negly, especially if you turn up late for a rendezvous, but once you break through the initial reserve you discover an enthusiastic young winemaker who is given a free hand by the proprietor to make quality wines from grapes harvested at low yields using organic methods. All work in the vineyards is manual; debudding, vendange vert are customary to limit yields. Wines are vinified by cépage and by parcel. Time of harvest is determined by tasting the grapes rather than technical analysis, the aim here being to obtain full flavor maturity. Whites from international varieties are IGP; the white La Clape is 70% Bourboulenc and 30% Grenache Blanc. Reds include Le Pavilion (mostly Cinsault and the only red IGP) and La Falaise (65% Syrah and 35% Grenache from La Clape). The top wines are L'Ancely (70% Mourvèdre, 20% Grenache, 10% Syrah, from La Clape), La Porte du Ciel (70% Syrah and 30% Grenache from La Clape), and Clos des Truffiers (80% Syrah, 20% Grenache, from St. Pargoire in the Hérault). Wines are matured in wood of various sizes, with the 225l barriques being replaced every two years, the 3000l barrels every 3 years, and the demi-muids every 5 years.

Château de Nouvelles

Nouvelle, 11350 Tuchan	*+33 4 68 45 40 03*
daurat-fort@terre-net.fr	*Jean-Rémy Daurat*
www.chateaudenouvelles.fr	*Fitou [map p. 82]*
	75 ha; 120,000 btl

Located in the eastern part of Fitou, the domain first made its reputation for its sweet wines from Rivesaltes, but today produces about two thirds dry red wine from Fitou. It has been in the family since the nineteenth century, and today is run by Jean Daurat together with his son Jean-Rémy. Vineyards fall into blocks on either side of the winery: elevations of 250m on schist to one side, lower at 150m with clay-limestone on the other. Plantings of black varieties are 40% Carignan, and 30% each of Grenache and Syrah. Fitou Augusta and the Fitou Vieilles Vignes age in cuve, while the top red, Gabrielle ages in barriques with one third new oak. From Rivesaltes there are the oxidative styles of Ambré and Tuilé, and also two cuvées from Muscat de Rivesaltes.

Domaine Ollier-Taillefer

Route de Gabian, 34320 Fos	*+33 4 67 90 24 59*
ollier.taillefer@orange.fr	*Luc & Françoise & Florent Ollier*
www.olliertaillefer.com	*Faugères [map p. 83]*
	37 ha; 140,000 btl

Brother and sister Luc and Françoise Ollier are the fifth generation at this family domain, where their parents started estate-bottling in 1977. Luc's son Florent joined them in 2020. Production is entirely Faugères AOP, almost three quarters red and a quarter rosé, with just a little white. Les Collines is the entry-level wine from Carignan, Grenache, and Syrah, Grande Réserve comes from the oldest vines, and Castel Fossibus is a GSM blend aged in barriques. In top vintages they also produce Rêve de Noé, a blend of 50% Mourvèdre aged in new barriques with 50% Syrah aged in 2-year barriques. The white Allegro is a blend of Vermentino and Roussanne, aged in vat. Grenache Doux is a sweet rosé, aged in vat. They also produce a Faugères eau de vie.

Mas Onésime

4 Chemin de la Crouzette, La Liquière, 34480 Cabrerolles	*+33 4 67 93 63 58*
olivier.villaneuva@masonesime.com	*Olivier.Villaneuva*
masonesime.com	*Faugères [map p. 83]*
	12 ha

Located in the hamlet of La Liquière, the property was bought by Olivier Villanueva's grandparents after the second world war. His parents expanded the vineyards to their present size and sent grapes to the coop. Olivier studied oenology and worked elsewhere before taking over in 1999. He started bottling his own wines in 2011, giving the estate the name of his grandfather. Vineyards are on the typical poor, pebbly schist of Faugères, at altitudes of 230-360m. Most of the cuvées are Faugères. L'Insoumis is a blend of Cinsault, Carignan, Syrah, and Grenache, aged in vat. Le Sillon is 70% Grenache with 10% each of Syrah, Mourvèdre, and Carignan, aged in vat. Le Paradis Caché is 45% Mourvèdre, 30% Syrah, 15% Grenache, and 10% Carignan, aged in barriques for 12 months. The white Faugères, Le Sillon Blanc, is Marsanne, aged in vat; the rosé, L'Insoumis, is 90% Cinsault and 10% Grenache. A red Vin de France is 100% Cinsault and a white is 100% Chardonnay.

Les Païssels

Rue des Cèdres, 34360 Babeau-Bouldoux	
contact@paissels.fr	*Vivien Roussignol*
www.paissels.fr	*Saint Chinian [map p. 83]*
	12 ha; 25,000 btl

Païssels are small poles made of chestnut, used to stake young bush vines. This was the name for the first cuvée, made from a single hectare of bush vines in 2011. Marie Toussaint and Vivien Rossignol are both oenologists, and after working in a variety of regions, retrieved Vivien's family's vineyards from the cooperative to start their own venture, starting with 1 ha. Another 2 ha were added in 2012, and the domain continued to grow. Vineyards are at the foot of the Montagne Noire, on soils of schist at 150-250m elevation surrounded by woods. The vines are old, from 30- to 100-years, pruned in gobelet (as free-standing bushes). They are being maintained by field-grafting replacements on to the existing roots when a vine dies. Le Banel, which is about half of production, has half each of Carignan and Grenache, and ages in cuve. The first cuvée was Les Païssels, from the original hectare of old vines, with 35% Carignan and 15% Grenache aged in stainless steel, and 35% Syrah and 15% Mourvèdre aged in 2-3-year barriques. Les Jalouses comes from a parcel of old Carignan, coplanted with 5% of a mix of other varieties. It ages in stainless steel. The rosé comes from Cinsault. The white is unusual: Touche Pas au Gibi is a blend of Grenache Gris and Gibi, a very old variety that they found in the Jalouses parcel: it's a female variety that does not self-pollinate, which is why it is all but extinct. It was propagated in a parcel of Grenache Gris, and the two varieties are cofermented after pressing whole bunches.

Château Pech Céleyran

Le Pech, 11110 Salles-d'aude	*+33 4 68 33 50 04*
saint-exupery@pech-celeyran.com	*Nicolas de Saint-Exupéry*
www.pech-celeyran.com	*La Clape [map p. 82]*
	96 ha

This family domain is now in its fifth generation, under Nicolas de Saint-Exupéry, who has been running the domain since 1998 together with his father Jacques. The estate extends over 145 ha, and includes garrigue and pine trees as well as vineyards. The upper part of the property has 44 ha used to produce wines of La Clape; plots lower down are used for IGP. Traditional grape varieties are planted for La Clape: Syrah, Grenache, Mourvèdre, and Carignan for the reds, Bourboulenc, Marsanne, Roussanne, and Grenache Blanc for the whites. Cuvée Cinquième Génération from La Clape comes in red and white; Cuvée Celeste describes red, white, and rosé. The red is GSM and ages in barriques. More international varieties are planted for the IGP, in which Cuvée Ombline has Bordeaux varieties, and there is also a series of monovarietals. The domain is well into oenotourism, with a new tasting room and accommodation.

Domaine Rimbert

place de l'Aire, 34360 Berlou	*+33 4 67 89 74 66*
domaine.rimbert@wanadoo.fr	*Jean-Marie Rimbert*
www.domainerimbert.com	*Saint Chinian [map p. 83]*
	27 ha; 90,000 btl

Starting from 4 ha, Jean-Marie has built up his holdings in more than 10 separate parcels, 70% on the Coteaux and 30% lower down in the valley. The domain occupies a tiny property just outside Berlou, where all available space was filled by a new barrel room and tasting room. Jean-Marie makes wines that interest him, and they are labeled as Vin de France or AOC depending on whether they conform with the appellation rules. A devotée of Carignan, he produces some monovarietal cuvées under the IGP. There are Vins de France with bright labels at an entry-level, with the more sophisticated reds under the St. Chinian-Berlou AOP. as well as a white St Chinian. For the AOP wines, two thirds are destemmed, there is a cuvaison of 3 weeks with punch-down, and the wine is aged in 3-6 year old oak. Jean-Marie started producing white St. Chinian soon after the appellation rules were changed to allow whites as well as reds, initially from 2 ha planted with Carignan Blanc and Marsanne, but with Grenache Blanc and Clairette added as more plantings came on line.

Domaine de la Rochelierre

8 Rue de la Noria, 11510 Fitou	*+33 6 14 69 65 07*
la.rochelierre@orange.fr	*Émilie & Jean-Marie Fabre*
www.domainedelarochelierre.com	*Fitou [map p. 82]*
	15 ha; 60,000 btl

Located in the village of Fitou, the Fabre family has been here for four generations. Jean-Marie took over in 1988. Viticulture isn't certified organic, but uses organic methods. Harvest is manual. All wines are fermented in stainless steel; some cuvées then age in barriques. Dry red wines are Fitou AOP; there are also cuvées in all three colors in IGP Pays d'Oc. There are also sweet wines from Rivesaltes, just across the border in Roussillon. In Fitou, Tradition and Privilège both have all four local varieties (typically 30% each of Carignan and Grenache with 20% each of Mourvèdre and Syrah 20%) both Tradition ages in vat and Privilège ages in barriques with one third new oak. Noblesse du Temps is 50% Mourvèdre with 30% Grenache and 20% Carignan, aged in new barriques. À Deux is a small cuvée based on equal Carignan and Grenache, aged in new barriques. From Rivesaltes there are two fortified sweet wines: Muscat de Rivesaltes (60% Muscat d'Alexandrie 60%, 40% Muscat à Petit Grains, aged in cuve), and Grenat (100% Grenache).

Domaine Sarrat de Goundy

46 avenue de Narbonne, 11110 Vinassan	*+33 4 68 45 30 68*
olivier@sarratdegoundy.com	*Olivier Calix*
www.sarratdegoundy.com	*La Clape [map p. 82]*
	70 ha

The family has been growing grapes here for four generations, and the domain as such was established in 2000 by Claude and Rosy Calix. Their son Olivier returned from studying art to take over in 2002, and left the cooperative to start producing estate wine. The first red from La Clape, Le Moulin, is 60% Syrah, 30% Grenache, and 10% Carignan (with carbonic maceration for the latter) and ages in cuve. A step up, Cuvée du Planteur is 50% Syrah, 30% Grenache, and 20% Mourvèdre, and ages in barriques with 15% new oak. The top reds are Combe aux Louves, 50% Mourvèdre with Syrah, Grenache, and Carignan, aged longer in barriques, and Mano À Mano, a Vin de France which ages terracotta jars, which Olivier introduced in 2014. Whites come from the usual local varieties, with Bourboulenc prominent, and there is also a range of rosés.

Mas du Soleilla

11100 Route de Narbonne-Plage, Narbonne	*+33 4 68 45 24 80*
vins@mas-du-soleilla.fr	*Christa Derungs & Peter Wildbolz*
www.mas-du-soleilla.fr	*La Clape [map p. 82]*
	22 ha; 85,000 btl

The domain was created in 2002 by Christa Derungs and Peter Wildbolz, originally involved in textiles in Switzerland. In 2018, it was purchased by Gerard Bertrand, who owns neighboring Château l'Hospitalet (see profile), and rents Château des Karantes (see profile) and is one of the largest wine producers in Languedoc. (L'Hospitalet and Mas du Soleilla were part of one property until they were separated in 2002 when the two domains were created.) The best known cuvées under the label of Mas du Soleilla are Les Chailles (90% old vines Grenache and 10% Syrah, aged in cuve), Les Bartelles (75% Syrah and 25% Grenache, aged in barriques), and Clôt de l'Amandier (80% Syrah and 30% Grenache from 60-year old vines, aged in barriques including new oak). Cuvée Sans Titre is an experimental wine that changes every year; in 2012 it was Cinsault, and in 2014 it was Syrah.

Abbaye de Sylva Plana

13, Ancienne Route Nationale, 34480 Laurens	*+33 4 67 24 91 67*
info@vignoblesbouchard.com	*H.-f., Nicolas & Charline Bouchard*
www.vignoblesbouchard.com	*Faugères [map p. 83]*
	54 ha; 140,000 btl

Abbaye de Sylva Plana, together with Domaine Deshenrys in IGP Côtes de Thongue, belongs to Vignobles Bouchard (no connection with Bouchard in Burgundy). As the name suggests, the domain goes back centuries to the era of the monasteries. Vineyards are on the classic schist of Faugères, and include 5 ha of very old vines that are cultivated biodynamically. There are four red Faugères, a rosé, and a white. In reds, entry-level Les Novices is Cinsault with some Grenache and Carignan, La Closeraie is mostly Grenache, some Syrah, and Carignan and Mourvèdre fermented by carbonic maceration, Le Songe de l'Abbé is predominantly Syrah, aged in barriques including new oak, and Le Part du Diable is a blend of all four varieties from the oldest vines, fermented in barrique and aged in wood cuves.

Terre des Dames

Route de Causses et Veyran, 34490 Murviel les Béziers	*+33 6 60 88 00 17*
terre.desdames@gmail.com	*Lidewij van Wilgen*
www.terredesdames.com	*Languedoc [map p. 83]*
	14 ha; 50,000 btl

Lidewij van Wilgen was a marketing executive in Amsterdam before she changed career and bought this estate in the Languedoc. She restored the vineyards, renovated the cellars, and rebuilt the house. Vineyards are in 25 small plots surrounded by the garrigue, on soils of clay, limestone, and flint. The wines are Languedoc AOP, except for two cuvées, The entry-level white, Le Blanc, is IGP Pays d'Oc, from 100% Grenache Blanc, aged half in cuve and half in barriques. La Diva Blanche is monovarietal Grenache Blanc from the oldest vines, aged in demi-muids with 50% new oak. La Diva rosé is a GSM blend aged in demi-muids. Production focuses on reds. La Dame is almost half of all production, and is 50% Grenache, 30% Carignan, and 20% Syrah, from 35-70-year-old vines, aged in concrete. La Diva is IGP Pays d'Oc, because in addition to 55% Syrah and 30% Grenache, which come from the best plots, it includes 15% Alicante from 100-year-old vines. It ages in oak vats for 12 months. L'Unique is described as having Burgundy-style aging: a blend of 80% Syrah from the oldest plots with 20% Grenache, it ages in demi-muids for 24 months.

West Languedoc

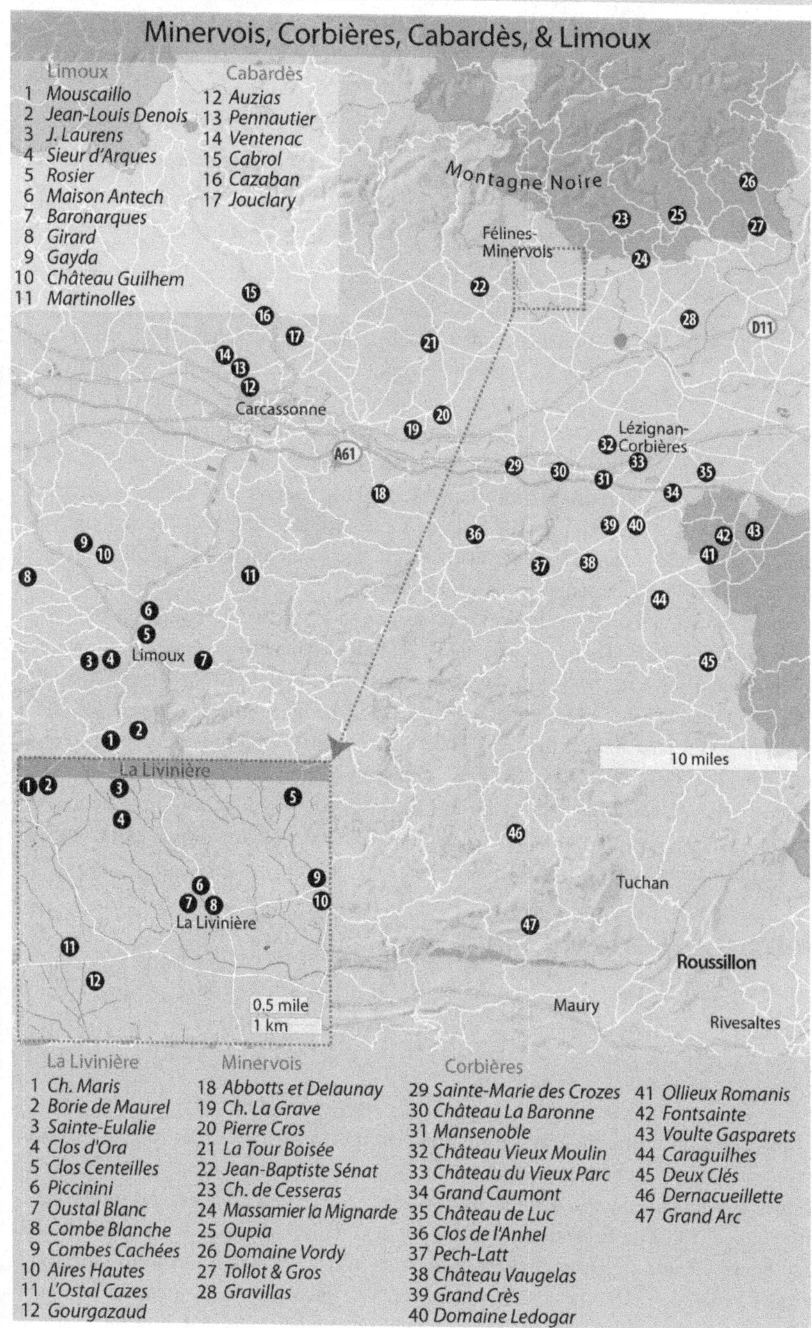

Château La Baronne *

21 rue Jean Jaurès, 11700 Moux	*+33 4 68 43 90 97*
info@chateaulabaronne.com	*Jean et Anne Ligneres*
www.chateaulabaronne.com	*Corbières [map p. 103]*
90 ha; 250,000 btl	*Corbières, Alaric*

The Lignères have the unusual characteristic of being medically qualified, although their main interest is now wine. The domain was founded by André and Suzette in 1957, and is now run by their three children. Visits start at the headquarters in Moux, where wines for all their three domains are bottled. Château La Baronne is the most important; nearby are Las Vals and Plo de Maorou. Vineyards lie between Moux and Fontcouverte under the lee of calcareous mountains, with elevations around 100-200 m making for late harvests. Black varieties are 90% of plantings. The winery has a mix of all sorts of cuves: concrete, stainless steel, and wood. There are also experiments with amphorae (made by a local potter from clay from the same terroir as the wines).

Vineyards are in Corbières, but several monovarietal cuvées are bottled as IGP Hauterive, including Notre Dame (Syrah), and Les Vals (Mourvèdre for red and Roussanne for white). The most interesting of the monovarietals is Pièce de Roche, from a 4 ha plot of Carignan planted in 1892. Carignan is a focus of the domain, occupying more than a third of the vineyard area. It figures in the blends under the Corbières AOP: Les Lanes (Grenache and Carignan), Les Chemins (Grenache, Syrah and Carignan), and Alaric (Syrah, Carignan, and Mourvèdre). There's a focus on low sulfur, and Les Chemins de Traverse is a cuvée bottled without added sulfur. "We are looking for light extraction," is how Paul Lignères describes the style.

Domaine Borie de Maurel *

rue de La Sallèle, 34210 Félines-Minervois	*+33 4 68 91 68 58*
contact@boriedemaurel.fr	*Michel Escande*
www.boriedemaurel.fr	*Minervois La Livinière [map p. 103]*
	35 ha; 120,000 btl

A young domain, Borie de Maurel was founded in 1989 by Sylvie et Michel Escande (who abandoned a nautical career) as part of the return to the land movement in the Languedoc. The domain is located in the heart of Minervois, by La Livinière, one of the Crus of the Languedoc. The Escandes started by buying 5 ha of vineyards and a rather dilapidated house. Steady expansion has made this one of the larger domains in the area, and the next generation, Gabriel and Maxime, are now involved. Vineyards are on steep slopes, and significant heterogeneity in the terroirs (roughly divided between warmer

sandstone and cooler limestone) is matched by the diversity of grape varieties, many vinified as monovarietals.

All the wines are under the Minervois label, coming from different varieties or blends: Rève de Carignan and Sylla (100% Syrah) use carbonic maceration for softening the flavor profile, while Maxime (100% Mourvèdre) and Belle de Nuit (100% Grenache) are vinified conventionally. The Sylla cuvée was the wine that made the reputation of the domain in the early nineties. The introductory wine, Esprit d'Automne, is a blend of Syrah, Carignan, and Grenache, while the Minervois La Livinière, La Feline, is a blend of two thirds Syrah with one third Grenache and a little Carignan; it's matured a third in barriques and two thirds in cuve. Most production is red, but there is a white, La Belle Aude, which is 90% Marsanne and 10% Muscat.

Domaine Gayda *

Chemin de Moscou, 11300 Brugairolles	*+33 4 68 31 64 14*
info@domainegayda.com	*Tim Ford & Vincent Chansault*
www.domainegayda.com	*IGP Pays d'Oc [map p. 103]*
	100 ha; 1,000,000 btl

"We always consider that we're the new guys on the block, but we've been here 16 years, and we've grown the winery to producing one million bottles, so maybe we're not so new now," says Tim Ford, a British expat, who founded the domain in 2013 together with winemaker Vincent Chansault and Anthony Record. They had met in South Africa the year before, and purchased a 12 ha plot of land southwest of Carcassonne to start their vineyard. Planting a wide range of varieties, they ignored the appellation system, and started producing both blends and varietal wines under the IGP Pays d'Oc. They also purchased 18 ha of vineyards in Roussillon, mostly on terroir of schist, with a continuing program. "We are now buying vineyards in Roussillon that are specific for us," Tim says. A purchase in Minervois La Livinière led to the production of the only AOP wine.

The range extends to 21 cuvees in white, rosé, and red. The Flying Solo entry-level wines are more or less conventional blends, 85% Grenache Blanc with 15% Viognier for white, and 60% Grenache with 40% Syrah for red. Vibrant aromatics make them typically southern. In whites, there are several varietal wines, including Sauvignon Blanc (grassy rather than herbaceous), Chardonnay (with a herbal character), and Viognier (somewhat perfumed). In reds, monovarietal wines include Syrah, Cabernet Franc (stern rather than vegetal), and Mourvèdre (tight and precise).

The main focus is Syrah, and the range of the domain can be followed through a series of Syrah varietals or blends. T'Air d'Oc is 100% Syrah, and without the Grenache is a little less obvious than Flying Solo. The IGP Pays d'Oc Syrah (without any other name) shows more grip, and is a little nutty, not quite earthy. Chemin de Moscou is the flagship (the name does not indicate left-wing leanings but is the name of the road leading to the domain) with 72% Syrah, 22% Grenache, and 6% Cinsault, sourced in La Livinière and Roussillon. With some depth to the palate, and an impression that it benefits from a little time to develop more flavor variety, this is the most "serious" wine of the domain. Produced in very small amounts, the top wine is a 100% Syrah, Villa Mon Rêve, from Minervois La Livinière; with exuberant aromatics reflecting ripe if not over-ripe fruits, this moves in the direction of the New World.

Château Guilhem *

1 Boulevard du Château, 11300 Malviès	*+33 4 68 31 14 41*
contact@chateauguilhem.com	*Bertrand Gourdou*
www.chateauguilhem.com	*Malepère [map p. 103]*
	Malepère, Clos du Blason
30 ha; 250,000 btl	*IGP Pays Cathare, Grand Vin Blanc*

This is the go-to domain for understanding the nature of Malepère, which is an unusual AOP for the Languedoc, growing Bordeaux varieties. The wines are more than 50% Merlot. When asked how this relates to climate and terroir, Bertrand Gourdou says, "I can't criticize, it was my grandfather who planted the first Merlot vines, which he selected in Bordeaux, in 1974." Château Guilhem is the oldest and largest estate in Malepère, founded in 1878, and Bertrand is the fifth generation.

Vineyards are on the Massif de Malepère at altitudes from 250 to 400m. Four different cuvées are based on Merlot, ranging from the entry-level Pot de Vin Rouge (IGP Pays d'Oc, 100% Merlot), to the Malepère AOP cuvées: Cuvée Prestige (half Merlot, the rest Cabernet Sauvignon, Cabernet Franc, and Malbec); Grand Vin Rouge (half Merlot, half Cabernet Franc); and the top-line Clos du Blason (60% Merlot, 20% each of Cabernet Sauvignon and Cabernet Franc).

Styles range from the light fresh entry-level wines to the richer and more structured impressions at the top. Grand Vin Rouge is quite weighty with some structure showing, Clos du Blason is more finely structured, both in a relatively fresh style, light rather than lush. Whites under the IGP Pays d'Oc label include Chardonnay, Sauvignon Blanc, blends of the two, and a blend based on Muscat. The Chardonnay shows the aromatics of the south, Sauvignon Blanc is a soft version of the variety, and the blend has the most concentration and smoothness.

Domaine Ledogar *

Place de la République, 11200 Ferrals lès Corbières	*+33 6 81 06 14 51*
xavier.ledogar@orange.fr	*Xavier Ledogar*
www.domaineledogar.fr	*Corbières [map p. 103]*
19 ha; 50,000 btl	*Vin de France, La Mariole*

Four generations of Ledogars have been making wine in Corbières, but it was only when Xavier Ledogar decided he wanted to become a vigneron that his father, André, decided to create his own domain (initially called Domaine Grand Lauze, renamed Domaine Ledogar in 2008). They purchased an old building in 1997, and made the first vintage in 1998. Xavier's younger brother Mathieu joined the domain in 2000. The domain is committed to producing natural wine, and as a result has run into the usual difficulties with the *agrément* for the AOP; so although 80% of their vineyards are in Corbières and 20% in IGP, some of the wines are labeled as Vin de France.

Within Corbières, plantings are mostly Carignan (11 ha), Mourvèdre (2.5 ha), Syrah (2.5 ha), or Grenache (2 ha); the rest consists of Macabeo and Cinsault, and a small amount of white varieties. Yields are low, at 25-35 hl/ha. In addition there are some IGP vineyards that André had planted with Cabernet Sauvignon and Marselan. There are some plots in Corbières of very old Carignan and Grenache, within which are some other old varieties of the area. The top wines of the domain come from Carignan or Carignan-dominated blends. Rather spicy, the Corbières is a conventional blend, but Tout Natur, a Vin de France blend of Carignan with Mourvèdre, would make a fine Corbières if it had the agrément. Coming from very old vines, La Mariole is a monovarietal Carignan with a rare precision.

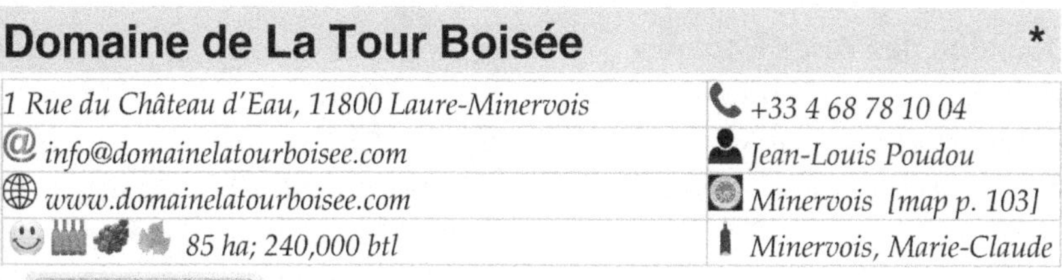

Domaine de La Tour Boisée *

1 Rue du Château d'Eau, 11800 Laure-Minervois	*+33 4 68 78 10 04*
info@domainelatourboisee.com	*Jean-Louis Poudou*
www.domainelatourboisee.com	*Minervois [map p. 103]*
85 ha; 240,000 btl	*Minervois, Marie-Claude*

This old family domain dates from 1826. A person of strong opinions ("AOC says something—it is controlled—but AOP is nothing, it is a trick to talk about Protégé"), current proprietor Jean-Louis Poitou, who took over in 1982, tries to maintain tradition, growing 17 grape varieties in his many parcels. "We can take a Burgundian approach and identify a place for each variety," he says. He's been trying to reintroduce some of the old Gris varieties that used to be grown in the area.

About 70% of production is red, with the rest divided between white and rosé; 60% of the wines are Minervois; the others, including monovarietals and some unusual combinations of varieties, are in one of the local IGPs. The difference is due more to the regulations of the AOPs and IGPs than quality. "Our IGP wines are worked in the same spirit as AOP with similar yields, 40 hl/ha for the IGP, and 30 hl/ha for the AOP." The whites of Minervois are blends of the usual southern varieties, but the IGP Coteaux de Peyriac is a Chardonnay. There's a range of red monovarietals in the IGP, but the most interesting wine here is the red Minervois Marie-Claude, a blend of Syrah, Grenache, and Carignan. A late harvest wine from Marsanne, Minervois Noble, has some botrytis as well as passerillage, and matures for ten years in old tonneaux. In addition to the wines that are labeled as Château Tour Boisée, there's also an entry-level line (including red, white, and rosé) under the label of Domaine Tour Boisée.

Profiles of Important Estates

Abbotts et Delaunay

32, avenue du Languedoc, 11800 Marseillette	*+33 4 68 79 00 00*
contact@abbottsetdelaunay.com	*Laurent Delaunay*
www.abbottsetdelaunay.com	*Corbières* *[map p. 103]*
	25 ha

Laurent Delaunay is the fifth generation of a family of wine merchants in Nuits St. Georges in Burgundy; after founding Bader, Clément in 1995, he specialized in the wines of Languedoc, and then in 2005 took over the winery created by Nerida Abbot near Carcassonne. There are three ranges of wines: varietal wines under IGP Pays d'Oc, AOP wines from appellations including Corbières and Minervois, and micro cuvées from high altitude vineyards. Alto Stratus is 100% Carignan Vin de France from 100-year-old vines, Cumulo Nimbus is a blend of Syrah and Grenache from Minervois, and Boréas is a blend of GSM and Carignan from Faugères. The micro cuvees age and 40% in stainless steel , and 60% in barriques with 30% new oak.

Domaine des Aires Hautes

12 chemin des Aires, 34210 Siran	*+33 4 68 91 54 40*
gilles.chabbert@wanadoo.fr	*Gilles Chabbert*
aires-hautes.pagesperso-orange.fr	*Minervois La Livinière* *[map p. 103]*
	30 ha; 135,000 btl

Already growing grapes in the Montagne Noire, Edmond Chabbert created the domain in 1938. His son René succeeded him, and in the next generation Gilles took over in 1995. The domain is located in the heart of Minervois, in the area known as Le Petit Causse. In traditional wines, Minervois Tradition is a blend of Carignan, Grenache, Syrah, and Cinsault, the Réserve is Minervois La Livinière and is mostly Syrah and Grenache with a small amount of Carignan, and the top wine, Clos de l'Escandil, is a GSM that is 50% Syrah, aged in barriques including one third new oak. Under IGP Pays d'Oc there are varietal wines from Malbec, Chardonnay, and Sauvignon Blanc.

Clos de l'Anhel

2 rue Montlauriers, 11220 Montlaur	*+33 4 68 76 16 23*
anhel@wanadoo.fr	*Sophie Guiraudon*
www.anhel.fr	*Corbières* *[map p. 103]*
	9 ha; 30,000 btl

"I am a winegrower of the zero generation," says Sophie Guiraudon. Sophie started by taking over 6 ha from a coop member who retired. Her partner Philippe Mathias managed Château de Pech-Latt (see profile) before joining her full time in their own domain (Philippe left Pech-Latt in 2017), where they produce only red wine. The four cuvées are based on a predominance of Carignan. Le Lolo d'Anhel is the easy-drinking entry-level wine, Les Autres is 100% Carignan (and therefore labeled as Vin de France), Les Terrasettes is the first "serious wine," and Les Dimanches is the top wine; with 70% Carignan and a proportion aged in barriques, it is regarded as showing unusual finesse (the name indicates that it should be saved for Sundays).

Maison Antech

Domaine de Flassian, Rue Dewoitine, 11300 Limoux	*+33 4 68 31 15 88*
courriers@antech-limoux.com	*Françoise Antech-Gazeau*
www.antech-limoux.com	*Limoux [map p. 103]*
	60 ha; 1,000,000 btl

This negociant is a family business that goes back six generations. The commitment to sparkling wines was made by brothers Georges and Roger, who took over in 1965. Since 1996, the Maison has been run by George's daughter, Françoise. Estate vineyards provide the major part of production, and are planted to 65% Mauzac, 15% Chenin Blanc, and 20% Chardonnay. There is a wide range of both Blanquette de Limoux and Crémant de Limoux, all from blends of the three varieties. The Blanquette cuvées have more than 90% Mauzac, while the Crémant cuvées have less than 10%. There is also a Chardonnay labeled under IGP Pays d'Oc.

Château Auris

Route du massif de Fontfroide, 11100 Narbonne	*+33 4 68 45 19 43*
axel.dewoillemont@maisonalbert.fr	*Jean-Claude Albert*
www.chateau-auris.com	*Corbières [map p. 82]*
	40 ha

The vineyards are part of an estate of 160 ha that once belonged to the Cistercian abbey of Fontfroide. Jean-Claude Albert bought the property in 2005. He also owns Domaine les Bugadelles at La Clape, and some wines are produced under the label of Maison Albert. A few miles inland from Narbonne, Château Auris is just south of the mountain of Fontfroide. Black grapes are grown on slopes of the mountain, where soils are based on sandstone, and white varieties are grown on the plain, where the soils vary from sand to clay. The Souffle d'Ange range has all three colors and ages in tank. In the Collection range, the red of Syrah, Grenache, and Carignan has the Syrah aged in barriques, the rosé is Grenache, Cinsault, and Syrah, and the white is Marsanne and Grenache Blanc. There are two other red cuvées: Les Terrasses de Béa has Syrah, Grenache, Carignan et Cinsault and ages in tank; A D'Auris is Syrah and Grenache, aged new and 1-year barriques for 12 months.

Château Auzias

Chemin de Paretlongue, 11610 Pennautier	*+33 4 68 47 28 28*
info@auzias.fr	*Nathalie & Dominique Auzias*
www.auzias.fr	*Cabardès [map p. 103]*
	110 ha; 600,000 btl

Founded by monks in the twelfth century on the site of a Roman villa, the domain is just off the Canal du Midi a mile north of Carcassonne, at the foot of the Montagne Noir. The Auzias negociant family bought the property in 1872, and still hold it today. This is one of the largest family domains in the Languedoc, with its vineyards in a single block in the 160 ha estate. Soils are calcareous clay. Wines fall under AOP Cabardès and IGP Cité de Carcassonne. IGP cuvées include Chardonnay-Viognier and Chardonnay-Sauvignon Blanc-Muscat blends, rosé from Grenache, and varietal Syrah with no added sulfur. Cabardès cuvées are blends of Syrah, Cabernet Franc, and Grenache, with Petits Messieurs coming from young (under 15-years old) vines, aged in concrete, and Mademoiselle from older vines (average age 25 years), aged half in concrete and half in barriques. The top wines are Instinct Terrien (60% Cabernet Franc and 40% Syrah) and Instinct Marin (60% Syrah and 40% Cabernet Franc), both aged 30% in barriques with the rest in concrete, and Gloria Mundi (50% Syrah and 50% Cabernet Franc) aged for 18 months in barriques.

Domaine de Baronarques

Lambert, 11300 Saint-Polycarpe	*+33 4 68 31 94 66*
caveau@domainedebaronarques.com	*Lionel Lerch*
www.domaine-de-baronarques.com	*Limoux [map p. 103]*
	45 ha; 100,000 btl

Under the name of Domaine de Lambert, the estate belonged to the Abbaye de Saint Polycarpe from 1650 until it passed into private hands after the Revolution in 1789. The 110 ha estate was bought by Château Mouton Rothschild in 1998, when the buildings were renovated and vineyards replanted. They gave it the name Domaine de Baron'Arques, which they simplified to Baronarques in 2015. Their first vintage was 2003. A new barrel room was built in 2018. Vineyards are on calcareous clay, at 250-350m altitude, planed 70% with Bordeaux varieties and 30% with local varieties for reds; only Chardonnay is used for whites. Cuvées follow the Bordeaux model of a grand vin and a second wine. The blend of the grand vin depends on the year but typically follows the balance of plantings, which means about three quarters Bordeaux varieties (Merlot usually makes up about half the total) and one quarter Grenache and Syrah. It ages in barriques with 25-50% new oak and 50-75% 1-2-year oak for 12 months. The blend is simplified for the second wine, which does not have Cabernet Sauvignon or Cabernet Franc, and again is about 50% Merlot. It ages for 6 months in 1-2-year barriques. The white ferments and ages for 8 months in barriques with a third each of new, 1-year, and 2-year. It's a sign of the times that the domain produces only still wine under Limoux AOP and not sparkling wine.

Domaine de Cabrol

RD118, 11600 Aragon	*+33 6 81 14 00 26*
cc@domainedecabrol.fr	*Claude Carayol*
domainedecabrol.fr	*Cabardès [map p. 103]*
21 ha; 60,000 btl	*Cabardès, La Dérive*

This has been a family domain for many generations. Just north of Carcassonne, it is a large estate of around 125 ha, with 21 ha of vines planted in individual plots each surrounded by woods and the garrigue. It's quite hilly, with steep paths through the woods between the vineyards, with an average elevation around 300m. Cabernet Sauvignon is planted where the soil is deepest, because it requires the most humidity, and Syrah is planted on the stoniest parcels, often facing south as they are hottest. Stony is a euphemism; the ground is covered with quite sizeable rocks, indicating the calcareous character of the terroir. All production is red in the Cabardès AOP except for a tiny amount of white wine labeled as Vin de France. The reds split into southern blends based on Syrah (Vent d'Est is a Syrah-Cabernet Franc blend) or more northern blends based on Cabernet Sauvignon (Vent d'Ouest is Cabernet Sauvignon with lesser proportions of Grenache and Syrah), but the best wine by far is La Dérive, which splits the difference and is an equal blend of Syrah and Cabernet Sauvignon. Coming from the best parcels, this is the only cuvée to be matured in wood, and spends two years in demi-muids. These are wines that are best enjoyed relatively young.

Château de Caraguilhes

11220 Saint Laurent de La Cabrerisse	*+33 4 68 27 88 99*
chateau@caraguilhes.fr	*Pierre Gabison & Etienne Besancenot*
www.caraguilhes.fr	*Corbières-Boutenac [map p. 103]*
	130 ha; 300,000 btl

Owned in the twelfth century by the Cistercian monks of the Abbaye de Frontfroide, this 600 ha estate has remained intact. The modern era started when winemaker Lionel Faivre returned from Algeria, took over the estate, and began organic production (very rare indeed at the time). In 1998, Lionel sold the estate to Pierre Gabison; Pierre took over completely in 2005. Vineyards are in a single block at 100-180m altitude, surrounded by 500 ha of garrigue. With such a large estate, there's variation in soil types, but they are generally calcareous and pebbly. From Corbières-Boutenac, L'Echappée Belle is 80% Carignan (going through carbonic maceration) and 20% Mourvèdre, aged in vat, Solus (Mourvèdre, Carignan, and Syrah, aged partly in concrete and partly in barriques), and Le Trou de l'Ermite (Carignan, Grenache, Syrah, Mourvèdre, aged in 2-3-year barriques). There are also two cuvées from Corbières and a 100% Cinsault IGP. White Vins de France are blends of Viognier, Marsanne, and Grenache Blanc, Corbières La Font Blanche is Roussanne, Grenache Blanc, and Vermentino, aged mostly in vat, and Solus is 80% Grenache Blanc, 20% Roussanne, aged in demi-muids.

Domaine de Cazaban

Chemin des Eclauzes, 11600 Villegailhenc	*+33 4 68 72 11 63*
info@domainedecazaban.com	*Emmanuel Taillez*
www.domainedecazaban.com	*Cabardès [map p. 103]*
	22 ha; 85,000 btl

The domain was created by Clément Mengus as an organic venture with 6 ha of vineyards in a 15 ha estate. After ten years, he sold the property to Emmanuel Taillez, formerly an industrialist. The domain produces Vin de France, IGP Pays d'Aude, and Cabardès. In a reversal of the typical cuvées elsewhere in Languedoc, the IGP has the local varieties (Jours de Vigne is Carignan and Grenache, while Demoiselle Claire is Grenache and Syrah), and AOP Cabardès has Atlantic varieties (Les Petites Rangées is

Syrah and Cabernet Franc, while the estate wine—"probably the most typical of the AOP" is Merlot and Syrah).

Domaine de la Cendrillon

La Cendrillon, Route de Narbonne, 11200 Ornai-	*+33 9 61 37 85 51*
info@lacendrillon.fr	*Hubert Joyeux*
www.lacendrillon.fr	*Corbières-Boutenac [map p. 82]*
	50 ha; 160,000 btl

Robert Joyeux is the seventh generation at this family estate, which dates from 1750. Robert began at the estate in 1993, when all grapes were sent to the coop, and he started estate-bottling in 2008. There's one white, one rosé, and four red cuvées. Classique is a GSM, with 45% Grenache and 40% Syrah, aged in cuve, while Inédite has the same varieties, but 50% Syrah and 35% Mourvèdre, aged in a mixture of wood and steel. The top wine, No. 1, is another play on these verities, with 60% Mourvèdre, 30% Syrah, and 10% Grenache, all from old vines, aged in foudres. As its name suggests, Atypique is quite different, with a blend of Marselan, Merlot, Mourvèdre, Grenache, and a dash of Petit Verdot, aged in stainless steel. The white, introduced in 2014, has Petit Manseng, Albariño, Verdejo, and Grenache Blanc and Gris. The rosé is Mourvèdre, Grenache, and Syrah.

Clos Centeilles

Chemin de Centeilles, 34210 Siran	*+33 4 68 91 52 18*
contact@closcenteilles.com	*Patricia Boyer Domergue & Cécile Domergue*
www.closcenteilles.com	*Minervois La Livinière [map p. 103]*
	13 ha; 60,000 btl

Patricia Boyer Domergue bought this property in 1990 in what later became the AOP of Minervois La Livinière at the west of the Languedoc. There were already some old vines, and she focused on planting ancient varieties, in conjunction with her husband Daniel, a professor of oenology. Today she runs the domain with her daughter Cécile. Clos Centeilles (the first cuvée when the domain was founded) is a conventional GSM. Campagne de Centeilles is based mostly on 50-year-old Cinsault. Carignanissime de Centeilles is a varietal Carignan from 60-100-year-old vines. La Part des Anges is a blend of old Carignan with younger Picpoul. Clos de Centeilles rouge includes some really obscure varieties—Picpoul Noir, Riveirenc, Morastel, and l'Oeillade. Guigniers de Centeilles is Pinot Noir. L'Erme de Centeilles is a sweet white from Grenache Blanc. All of the wines have élevage of 18-24 months in cuve.

Château de Cesseras

5 Chemin de Minerve, 34210 Cesseras	*+33 4 68 49 35 21*
domainecoudoulet@gmail.com	*Pierre-André Ourna*
www.Domainecoudoulet.com	*Minervois La Livinière [map p. 103]*
	94 ha; 200,000 btl

Château de Cesseras is part of Domaine de Coudoulet, a very large domain, with 20 ha in Minervois, including a large part in La Livinière. It's been a family estate since 1840, and estate bottling started after Pierre-André Ornac took over in 1985, now helped by his nephew Guillaume. The Coudoulet estate as a whole produces a large amount of white wine, but Château de Cesseras is known for its reds from Minervois and La Livinière. When Pierre-André took over, it was planted with Aramon and Carignan, but now the top wine from La Livinière is 70% Syrah with 30% from Carignan, Grenache, and Mourvèdre. The wine is powerful with high alcohol, as typical for the region, but fruits are cut by a sense of the garrigue, and the smooth palate conveys elegance.

Les Clos Perdus

17 Rue du Marché, 11440 Peyriac-de-Mer	*+33 6 88 45 02 77*
lesclosperdus@hotmail.com	*Paul Old*
www.lesclosperdus.com	*Corbières [map p. 82]*
	20 ha

The name describes the philosophy of the project—Les Clos Perdus means 'the lost parcels'—and it was founded by Paul Old and Hugo Stewart in 2003 with 1.5 ha at the far east of Corbières, in the area known as Corbières Maritimes for its proximity to the sea. Over the years they accumulated more parcels, now 32 altogether, extending from farther west in Hautes Corbières and farther south in the Agly valley in Roussillon. The parcels usually have rather old vines, often in poor shape to start off with. Hugo left the project, but Paul continues to make the wines. Mire La Mer is a blend from 65% 40-year-old Mourvèdre, 30% 110-year-old Carignan, and 5% Grenache, on heavy clay and limestone in Corbières Maritimes. Prioundo is blend of 80% Grenache and 20% Cinsault from 30-year-old vines at high altitude in Hautes Corbières. L'Extrême red is 75% Grenache and 25% Syrah from schist terroir in the Agly valley. Whites come from the Agly valley: L'Année Blanc is 85% Macabeu (Viura) and 30% Grenache Gris, both from 60-70-year-old vines with 5% Muscat; L'Extrême is 70% Grenache Gris, 25% Grenache Blanc, and 5% Grenache, from 120-year-old vines. The numbered cuvée—cuvée 151 from 2017, 141 from 2016 and so on, going back—is the first cuvée made at Clos Perdus, mostly Corbières Maritimes, but sometimes including lots from Hautes Corbières, and is 50% Carignan, 35% Grenache, and 15% Mourvèdre, aged only in stainless steel. The other wines mostly age in stainless steel with some use of 400- or 500-liter oak barrels.

Domaine la Combe Blanche

Ancien Chemin du Moulin de Rigaud 3, 34210 La Livinière	*+33 6 80 43 40 61*
contact@lacombeblanche.com	*Guy Vanlancker*
www.lacombeblanche.com	*Minervois La Livinière [map p. 103]*
	12 ha; 40,000 btl

Guy Vanlancker left a teaching career in Belgium 1981 to make wine in the Languedoc. He founded Domaine Combe Blanche in 2000. His main production is La Livinière, but he is also notable for a range of IGP monovarietal wines, including Roussanne, Pinot Noir, Tempranillo, and Cinsault. In addition to an entry-level Minervois, there are three cuvées from La Livinière. La Galine is the benchmark, from 40% Syrah, 40% Grenache, and 20% Carignan. La Chandelière increases the proportion of Syrah to 75%; the rest is Grenache. Both are spicy and nutty, with a sense of power accentuated by high alcohol (as much as 15%) but Chandelière (a small production of only 2,000 bottles) is distinctly more powerful. Under the separate label of Clos du Causse (because he does not own the vineyard, which is a couple of miles away near Félines Minervois), Guy makes another cuvée from La Livinière. Clos du Causse is a contrast with the wines under the Combe Blanche label; although it has less Syrah (25%) and more Grenache (75%), instead of being more powerful, it is instead more elegant, quite smooth with an unusual sense of finesse for the Languedoc.

Combes Cachées

Chemin Calle, 34210 Fourquevaux	*+33 6 72 88 65 10*
lescombescachees@gmail.com	*Michel Pousse*
www.les-combes-cachees.fr	*Minervois La Livinière [map p. 103]*
	15 ha; 50,000 btl

The domain takes its name from three plots hidden in the garrigue. It's a collaboration between three friends from the same village, Michel Pousse, Xavier Michelin, and François Aumonier, as something of a retirement activity. They started with 8 ha in 2015, and the project grew as their families joined in. There are now more than 18 separate parcels, dispersed in Minervois. Most of the production is a blend of Syrah and Grenache from Minervois or Minervois La Livinière, which ages for 12 months in barrique. A large part of La Livinière was at first declassified to Minervois, but the balance has shifted towards producing more La Livinière. There is also a small production of white Minervois. Under IGP Pays d'Oc there are varietal cuvées of Viognier, Malbec, and Pinot Noir each from small specific plots. Wines are sold as Domaine Les Combes Cachées in France and as Domaine Michelin - Les Combes Cachées elsewhere.

Domaine Pierre Cros

20 Rue du Minervois, 11800 Badens	*+33 4 68 79 21 82*
dom-pierre-cros@sfr.fr	*Piere Cros*
www.vinparleur.net/-pierre-cros-58	*Minervois [map p. 103]*
	28 ha

A few miles east of Carcassonne, the domain covers about 50 ha, on poor, shallow, clay-calcareous soils. Half the estate is planted with vines, the other half with almond and olive trees on scrubland. A former rugby player, Pierre Cros has a collection of old vines, including some less common varieties. There are plantings of Carignan from 1905, Piquepoul Noir from 1910, Alicante from 1927, and Aramon from 1930. The family owned some parcels of vines, but Pierre is the first to be a grower and wine producer. The major cuvées are the red Tradition, a blend of the local black varieties, aged in cuve, and Les Aspres, a Syrah aged in barrique. The Vieilles Vignes comes from the century-old Carignan. There are blends in both red (Les Mal Aimés) and rosé (Partouse) from the old varieties: Alicante, Aramon, Piquepoul Noir, Morrastel, Rivairenc, and Carignan.

Domaine Jean-Louis Denois

Bordelongue, 11300 Roquetaillade	*+33 4 68 31 39 12*
jldenois@orange.fr	*Jean-Louis Denois*
www.jldenois.com	*Limoux [map p. 103]*
	35 ha; 200,000 btl

Jean-Louis Denois is somewhat of an iconoclast. He comes from six generations of winemakers in Champagne, but decided to make sparkling wine in the south, after working at various countries in the New World. He likes the clay and limestone terroir in Limoux, but does not like the local grape variety, Mauzac, which he ripped out to replace with Pinot Noir and Chardonnay. He tried to plant Riesling and Gewürztraminer, but was blocked by the authorities. His bone of contention is that the appellation rules in Limoux prevent him from making the best sparkling wine. His first property in Limoux was Domaine de l'Aigle, which he sold, although he kept some of the first plots he planted in 1988 with Chardonnay and Pinot Noir clones from Champagne; now he makes wine under his own name from 70 different plots. There are 10 ha, mostly Chardonnay in Roquetaillade, 3 ha of Pinot Noir in the next village, and a series of small plots of old vines around Fenouillèdes in the Upper Agly valley, relatively high at up to 400m. The Pinot Noir Village cuvée ages in used 500-liter barrels; the Grand Vin cuvée is a selection of the best lots from the higher plots, fermented in barrels, and then aged in used 500-liter barrels. Sainte Marie is Chardonnay (the 2016 vintage included some Chenin Blanc), fermented with no added sulfur in 3-year 500-liter barrels, and then aged for 9 months in the barrels. There are some less conventional cuvées: La Boulzane is 90% Chardonnay and 10% Muscat. There are also Cabernet Sauvignon, aged conventionally in oak, and the Amphores cuvée, which is Cabernet Sauvignon aged exclusively in amphorae for 9 months. The main weight, of course, is on sparkling wine. Tradition Extra Brut is the flagship cuvée, a blend of Pinot Noir and Chardonnay, with dosage of 5 g/l, going back to Jean-Louis's first production in the region. Rosé Brut is 100% Pinot Noir, with dosage of 7 g/l. Sainte Marie Extra Brut is Blanc de Blancs from old vines Chardonnay, fermented in oak, with malolactic fermentation blocked. Eclipse comes from a blend of Pinot Noir and Chardonnay fermented and aged in barrique, and is extra brut with 5 g/l dosage. Less conventionally, Classique Brut comes from a blend of Pinot Noir, Syrah, and Chardonnay with 7 g/l dosage; and the Blanc de Noirs Bulles de Syrah is certainly an unusual concept. The domain itself is not open, but the wines can be found at Vina et Terra in Limoux.

Domaine de Dernacueillette

15 Rue Fleurie, 11330 Dernacueillette	*+33 6 70 79 38 46*
domaine.de.dernacueillette@gmail.com	*Guillaume Boussens*
www.domainededernacueillette.fr	*Corbières [map p. 103]*
	25 ha; 35,000 btl

One of the highest estates in Hautes-Corbières, with vineyards at up to 600m, the property was taken over by Guillaume Boussens in 1999. The seventeenth century winery building was renovated and the vineyards were restructured and extended. Guillaume sent grapes to the cooperative until 2003, when he produced the first domain wine. Vineyards are mostly on schist, but there are also plots with iron-rich or calcareous clay. The AOP Corbières is 55% Syrah, 35% Carignan, and 10% Grenache from a blend of terroirs, aged in vat. Anne Fleur is a similar blend, but ages for 26 months in foudre. Château les Hauts de Dernacueillette has 50% Syrah with 25% each of Carignan and Grenache, from vineyards of the Chateau that dates from the thirteenth century and dominates the village. Passionément Cuvée Jacques increases the Syrah to 70%. They age in vat.

Domaine Des Deux Clés

1 Avenue Saint-Victor, 11360 Fontjoncouse	*+33 4 34 44 23 55*
info@domaine-des-deux-cles.com	*Gaëlle & Florian Richter*
fr.domaine-des-deux-cles.com	*Corbières* *[map p. 103]*
	14 ha

Gaëlle qualified as an oenologist in Dijon and Florian studied wine business at Geisenheim. They met while working at Maison Champy in Beaune in 2009, worked at vineyards in France, Italy, Germany, and New Zealand, and came to the Languedoc in 2012. It took three years before they were able to find and purchase their own vineyards (originally called Val Auclair), which are dispersed over several valleys near Fontjoncouse, at elevations of 250-350m, often facing northeast, which means that temperatures are cooler than average for the region. Soils vary from calcareous clay to schist and quartz. The plots have densely planted old vines, some almost a century old, and have to be worked manually. Whites follow Burgundian precepts, and are fermented and aged in barriques. Reds are fermented as a mix of whole clusters and destemmed berries. Clés En Main is a Vin de France from a third each of Syrah, Grenache, and Carignan (planted in 1950), aged in stainless steel. IGP Vallée du Paradis is 70% Carignan and 30% Grenache, cofermented, and aged in barrique. Corbières is 50% Carignan with 25% each of Grenache and Syrah, which are cofermented, aged mostly in concrete with a small proportion in barrique. The Corbières white is 80% Macabeu, 15% Grenache Blanc, and 5% Vermentino, fermented after whole bunch pressing. A Vin de France white, Jeu de Clés, is Roussanne.

Clos du Gravillas

Le Village, 34360 Saint Jean de-Minervois	*+33 4 67 38 17 52*
nicole@closdugravillas.com	*Nicole Bojanowski*
www.closdugravillas.com	*St. Jean-de-Minervois* *[map p. 103]*
	7 ha; 30,000 btl

John Bojanowski is American, Nicole comes from Béziers, and they more or less constructed this domain themselves from the ground up in 1999. Soils are calcareous, at an elevation of 300m. Today there are 15 cuvées, but the heart of the domain is in Carignan, with the oldest vines dating from 1911. The old plot also has Grenache Gris. They planted Syrah, Mourvèdre, and other varieties, bringing the number of cépages to 15. Lo Veilh comes from 2 ha of Carignan planted between 1911 and 1970; as a varietal Carignan, it's labeled as IGP. Sur La Lune is a blend of 40-80-year-old Carignan and Syrah with a little Carignan. L'Inattendu is a Grenache Blanc. The stated objective is elegance rather than power.

Château Sainte-Eulalie

Lieu-dit Sainte Eulalie, 34210 La Livinière	*+33 4 68 91 42 72*
info@chateausainteeulalie.com	*Isabelle & Laurent Coustal*
www.chateausainteeulalie.com	*Minervois La Livinière* *[map p. 103]*
	40 ha; 200,000 btl

The domain was established in the early twentieth century, and purchased by Laurent and Isabelle Coustal, both oenologues, in 1996. Isabelle is now President of the La Livinière growers' association. The vineyards are all in one holding around the winery, at altitudes of 200-250m in La Livinière. Soils are pebbly, with clay, chalk, and manganese; vineyards mostly predate the purchase, except for 2 ha of Syrah planted in 2000. There are reds from Minervois and Minervois La Livinière, rosé from Minervois, and a white IGP. Under Minervois, Plaisir d'Eulalie is a GSM that ages in cuve, and Prestige d'Eulalie is a GSM with almost half Syrah that ages in cuve and barriques. Under La Livinière, there are two cuvées. Grand Vin comes from a third each of very old Carignan and Grenache and a third of Syrah planted in the eighties. It has no oak. "We wanted to make a wine that keeps the fruit, so it ages in concrete for only 6 months," Isabelle says. It's light and approachable, but doesn't have the interest of La Cantilène, which comes from 55% Syrah, 30% Carignan, and 15% Grenache, and ages in a mix of concrete and barriques, which include some new oak.

Domaine de Fontsainte

11200 Boutenac	*+33 4 68 27 07 63*
earl.laboucarie@fontsainte.com	*Bruno Laboucarié*
www.fontsainte.com	*Corbières-Boutenac [map p. 103]*
	56 ha; 180,000 btl

The family has been involved in winemaking since the seventeenth century, and Yves Laboucarié established the domain in the Cru of Boutenac in 1971. His son Bruno took over in 1995. Vineyards are south-southeast facing adjacent to a large pinewood forest. Vineyards are broken up into many parcels, with an average altitude of 95m. Plantings are more than half Carignan. The modern cellar operates by gravity-feed. The domaine red is 60% Carignan, 30% Grenache, and 10% Syrah, made by carbonic maceration. Yves introduced the cuvées Gris de Gris (a rosé de saignée from five varieties based on 70% Grenache and Grenache Gris) and La Demoiselle (a blend (of 60% 115-year-old Carignan with Grenache and Mourvèdre from the Demoiselle parcel, fermented by carbonic maceration), and Bruno introduced Le Clos du Centurion (the same blend as the domain red, but coming from the best parcels, and aged in barrique).

Domaine Girard

Lieu dit La, Chemin de la Garriguette, 11240 Alaigne	*+33 4 68 69 05 27*
domaine-girard@wanadoo.fr	*Jean-François Girard*
www.domaine-girard.eu	*Malepère [map p. 103]*
	38 ha

This family estate is now in its fifth generation under Philippe Girard, who started estate-bottling when he took over in 2000, joined by his brother Jean—François in 2004. The domain is located in the medieval village of Alaigne. Vineyards are at 350-450m elevation, among the most northern in Languedoc. The reds vary between traditional and novel. Malepère Tradition is 60% Merlot and 40% Cabernet Franc, aged in cuve. There are two varietal Pinot Noirs under IGP Pays d'Oc, one aged in cuve, and Pech Calvel, aged in 500-liter barrels. Whites are all Chardonnay, with an AOP Limoux, Las Salvios, and the IGP Pays d'Oc, Elevé Sur Les Fines aged in 500-liter barrels, and the IGP Classique aged in cuve. There are also rosé and Crémant de Limoux.

Château de Gourgazaud

Hameau Gourgazaud, 34210 La Livinière	*+33 4 68 78 10 02*
contact@gourgazaud.com	*Annick Tiburce*
www.gourgazaud.com	*Minervois La Livinière [map p. 103]*
	75 ha; 350,000 btl

The Piquet family started by trading in wine in the nineteenth century. Roger Piquet started negociant Chantovent in 1953, and purchased the estate in 1973. Originally it consisted of 67 ha at the base of the Montagne Noir, in what is now the Minervois Cru of La Livinière, planted with Aramon and Cinsault. Roger's daughters Chantale Piquet and Annick Tiburce took over in 2005 and now focus on modern varieties. The blends from the AOP are Syrah with some Mourvèdre. Cuvée Mathilde is Minervois; the Réserve is Minervois La Livinière, and is aged in new barriques. Quintus is almost entirely Syrah, with just 5% Mourvèdre, and is IGP Pays d'Oc to give more flexibility in production. Pater Familias comes from 70-year old Grenache. The Cabernet Sauvignon is a monovarietal. The whites are mostly varietals in IGP Pays d'Oc, with two cuvées of Viognier, Chardonnay aged in either cuve or barriques, a Chardonnay-Viognier blend, and a Sauvignon Blanc.

Domaine du Grand Arc

15 Chemin des Métairies du Devez, 11350 Cucugnan	*+33 4 68 45 01 03*
info@grand-arc.com	*Nicolas Schenck*
www.grand-arc.com	*Corbières [map p. 103]*
	25 ha; 65,000 btl

Bruno Schenk was an engineer in Alsace before he bought the property in 1995. At first he sent grapes to the cooperative, but then he started to produce his own wine. Vineyards are at 250-600m elevation on calcareous clay, with some sandstone, near Cucugnan in an isolated valley of the Massif des Corbières, overlooked by the castles at Quéribus and Peyrepertuse. (The vineyards are high enough that Bruno was once advised it would be too cool for red wine.) Nicolas has now taken over from his father. The red Corbières range starts with Cuvée des Quarante (Carignan, Grenache, and Syrah), then there are La DéSyrahble (80% Syrah and 20% Grenache), En Sol Majeur (60% Grenache and 40% Syrah), and La Thébaïde (Cinsault, Grenache, Syrah, and Mourvèdre from the highest plots on Mont Tauch). Six Terres Sienne (Syrah, Carignan, and Grenache) is the only cuvée to have any oak exposure. Aux Temps d'Histoire is basically Carignan.

Château du Grand Caumont

D261, 11200 Lézignan Corbières	*+33 4 68 27 10 82*
flb.rigal@wanadoo.fr	*Françoise Rigal*
www.grandcaumont.com	*Corbières [map p. 103]*
	96 ha; 350,000 btl

One of the largest domains in the region, the property was once a Roman estate covering 1,000 ha. The estate was owned by King Charles in the ninth century, burned to destruction in the French Revolution in 1789, and then bought in 1850 by Auguste Sarda who reconstructed buildings and planted vines. Founder of the present owners, Louis Rigal purchased the 150 ha property in 1906, and it passed to his son in 1945 and then to his granddaughter Françoise in 1980. Françoise introduced estate-bottling. Her daughter Laurence took over in 2003. Production is 70% Corbières from traditional blends and 30% IGP focusing on varietal wines. AOP Corbières cuvées are mostly blends with more or less equal Carignan and Syrah which are partly destemmed, and a small proportion of Grenache: Spéciale ages in vat, Réserve de Laurence has 10% aged in barriques, Impatience ages 40% in barriques, and Capus Monti is 60% Syrah with 40% from 80-year-old Carignan, aged entirely in new barriques. Impatience Blanc is 80% Grenache Blanc and 20% Vermentino, aged with 50% in new barriques. The IGPs have varietal Cabernet Sauvignon, Merlot, and Syrah.,

Domaine du Grand Crès

11200 26 rue Sainte Elizabeth, Fabrezan	*+33 9 61 48 72 67*
grand.cres@outlook.fr	*Hervé Leferrer*
www.domainedugrandcres.fr	*Corbières [map p. 103]*
	15 ha; 50,000 btl

Hervé Leferrer worked at INAO, and then at Domaine de la Romanée Conti, before buying 5 ha in Corbières in 1989. The domain started by producing Corbières: the entry-level Le Junior has equal Grenache and Syrah and is bottled after a brief period in cuve, Le Senior is Syrah, Grenache, and a little Cinsault, aged mostly in cuve with a fraction in barriques, and the top AOP is Cuvée Majeure, 90% Syrah and 10% Grenache, aged in barriques followed by cuve. The white is a blend of Roussanne and Viognier. A purchase of 2 ha of Cabernet Sauvignon in 2006 makes an entry-level AOP Languedoc, Le Cabernet. However, the top wine (and by far the most expensive), is Cressaïa, a Vin de France from varying proportions of Grenache, Cabernet Franc, Syrah, and Marselan.

Château la Grave

La Grave, 11800 Badens	*+33 4 68 79 16 00*
info@chateau-la-grave.net	*Jean Francois Orosquette*
www.chateau-la-grave.net	*Minervois [map p. 103]*
	100 ha; 500,000 btl

When Jean Francois Orosquette's parents bought this estate in the west of Minervois in 1970, it was planted with Aramon, Alicante, and Carignan. The Carignan is still there, but the other black varieties are now Syrah, Grenache, and Mourvèdre, planted on the dry soils in the south part of the estate. To the north there is more clay, and whites are planted, including the traditional varieties of Macabeu, Grenache Blanc, and Marsanne. The original vineyard of 45 ha in Badens has expanded to 62 ha, and the other vineyards are in the next village. There is more white than usual for producers in Minervois, around 15%. Under the IGP des Hauts de Badens the wines are mostly monovarietals, including Cabernet Sauvignon, Merlot, Chardonnay, Sauvignon Blanc, and a Chardonnay-Sauvignon blend. The grapes varieties for Minervois are based on Grenache and Syrah, with a little Carignan and Mourvèdre. Under Minervois AOP, Ô Marie is Grenache with a little Syrah, Tristan et Julien is a Grenache-Syrah blend, Expression Red is mostly Syrah and also includes the vieilles vignes Carignan, and the top wine is the GSM Privilège Red, which ages in oak, with barrels coming from Privilège White, which is Macabeu and Grenache Blanc, aged in new barriques.

Anne Gros & Jean-Paul Tollot

rue du Couchant, Cazelles, 34210 Aigues-Vives	*+33 3 80 61 07 95*
domaine-annegros@orange.fr	*Anne Gros & Jean-Paul Tollot*
www.tollot-gros.com	*Minervois [map p. 103]*
	18 ha; 80,000 btl

Jean-Paul Tollot and Anne Gros have long antecedents in Burgundy, Jean-Paul from Domaine Tollot-Beat in Chorey-lès-Beaune, and Anne from Domaine Anne Gros in Vosne Romanée. They do not work together in Burgundy, but set up this joint project in the Languedoc in 2008. " Jean-Paul and I had all this experience but had never worked together," she said at the time. Vineyards are all around the village of Les Cazelles, at elevations from 200m up. They described vinification as 'Burgundian,' which means everything is fully destemmed. The range starts with cuvées aged in stainless steel, moves through mixed aging in stainless steel and barriques, and ends up with barriques. Almost half of production is La 50/50, a blend of Grenache, Syrah, and Carignan. La CinsO is Cinsault, La Grenache 8 is Grenache, L'O de la Vie is Syrah. These are all aged in stainless steel, and are Vin de France or IGP. Les Fontanilles is a Minervois blend of Syrah, Grenache, Carignan, and Cinsault, from sandstone and calcareous clay, aged half in stainless steel and half in barriques. La Ciaude has Syrah, Grenache, and 50-100-year old Carignan, from limestone terroir, aged 80% in barriques and 20% in stainless steel. Les Carrétals is Carignan and Grenache planted in 1909, aged in barriques. One unusual cuvée is the IGP Les Combettes, from Marselan (a cross between Cabernet Sauvignon and Grenache), aged entirely in barriques.

Château Jouclary

D35, Route de Villegailhenc, 11600 Conques-sur-Orbiel	*+33 4 68 77 10 02*
chateau.jouclary@orange.fr	*Pascal Gianesini*
www.chateau-jouclary.com	*Cabardès [map p. 103]*
	60 ha; 150,000 btl

Just a few miles north of Carcassonne, in AOP Cabardès where there is some Atlantic influence, the domain is planted with Cabernet Franc, Merlot, Syrah, and Grenache for red wines. It takes its name from Guilhaume Jouglary, Consul of Carcassonne in 1532. Robert Gianesini bought the domain in 1969, when it had only 30 ha. After his son Pascal joined him in 1990, they more or less doubled its size. Half the vineyards are in Cabardès on calcareous clay; the other half are in IGP Pays d'Oc, on deeper soils. Tradition is a blend of all four black varieties, aged in concrete. Les Amandiers is Merlot, Syrah, and Grenache, aged in 1-2-year barriques for 12 months. Cuvée Guilhaume is the top red, a blend of the same varieties selected from the best lots, aged for 12 months in new barriques. There is a 100% Merlot aged in vat. Whites are all 100% varietals, Chardonnay, Sauvignon Blanc, and Viognier, aged in vat.

Château de Lastours

11490 Portel-des-Corbières	*+33 4 68 48 64 74*
contact@chateaudelastours.com	*Thibaut de Braquilanges*
www.chateaudelastours.com	*Corbières [map p. 82]*
	100 ha; 400,000 btl

The Château de Lastours has a dual identity: originally an inn for travelers on the ancient Via Domitia between Narbonne and Spain (called Castrum de Turribus before it changed to its present name), it is an 850 ha estate that includes not only vineyards and 10 ha of olive trees, but a testing ground for 4x4 vehicles and motor sport teams. The property declined after the second world war, and was bought by the Allard family in 2004. Located in the Corbières Maritimes, elevations go up to 300m. Vineyards were replanted under the new ownership with traditional varieties. The wines are all Corbières AOP. The entry level range, La Bergerie de Lastours, and the mid-level range, Château de Lastours, each come in all three colors. The top red is La Grande Reserve, a blend of Syrah, Grenache, Mourvèdre, and Carignan, aged in new and 1-year barriques.

Domaine J. Laurens

Les Graimenous, 11300 La Digne d'aval	*+33 4 68 31 54 54*
contact@jlaurens.fr	*Jacques Calvel*
www.jlaurens.fr	*Limoux [map p. 103]*
	40 ha; 450,000 btl

Coming from Champagne, Michel Dervin created the domain in the 1980s, producing Blanquette de Limoux. Jacques Calvet, who worked in computing but was originally from the Pyrenees, took over in 2002. He expanded the vineyards, modernized the winery, and now focuses more on Crémant than Blanquette de Limoux. Henri Albrus is the winemaker. The Blanquette is 90% Mauzac and 10% Chardonnay, and comes in brut and demi-sec. La Méthode Ancestrale is 100% Mauzac that goes through only a single fermentation. The Crémants include Les Gramenous (60% Chardonnay, 30% Chenin, 5% Mauzac, and 5% Pinot Noir), La Matte (Chardonnay and Chenin Blanc with very little Mauzac, and given longer aging, 24-36 months on the lees before disgorgement), and Le Clos des Demoiselles (a special selection from 60% Chardonnay, 25% Chenin Blanc, and 14% Pinot Noir). La Rosé No. 7 has the same blend.

Château de Luc

1 Rue Du Château, 11200 Luc-Sur-Orbieu	*+33 4 68 27 10 80*
info@famille-fabre.com	*Louis Fabre*
www.famillefabre.com	*Corbières [map p. 103]*
	360 ha

Château de Luc is the headquarters of the Fabre family, which owns five domains in Languedoc: Château de Luc itself, Grand Courtade (near Beziers), Tour de Rieux (Minervois), Château Coulon (the first property they acquired, in Corbières), and Château Fabre Gasparets (Corbières-Boutenac). The Fabre family has been in the region since 1711: Louis Fabre took over in 1982, and in 2014 his daughters and niece, Clémence, Paule and Jeanne, joined the domain. Château de Luc produces varietal Viognier and

Syrah under IGP Pays d'Oc, the red Languedoc Orangerie de Luc (Grenache and Syrah from Lézignan), and Les Jumelles range (red from Cinsault, Grenache, and Mourvèdre) as well as white and rosé. The top wine is Veredus, Carignan, Mourvèdre, Syrah, and Grenache, aged for 12 months in barriques.

Maxime Magnon

125 avenue des Corbières, 11360 Durban Corbières	*+33 4 68 45 84 71*
maxime.magnon@orange.fr	*Maxime Magnon*
18 ha; 28,000 btl	*Corbières* *[map p. 82]*

Maxime Magnon comes from Burgundy, and worked with Jean Foillard in Beaujolais, before he bought vineyards in Corbières, presently comprising 9 separate plots in the Hautes Corbières, at elevations up to 500m. Many of the vines are old, with an emphasis on Carignan. There's a monovarietal Carignan, Campagnès, from 100-year old vines, and several other cuvées blended from Carignan and Grenache, with smaller amounts of Cinsault or Syrah. Rozeta comes from coplanted old vines of Carignan, Grenache, and Cinsault, and the varieties ferment together., In blends, La Démarrante has a majority of Carignan with Grenache and Syrah, while Cuvée Rose is 90% Grenache and 10% Cinsault. The white La Bégou comes from Grenache Gris and Blanc and Carignan Gris. The rosé Métisse is Grenache, Cinsault, and Carignan. The reds age in used barriques.

Château Mansenoble

15 Avenue Henri Bataille, 11700 Moux	*+33 4 68 32 56 12*
info@chateaumansenoble.com	*Alexandre Chekalin & Tatiana Korulchuk*
chateaumansenoble.com	*Corbières* *[map p. 103]*
	22 ha; 60,000 btl

Belgian Guido Jansegers worked at an insurance company for his day job, and as a wine journalist on the side—he is known as the Nose of Belgium—until in 1992 he established this vineyard in Corbières. He chose the northern part of the area, close to the Montagne d'Alaric, to get cooler conditions for producing more elegant wines. The Corbières cuvée Montagne d'Alaric is a blend of Syrah, Grenache, and Carignan, and ages in cuve; Réserve du Château, also includes Mourvèdre and half ages in one-year barriques. Cuvée Marie-Annick has the same blend as the Réserve, but is a selection made only in the best years. Le Nez is an IGP Coteaux de Miramont that includes Merlot, Cabernet Sauvignon, and Carignan. Guido recently sold the estate, but remains involved as a consultant.

Château Maris

RD 52 Route de Pépieux, 34210 La Livinière (cellars) *Grand Café Occitan, 7 rue de l'Occitanie, 34210 Felines Minervois (boutique)*	*+33 4 68 91 42 63*
hannah@chateaumaris.com	*Hannah Egea*
www.chateaumaris.com	*Minervois La Livinière* *[map p. 103]*
	45 ha; 200,000 btl

This is an old domain, but took on a new character when Englishman Robert Eden (known as Bertie) bought it in 1997. He had worked at vineyards in Australia, Italy, and elsewhere in France before settling on Minervois for his own domain. He built an eco-winery with bricks made of hemp straw and a green roof. Vineyards are in many separate plots, and the focus is on wines from individual parcels. For example, from the La Livinière Cru, Amandiers is Syrah from a 1 ha parcel of the oldest vines, Dynamic is also Syrah from a small parcel of the best vines, and Les Planets is Syrah from a 3 ha parcel with more clay. There are also cuvées from Grenache and Carignan (Les Anciens comes from 90-year-old vines), and Syrah-Grenache blends. There's also a little white and rosé. The style follows Australian antecedents and is rich and powerful, with alcohol levels often pushing 15%.

Château de Martinolles

11250 Saint Hilaire	*+33 4 68 69 41 93*
info@martinolles.com	*Jean-Claude Mas*
www.martinolles.com	*Limoux [map p. 103]*
	60 ha; 350,000 btl

The domain was owned by three generations of the Vergnes family from 1926 until 2011, when it was sold to a major Languedocian negociant, Paul Mas. The domain is in a forested estate in Limoux, and makes a wide variety of wines, about two thirds white. The sparkling wine is Blanquette de Limoux from Mauzac and Crémant de Limoux, from Chardonnay, Chenin, and Mauzac. There are white wines under IGP Pays d'Oc from oak-fermented Chardonnay and also a white Mauzac, and red Limoux is based on Bordeaux varieties plus Syrah. There is a Pinot Noir under IGP Pays d'Oc.

Château Massamier la Mignarde

Massamier La Mignarde, 11700 Pépieux	*+33 4 68 91 64 55*
frantz.venes@massamier-la-mignarde.com	*Frantz Vènes*
www.massamier-la-mignarde.com	*Minervois [map p. 103]*
	70 ha; 100,000 btl

Named after a Roman legionary who once owned the land, the domain goes back to Roman times, and has a villa and extensive gardens. It has been in the Vènes family for 300 years, and Frantz Vènes took over from his father in 1998. "Viticulture is certainly not conventional, nor is organic or biodynamic," Frantz says. He follows a syntropic model, a type of agriculture using groups of plants that are complementary, organized to maximize sunshine exposure and the nutrient cycle, with a permanent cover crop to stop erosion and support the soil. Most cuvées are made by carbonic maceration. The best known cuvée is Domus Maximus, a blend of 80% Grenache and 20% Syrah, named for the Roman legionnaire, which ages in new barriques. Tènement des Garouilhas, which is 60% Syrah, 20% Carignan, and 20% Grenache, also ages in new barriques. Aubin, which is half Grenache and quarter each of Syrah and Carignan, ages in used barriques. Under IGP Coteaux de Peyriac there are monovarietal wines from Carignan and Cinsault.

Domaine de Mouscaillo

4 rue du Frêne, 11300 Roquetaillade	*+33 6 87 07 02 36*
info@mouscaillo.com	*Camille & Thomas Fort*
www.mouscaillo.com	*Limoux [map p. 103]*
	7 ha; 30,000 btl

Marie-Claire and Pierre Fort founded the domain in 2004; now the next generation, Camille and Thomas are in charge. Vineyards are at 400m altitude, giving freshness. The Limoux Blanc is effectively Chardonnay (it has 1% each of Chenin Blanc and Mauzac); it ferments and ages with battonage in demi-muids, with new oak used only when it's necessary to replace a barrel. A varietal Pinot Noir comes from a single parcel. There's a Crémant from 70% Chardonnay, 20% Pinot Noir, and 10% Chenin Blanc, fermented and aged for 8 months in old barriques before the second fermentation, followed by 18 months aging before disgorgement. "We want a slightly different product, we have vinified it like a (still) white wine," they say. The rosé Crémant is Pinot Noir and Chardonnay.

Château Ollieux Romanis

Montséret Tm 14, 11200 Lézignan Corbières	*+33 4 68 43 35 20*
contact@chateaulesollieux.com	*Pierre Bories*
www.chateaulesollieux.com	*Corbières* *[map p. 103]*
	149 ha; 750,000 btl

Located in the Massif de Pinada, in Corbières-Boutenac, the domain originated as a farm in the Roman era. In the Middle Ages it became part of the Abbaye de Fontfroide. Vines were first planted in the eleventh century; viticulture became the main activity in the eighteenth century. In 1872 the domain was divided into Ollieux Romanis and Château des Ollieux. François Bories bought Ollieux Romanis in 1978, and then in 2006 he bought Château des Ollieux, reuniting the two parts, making it one of the largest family-owned domains in Languedoc. His son Pierre, who now runs the domain, joined in 2001. The range of Corbières starts with the Cuvée Classique (in all three colors), and then moves to Cuvée Prestige (a red blend of Carignan, Mourvèdre, Syrah. and Grenache, aged in barriques, and a white blend of Roussanne, Grenache Blanc, and Marsanne, aged in demi-muids). The top wines are selected from special parcels. Atal Sia is Carignan, Grenache, and Mourvèdre, from 60-100-year-old vines, aged in stainless steel. Cuvée d'Or also has some Mourvèdre, selected from the best plots of 40-80-year-old vines on slopes of red sandstone, aged in barriques. Alba is 60% Grenache and 40% Cinsault, from 50-70-year-old vines, aged in stainless steel. There is also an Alba rosé (Cinsault, Grenache and Grenache Gris).

Clos d'Ora

34210 La Livinière	*+33 4 68 45 57 55*
vins@gerard-bertrand.com	*Gérard Bertrand*
www.gerard-bertrand.com	*Minervois La Livinière* *[map p. 103]*
	9 ha

Clos d'Ora is Gérard Bertrand's attempt to make a high-flying wine from Minervois. His flagship property is Château l'Hospitalet (see profile) at La Clape near Narbonne, and he owns many other properties in the Languedoc. Clos d'Ora is in fact a *clos* , a 9 ha vineyard enclosed by stone walls at 220 m elevation. Soils are chalk, sandstone, and marl. The wine is a blend of Carignan (whole bunches), with Syrah, Mourvèdre, and Grenache (all destemmed). It ages for 12 months in barriques. All about black fruits, the wine is unusually smooth and glossy with an unusually polished impression for the Languedoc; it's one of the most expensive wines by far for the region.

Domaine de L'Ostal

Tuilerie Saint Joseph, 34210 La Livinière	*+33 4 68 91 47 79*
fdarmaillacq@lostalcazes.com	*Fabrice Darmaillacq*
www.jmcazes.com/en/domaine-lostal-cazes	*Minervois La Livinière [map p. 103]*
	60 ha; 250,000 btl

Jean-Michel Cazes of Château Lynch Bages in Bordeaux bought this property on the edge of the Montagne Noir in 2002. Two neighboring properties were combined to make an estate of 150 ha, including 25 ha of olive groves as well as the vineyards, which were largely replanted, and a new cellar was constructed in the Tuilerie Saint-Joseph (a former tile factory). There are four wines. White and rosé are IGP Pays d'Oc. Estibals is the Minervois and is 42% Syrah, 36% Carignan, 12% Grenache and 10% Mourvèdre. The Grand Vin (echoes of Bordeaux here) is Minervois La Livinière, and is 90% Syrah with 10% Grenache. Both wines age in barriques previously used at Lynch Bages.

Château d'Oupia

4 place du Château, 34210 Oupia	*+33 4 68 91 20 86*
chateau.oupia@aliceadsl.fr	*Marie-Pierre Iche*
www.chateauoupia.fr	*Minervois [map p. 103]*
	63 ha; 300,000 btl

The domaine is located in a thirteenth century château. It was bought by Romain Iché in 1860, and his grandson André Iché made wine there from 1969 until his death in 2007. The story goes that he sold the wines in bulk to local negociants until a visiting winemaker from Burgundy tasted the wines and persuaded André to bottle them himself. His daughter Marie-Pierre made the wine with him from 1996, and took over in 2007. Vineyards are divided between 37 ha in Minervois (around the château) and 26 ha in IGP de l'Hérault. There wines are almost all red (there is one rosé), with the best-known being entry-level Les Hérétiques (Carignan with half fermented conventionally and half by carbonic maceration), and the top wines Cuvée des Barons, and Nobilis, both a blend of 60% Syrah with 40% Carignan, aged in barriques.

Domaine L'Oustal Blanc

Chemin de Condomine, 34210 La Livinière	*+33 6 03 61 02 31*
earl.fonquerle@wanadoo.fr	*Isabel Fonquerle*
8 ha; 40,000 btl	*Minervois La Livinière [map p. 103]*

Claude Fonquerle spent ten years in Châteauneuf-du-Pape, followed by ten years in Ventoux, and then returned in 2002 to Minervois with his wife Isabelle to create his domain. Time spent in the Rhône showed in the initial engagement of Philippe Cambie from Châteauneuf as consulting oenologist (until 2006). The Naïck cuvées are Vins de France, because the varieties do not conform with the AOP (the red is dominated by Cinsault, the white is Grenache Gris), and "K" is a Carignan (also Vin de France). The Minervois, Giacosa, is 65% Grenache, with the rest Syrah and Carignan, and the top wine, Minervois La Livinière, Prima Donna, is 40% Syrah and 60% Grenache. The cellars are located in La Livinière, but the bureau (where wines can be tasted and purchased) is some miles to the east, near St. Chinian.

Château de Pech Latt

11220 Lagrasse	*+33 4 68 58 11 40*
louismax@louis-max.fr	*Lise Sadirac*
louismax.bio	*Corbières [map p. 103]*
	165 ha; 500,000 btl

Vines are supposed to have been first planted here in 784 by the monks of the Abbey of Lagrasse. Reached by a narrow track from the village, the estate covers 340 ha, and was bought by Burgundian negociant Louis Max in 1999. It is a major part of his holdings, which amount to 230 ha in Burgundy and the South. Philippe Mathias was the winemaker for twenty years, with a small (9 ha) biodynamic estate of his own nearby, Clos de l'Anhel (see profile). Lise Sadirac, formerly the assistant winemaker, took over in 2017. The Pech Latt vineyards are in a single large plot, and almost half the vines are Carignan. Wines used to be divided into the major (85%) cuvée, Tradition, and Vieilles Vignes, and other Corbières, but now there is a range characterized by predominant varieties, with Le Roc (Carignan), Le Charlemagne (Grenache), La Chapelle (Syrah) and the wider blend of Le Précieux.

Château de Pennautier

11610 Pennautier	*+33 4 68 72 65 29*
contact@lorgeril.com	*Nicolas de Lorgeril*
www:chateaudepennautier.com	*Cabardès [map p. 103]*
	350 ha; 1,800,000 btl

Built in 1620 along the lines of Versailles with profits from constructing the Canal du Midi, the Château de Pennautier is a Monument Historique de France, and a major tourist attraction, with an extensive park surrounding the Château. Still in the hands of descendants of the original family, it has been run since 1987 by Nicolas and Miren de Lorgeril, who are the tenth generation. They also own some other, smaller estates in the region, and produce negociant wines under the label of Maison Lorgeril. Most of the vineyards were replanted in the 1960s, extending up the hillsides to 200-400m. This is the largest estate in Cabardès, with about two thirds of the vineyards in the AOP, and the rest in IGP Pays d'Oc. The cuvées from Cabardès include Terroirs d'Altitude (a classic Cabardès mix of varieties from the highest altitude vineyards, aged partly in cuve and partly in barrique), Série Limitée (a rosé de saignée), and Esprit de Pennautier (50% Merlot, 10% Cabernet Sauvignon, and 40% Syrah, aged half in barriques). The top white is an IGP, Le Rêve de Pennautier, a Chardonnay aged in barriques.

Domaine Piccinini

14 route des Meulières, 34210 La Livinière	*+33 6 87 04 48 47*
domainepiccinini@orange.fr	*Jean-Christophe Piccinini*
www.domainepiccinini.com	*Minervois La Livinière [map p. 103]*
	40 ha; 120,000 btl

Maurice Piccinini was president of the cooperative in La Livinière, and instrumental in the creation of the AOP. His son Jean-Christophe was the driving force in creating the family domain in 1997, and now runs it alone after Maurice's retirement. From Minervois there are Les Belles Vues (Grenache, Syrah, and Carignan, aged in cuve) and the selection Clos Angely (70% Syrah, 15% Grenache, 15% old Carignan, aged in barriques). The top red is the Minervois La Livinière, Line et Laëtitia (40% each of Syrah and Mourvèdre with 20% Grenache), aged in barriques. The white Minervois Les Belles Vues is Grenache Blanc, Roussanne, and Muscat.

Domaine Rosier

Rue Farman, 11300 Limoux	*+33 4 68 31 48 38*
domaine-rosier@wanadoo.fr	*Michel Rosier*
domaine-rosier.com	*Limoux [map p. 103]*
	35 ha; 650,000 btl

Michel Rosier came from Champagne in 1982 to establish his domain at Villelongue-d'Aude, a fortified village in the west part of Limoux. Michel's son Nicolas joined him in 2010. Vineyards are at 300-450m elevation; Michel restructured them by pulling out the plantings of Aramon and replanting with Chardonnay, Chenin Blanc, Mauzac, and Pinot Noir. The first cuvée was Blanquette de Limoux, on a small basis of 6,000 bottles. In 1985 the cellars moved to Limoux as the cellars in the village had become too small. Following the model of Champagne, Michel now produces many cuvées of Blanquette and Crémant de Limoux from grapes sourced from 12 growers, in an ultra-modern winery.

Domaine Sainte-Marie des Crozes

50 Avenue des Corbières, 11700 Douzens	*+33 6 59 00 67 90*
d.alias11@orange.fr	*Christelle Alias*
www.saintemariedescrozes.com	*Corbières [map p. 103]*
	140 ha; 150,000 btl

Located in the most northern part of Corbières, at the base of Mont Alaric (the mountain running from Carcassonne to Lézignan), the domain has been in the Alias family for five generations. Bernard and Dominique took over in 1997 and replanted the vineyards; they handed over to their daughter Christelle in 2012. Vineyards are on calcareous clay terroir at the base of the mountain, surrounded by the garrigue. The philosophy here is a little different. "Many producers have a range extended from tradition to prestige, we don't follow this rule at all, we have 11 cuvées in completely different styles, but with the common feature of drinkability." There are wines from local varieties under Corbières AOP, but also unusual varietals under IGP Pays d'Oc. "We make a Pinot Noir (En Rébellion) with the accent of the south, a Sauvignon Blanc (Le Clandestin) with notes of grapefruit from Occitan, and Cabernet Franc (L'Outsider) which is frankly northern in style." IGP also includes a varietal Carignan. There is an almost equally diverse range of Corbières, from the overtly fruity Les Pipelettes (Cinsault, Syrah, and Grenache, aged in vat) to Timeo Rouge (GSM plus Carignan and Cinsault, fermented in new 500-liter barrels and then aged in the same barrels). The mix of grape varieties reverses from Les Mains sur les Hanches (85% Grenache and 15% Syrah) to Hector et Juliette (90% Syrah and 10% Grenache). Whites are blends of a majority of Roussanne with minority of Grenache Blanc; Premier Pas sur la Lune ages in vat, while Milo Blanc (previously known as Timeo Blanc) ages half in barriques.

Domaine Jean-Baptiste Senat

12 rue de L'Argent Double, 11160 Trausse-Minervois	*+33 4 68 79 21 40*
charlotte@domaine-senat.com	*Jean-Baptiste Sénat*
www.domaine-senat.com	*Minervois [map p. 103]*
	17 ha; 70,000 btl

Jean-Baptiste Senat returned from being a student in history and politics in Paris to take over the neglected vineyards of his mother's family in 1995. He renovated the cellars and made his first vintage the following year. Vineyards are on the slopes of the Montagne Noire, spread over a few miles with two types of terroir: clay-calcareous, and siliceous. The wines are almost all blends: "It's only when you mix one grape variety with another that they reveal their true richness," Jean-Baptiste says. The range starts with Aude IGP: the white, Aux Amis de Ma Soeur, is 70% Grenache Blanc and 30% Grenache Gris, aged in barrique; the red, Hors Champs, is 70% Grenache and 30% Syrah, aged in cuve. Amalgame is an unusual blend of all three varieties of Grenache, Noir, Gris, and Blanc. Arbalète et Coquelicots is the simplest Minervois, 80% Grenache and 20% Carignan, aged in cuve. La Nine is 60% very old vines Carignan, 20% Grenache, 10% Cinsault, and 10% Syrah, aged two thirds in cuve and one third in barriques. Le Bois des Merveilles is equal Grenache and Carignan, aged in barriques.

Sieur d'Arques

Avenue du Mauzac, 11300 Limoux	*+33 4 68 74 63 00*
boutique1@sieurdarques.com	*Sylvia Feraud*
www.sieurdarques.com	*Limoux [map p. 103]*
	1658 ha; 9,200,000 btl

Founded in 1946, Sieur D'Arques is a huge cooperative. Located in Limoux, of course it produces sparkling wine, but Blanquette de Limoux and Crémant de Limoux are only a quarter of production. There are still wines from Limoux and a large range from IGP Pays d'Oc. The coop has moved towards quality with its Toques et Clochers line. However, Sieur d'Arques is best known for producing the Red Bicyclette brand for sale in the United States by Gallo, and became mired in scandal when it was discovered in 2010 that that they sold more fake Pinot Noir for inclusion in the brand than was actually produced in the whole Languedoc region.

Château Vaugelas

126 La Plaine-Sud, 11200 Camplong-d'Aude	*+33 4 67 93 10 10*
bonfils@bonfilswines.com	*Laurent Bonfils*
bonfilswines.com	*Corbières [map p. 103]*
	155 ha; 1,000,000 btl

The Bonfils family started making wine in Algeria in 1870. When they returned to France in 1962, they settled in the Languedoc. Their first property was Domaine de Lirou, and now Jean-Michel Bonfils and his three sons, Olivier, Laurent, and Jérôme, own 16 properties in the Languedoc and one in Bordeaux, with 1,200 ha of vineyards. In 2000, they bought Château Vaugelas, between Mont Alaric and the Montagne Noir, in the northern part of Corbières. Before the French Revolution, it was owned by the Benedictine monks of the Abbaye de Lagrasse. The vineyards are in a single block. The four red cuvées in

Corbières AOP all have Syrah as the majority grape variety, followed by Grenache, with smaller amounts of Carignan and Mourvèdre. All age in barriques. the top cuvée is 140, from the oldest grapes. The rosé comes from Grenache and Syrah, the white is Grenache, Vermentino, and Marsanne, and they age in vat.

Maison Ventenac

4, rue du Jardin, 11610 Ventenac-Cabardès	*+33 4 68 24 93 42*
accueil@maisonventenac.fr	*Olivier Ramé*
www.maisonventenac.fr	*Cabardès [map p. 103]*
	160 ha; 1,000,000 btl

Some confusion is possible here, because the house is known variously as Maison Ventenac or Domaine Ventenac, and labels its top wines as Château Ventenac, which is quite different from the Château de Ventenac in Minervois which is a cooperative. There are also small production runs of special cuvées, labeled as Les Dissidents from Maison Ventenac, or Famille Maurel from the neighboring village (Moussoulens). Located at the foot of the Montagne Noir, the domain is one of the two largest in Cabardès (the other is Château Pennautier: see profile). It was founded in 1973 by Alain Maurel and his father, and has been run since 2010 by Alain's daughter Stéphanie and her husband Olivier Ramé. The approach is modernist, with all the latest equipment in the cellars. Wines are aged variously in concrete, demi-muids, foudres, or amphora, barriques having been abandoned in the search for greater finesse. The AOP wines follow the rules of at least 40% of Atlantic varieties (Cabernet and Merlot) and 40% of Mediterranean varieties (Grenache and Syrah). There are also IGP Pays d'Oc wines with the same varieties, including monovarietals, in proportions not allowed by the AOP.

Château Vieux Moulin

Rue de Madone, 11700 Montbrun-des-Corbières	*+33 4 68 43 29 39*
contact@vieuxmoulin.net	*Alexandre & Laurence They*
www.vieuxmoulin.net	*Corbières [map p. 103]*
	29 ha; 110,000 btl

The estate is almost two hundred years old, and Alexandre was the seventh generation of the They family when he took over in 1997. "My terroir is the heart of the Corbières. The land is hot, and dry, which can be hard, but also rewarding. In many ways, it resembles the Carignan grape, which is the emblematic grape variety of this region," he says. The Corbières reds are varying blends of Carignan, Grenache, Mourvèdre, Syrah, and Cinsault. Terre de'Éole is a Vin de France with an unusual blend of Carignan and Cabernet Sauvignon. There's a series of natural wines, also Vin de France, Natura Humana (Carignan and Syrah), Natura Soli (100% Carignan), and Easy Rider (Carignan and Cinsault), a Pet Nat (lightly sparkling), and Pulp (an orange wine),

Château du Vieux Parc

1 Avenue des Vignerons, 11200 Conilhac Corbières	*+33 4 68 27 47 44*
contact@chateau-vieuxparc.fr	*Guillaume Panis*
www.chateau-vieuxparc.fr	*Corbières [map p. 103]*
	70 ha; 160,000 btl

The family has been here for six generations, selling wine in bulk until Guy Paris took over in the 1960s and started estate-bottling. Guillaume Paris joined the domain in 2005. Vineyards are on calcareous clay and pebbly terraces, facing due south. There are 40 ha in Corbières and 30 ha in IGP Pays d'Oc. Cuvée l'Air de Rien is the entry-level AOP range in all three colors. Sélection Rouge is a blend of four varieties, including old Carignan that goes through carbonic maceration; Sélection Blanc is a third each of old vines Grenache Blanc, Roussanne, and Vermentino. They age in barriques with new oak. Cuvée Ambroise has 80% Syrah and 20% Mourvèdre, Cuvée Ethan reverses the proportions, and both age for 18 months in new barriques. IGP includes bag-in-box, Les Amandiers (Merlot , Syrah, and Grenache) and a 100% Marselan (a cross between Grenache and Cabernet Sauvignon).

Domaine Vordy

Mayranne, 34210 Minerve	*+33 4 68 91 80 39*
vordy.didier@wanadoo.fr	*Didier Vordy*
www.domainevordy.com	*Minervois* *[map p. 103]*
	22 ha; 40,000 btl

Didier and Hélène Vordy gave up their jobs in 1994 to return home and take over the family vineyards. Their son Thibaut has now joined the domain. Located in the hamlet of Mayranne, vineyards are all in the Minervois AOP. Plantings are all the traditional varieties of the Languedoc, black varieties except for 1.5 ha of whites. There are two cuvées of white Minervois (which is relatively unusual): both are 80% Grenache Blanc and 20% Roussanne, but Pégounels ages in cuve while Los Gals Blanc ages in barriques. The rosé is a third each of Cinsault, Syrah, and Grenache. There are no less than six red cuvées. The entry-level Minervois is 70% Carignan with 15% each of Syrah and Grenache. Louise is 60% Syrah with 20% each of Grenache and Carignan. They age in cuve. A step up in varieties and vinification, Alice is a GSM with a third of each variety, aged in barriques, while Françoise is a quarter each of the GSM trio plus Carignan, aged equally in cuve barriques. The top wines are René, half Grenache and half Mourvèdre, and Los Gals Rouge, half 100-year-old Carignan, half Grenache, both aged in barriques.

Château la Voulte Gasparets

Hameau de Gasparets, 11200 Boutenac	*+33 4 68 27 07 86*
chateaulavoulte@wanadoo.fr	*Patrick & Laurent Reverdy*
www.lavoultegasparets.com	*Corbières-Boutenac* *[map p. 103]*
	63 ha; 260,000 btl

This has been a family domain for six generations, today run by Patrick Reverdy and his son Laurent. It is one of the reference domains in Corbières, and the specialty is Carignan, usually vinified by semi-carbonic maceration to be a soft and fruity component of the blend. Une Fois de Plus is AOP Corbières, a little unusual in its composition of 90% Mourvèdre and 10% Carignan. Cuvée Réservée is a more conventional Corbières: 50% Carignan, with GSM for the rest. Romain Pauc is the top red, a Corbières Boutenac with the same varieties as Cuvée Réservée, but aged exclusively in barriques with 20% new oak. The white Corbières is half Vermentino, with a mix of several other varieties for the rest; Cuvée Bj is 90% Roussanne with 10% Grenache Blanc.

Roussillon

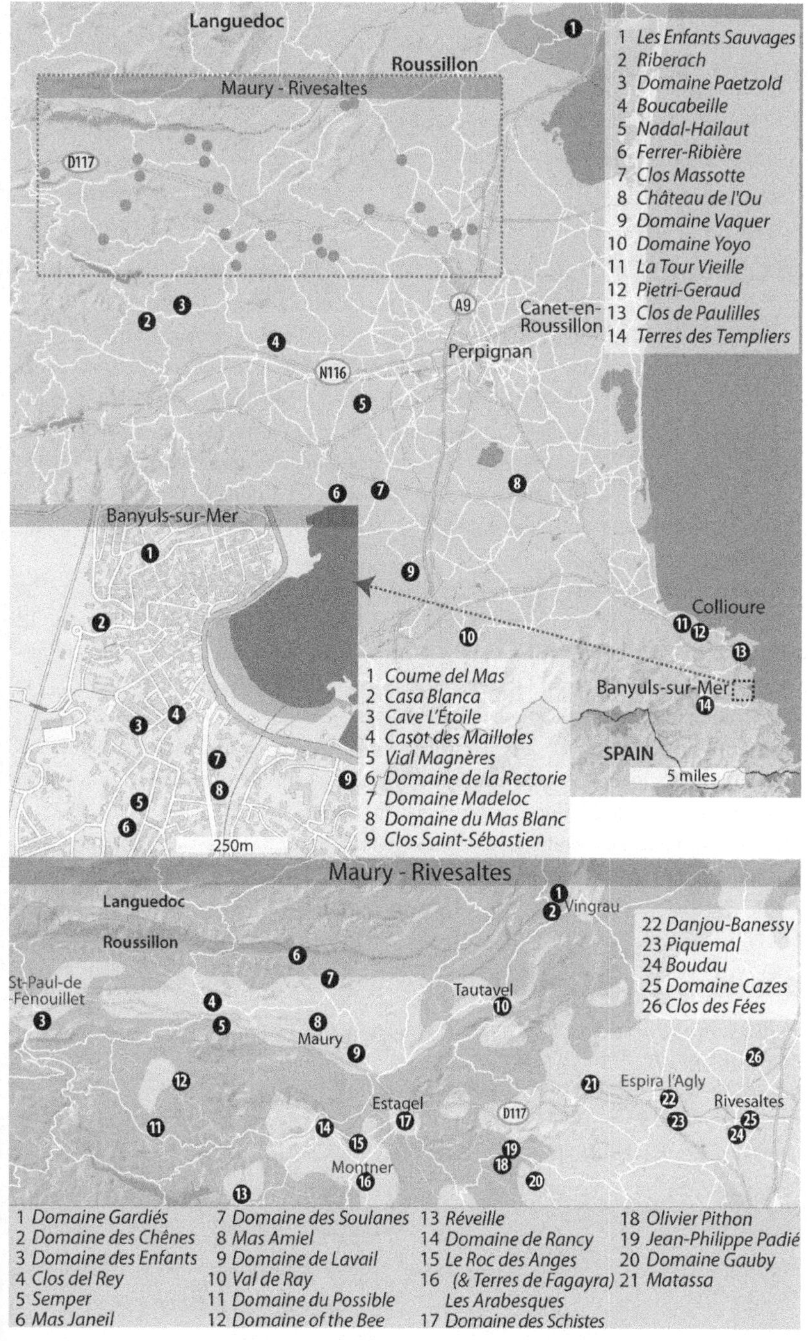
Languedoc
Roussillon
Maury - Rivesaltes
D117
A9
N116
Canet-en-Roussillon
Perpignan
1 Les Enfants Sauvages
2 Riberach
3 Domaine Paetzold
4 Boucabeille
5 Nadal-Hailaut
6 Ferrer-Ribière
7 Clos Massotte
8 Château de l'Ou
9 Domaine Vaquer
10 Domaine Yoyo
11 La Tour Vieille
12 Pietri-Geraud
13 Clos de Paulilles
14 Terres des Templiers
Collioure
Banyuls-sur-Mer
SPAIN
5 miles
Banyuls-sur-Mer
1 Coume del Mas
2 Casa Blanca
3 Cave L'Étoile
4 Casot des Mailloles
5 Vial Magnères
6 Domaine de la Rectorie
7 Domaine Madeloc
8 Domaine du Mas Blanc
9 Clos Saint-Sébastien
250m
Maury - Rivesaltes
Languedoc
Roussillon
Vingrau
St-Paul-de-Fenouillet
Tautavel
Maury
Estagel
Montner
D117
Espira l'Agly
Rivesaltes
22 Danjou-Banessy
23 Piquemal
24 Boudau
25 Domaine Cazes
26 Clos des Fées
1 Domaine Gardiés
2 Domaine des Chênes
3 Domaine des Enfants
4 Clos del Rey
5 Semper
6 Mas Janeil
7 Domaine des Soulanes
8 Mas Amiel
9 Domaine de Lavail
10 Val de Ray
11 Domaine du Possible
12 Domaine of the Bee
13 Réveille
14 Domaine de Rancy
15 Le Roc des Anges
16 (& Terres de Fagayra) Les Arabesques
17 Domaine des Schistes
18 Olivier Pithon
19 Jean-Philippe Padié
20 Domaine Gauby
21 Matassa

Coume del Mas *

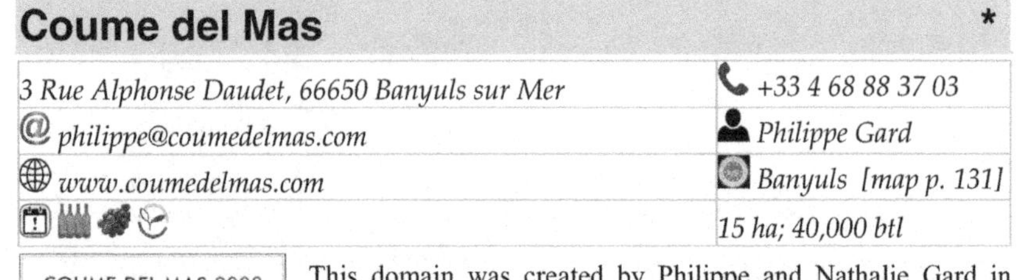

3 Rue Alphonse Daudet, 66650 Banyuls sur Mer	*+33 4 68 88 37 03*
philippe@coumedelmas.com	*Philippe Gard*
www.coumedelmas.com	*Banyuls [map p. 131]*
	15 ha; 40,000 btl

This domain was created by Philippe and Nathalie Gard in 2001 (after Philippe consulted for several domains in Chablis and Pomerol), when they purchased vineyards mostly around the lieu-dit of Coume del Mas, but with outlying plots scattered all over the hills surrounding Banyuls-sur-Mer. The domain expanded from its original 2 ha to its present thirty parcels. The focus was to find old vines, and the majority of plantings are old bush vines of Grenache. The domain produces both the VDN (sweet) Banyuls and also the dry style of Banyuls Blanc, dry red under the Collioure AOP, and a rosé.

Altogether there are about eight cuvées; sweet wines are about 20% of production. The flagship wine is Quadratur, a blend of Grenache, Carignan and Mourvèdre that spends 12 months in oak. By contrast, Schistes is a monovarietal old vines Grenache that is fermented and matured exclusively in stainless steel. Given the amount of manual (or equine) labor required to maintain the vines, the Coume del Mas domain has now reached its size limit, but has become quite a wide-ranging enterprise as another set of wines comes from Mas Christine, a separate property leased nearby in the Côtes de Roussillon appellation. In addition. Philippe runs a negociant business, Tramontane Wines, in association with winemaker Andy Cook, who is also a partner in Mas Christine. The Consolation range comes from selections from Coume del Mas, Mas Christine and other sources.

Famille Pierre Galllard *

Domaine Cottebrune, Route de la Chaudière, Lieu-dit La Liquière, 34480 Cabrerolles / Domaine Madeloc, 1 Avenue Gén de Gaulle, 66650 Banyuls sur Mer, France	*+33 4 68 88 38 29*
vinsp.gaillard@wanadoo.fr	*Elise Gaillard*
www.domainespierregaillard.com	*Collioure [map p. 131]*
	Domaine Maledoc, Collioure, Crestall
42 ha; 85,000 btl	*Domaine Maledoc, Collioure, Tremadoc*
	Domaine Maledoc, Banyuls, Cirera

Best known for his wines in the Northern Rhône, Pierre Gaillard explains that he expanded into Languedoc and Roussillon, "Just for pleasure, around here it is all Syrah, I wanted the experience of other varieties. Here we could not expand. My passion is to understand terroir." Domaine Cottebrune is the estate of 13 ha in Faugères, "but there is extra land for planting;" Domaine Maledoc is in Banyuls, with 29 ha, and produces both dry wines under the AOP Collioure and sweet wines under AOP Banyuls. All the estates are on steep hillsides, with terroirs based on schist.

The whites in both Faugères and Collioure are based on blends of Grenache (Blanc or Gris) with Roussanne and Vermentino, and tend towards a fruity balance. In Faugères, Le Cairn comes from warmer terroir than Les Moulins, but curiously makes a more mineral impression. In reds, Transhumance is a blend of Grenache and Syrah and shows a traditional palate, while Parole de Berger is a blend of Syrah and Mourvèdre making a more modern impression.

In Collioure, Serral is a blend of Grenache, Mourvèdre, and Syrah showing an elegant style, while Crestall is a blend of Mourvèdre and Syrah showing purity and precision of fruits. There are three sweet wines from Banyuls: Aspodèles is an unusual white, made from Grenache Gris and Tourbat, with an elegant balance that is not too sweet, while Cirera is a modern style from 100% Grenache, pure and sweet with just a hint of oxidative character, and Robert Pages is the full traditional style, matured in glass bon-bons, and blended across vintages. While true to their appellations, the elegant style for which Pierre is known in the northern Rhône carries over to these wines of the south.

Domaine Gardiés *

Chemin de Montpins, 66600 Espira de L'Agly	*+33 4 68 64 61 16*
domgardies@wanadoo.fr	*Jean Gardiés*
www.domaine-gardies.fr	*Côtes du Roussillon Villages [map p. 131]*
	40 ha; 100,000 btl

Jean Gardiés took over the family domain in 1990. Previously the wine had been sold off in bulk, but he started bottling in 1993. A new wooden winery was built at Espira de l'Agly in 2006. Vineyards are located in two somewhat different terroirs, on the chalky-clay soils of Vingrau (where the family originated), and the black schist of Espira de l'Agly north of Perpignan. The older vines are at Vingrau, with newer plantings at Espira de l'Agly. The major plantings are black varieties, on the south- and east-facing slopes, with some white varieties on north-facing slopes in Vingrau at higher altitudes to retain freshness. Black varieties are Grenache and Carignan; whites are Grenache Blanc and Roussanne.

There are four series of wines. The introductory wines, red, rosé, and white, are Côtes du Roussillon, blended from various holdings, while both red and white Le Clos des Vignes come specifically from Vingrau (the red is a Côtes du Roussillon Tautavel). The top of the line reds come from lower yields; La Torre is based on a blend dominated by

Mourvèdre from Espira de l'Agly; and Les Falaises is dominated by Carignan from Vingrau. Although production has decreased, there is also a series of sweet wines from Rivesaltes, including a Muscat de Rivesaltes: "These sweet wines are a difficult sell outside of France, which is a pity as it's a unique tradition to the Roussillon," Jean says. Most of the wine is sold to restaurants in France.

Domaine Gauby ***

La Muntada, 66600 Calce	*+33 4 68 64 35 19*
domainegauby@outlook.fr	*Gérard Gauby*
www.domainegauby.fr	*IGP Côtes Catalanes [map p. 131]*
	Muntada
43 ha; 90,000 btl	*Coume Gineste*

The entrance to Domaine Gauby is an intimidating one-car-wide track along the ridge above a valley just outside Calce, 30-40 km northwest of Perpignan, at an elevation around 350-450 m. Half of the valley is given over to vineyards, the other half remaining in its natural state to maintain the ecosystem: "We practice polyculture, I don't believe in monoculture. We've planted cereals, olive trees, and almond trees," says Gérard Gauby. In 2003, winemaking moved from a garage in the town of Calce to a purpose built chai under the family house in the middle of the valley. Soils are based on deep, friable schist at the bottom of the valley with calcareous components higher up. Plantings are two thirds red.

The whites are IGP Côtes de Catalanes and the reds are AOP Côtes du Roussillon Villages. Tasting here is an exercise in understanding extreme precision and elegance, reinforced by moderate alcohol, rarely above 12.5% yet always fully ripe. When tasting, Gérard instructs you not to swirl the wine but to let the complexity of the aromas "montent tranquillement."

The whites are remarkable for their freshness. The Vieilles Vignes white comes from a blend based on Macabeo and Grenache Blanc, with vines aged from fifty to a hundred years. The top white wine is Coume Gineste, an equal mix of Grenache Blanc and Gris, from terroir based on pure schist. "This is a wine for those who don't understand minerality; after tasting this they will understand minerality," Gérard says. There's also an orange wine (white wine made with red wine methods), La Roque, entirely from Muscat. "This is the oldest variety in the world and we are working it like the Greeks and Romans. We have rediscovered Muscat," Gerard claims.

The reds extend from the classic blend of Vieilles Vignes, to the Grenache-based La Roque from old vines. Coume Gineste comes from friable schist, and Muntada comes from the same terroir as La Roque but is based on Syrah. The deepest red is La Founa, based on a complex mix of prephylloxera vines. Almost nothing here is less than exceptional for the region.

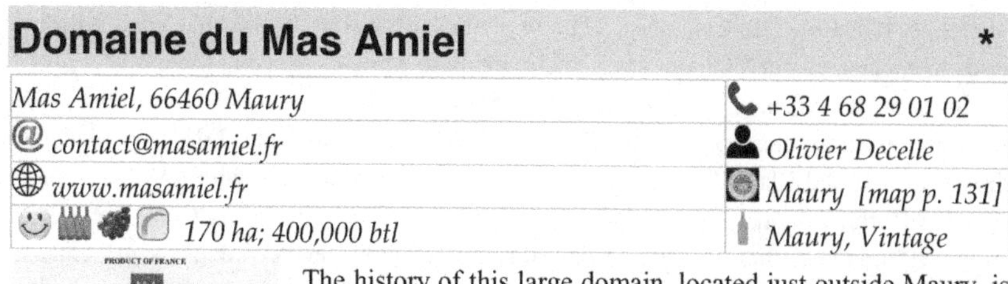

Domaine du Mas Amiel *

Mas Amiel, 66460 Maury	*+33 4 68 29 01 02*
contact@masamiel.fr	*Olivier Decelle*
www.masamiel.fr	*Maury [map p. 131]*
170 ha; 400,000 btl	*Maury, Vintage*

The history of this large domain, located just outside Maury, is somewhat chequered; won in a game of cards from the Bishop of Perpignan in 1816, it became the property of a bank when the owners were ruined in 1909, and then in 1999 was sold to Olivier Decelle (former owner of a frozen food retailer), who has set about renovating the vineyards (several hectares are replanted each year) and chais. Its fame was established for sweet fortified wines, but in the past couple of decades it has been making a transition to a point at which half the wines are dry. The old cellar is used for maturing traditional wines, but there is now a new cellar with temperature-controlled cuves for the new lines of dry wines. The vineyards are on slopes surrounding the winery, generally on soils of schist.

There are dry whites and reds under the AOP Côtes de Roussillon; and recently four cuvées of dry red wines from old vines and single vineyards have been introduced under the new Maury Sec label. The sweet wines divide into the modern Vintage line and the traditionally oxidative Classique line. Oxidative wines start out with a year in glass demi-johns in the sun, and then mature in large foudres. Vintage-dated VDNs are produced about once every decade; other Classique wines come from a blend of two or three vintages, and are labeled by their average age as 15-year or 20-year. Although no longer in fashion, the sweet wines remain a benchmark; the dry wines have yet to catch up.

Domaine Olivier Pithon *

Chemin de Montner, 66600 Calce	*+33 4 30 44 85 71*
olivierpithon@live.fr	*Olivier Pithon*
www.domaineolivierpithon.com	*IGP Côtes Catalanes [map p. 131]*
20 ha; 100,000 btl	*Côtes Catalanes, Le Clot*

"My family were vignerons in the Loire, and I never thought of doing anything else," says Olivier Pithon. "After studying wine in other regions, I looked for vines, and I liked the varieties and area here at Calce." The winery entrance is a garage door in what looks like a residence in the main street of Calce, but inside is a small winemaking facility, crammed with equipment. Starting with 7 ha the first year, the domain has slowly expanded, and now includes white grapevines as well the original black.

The vineyards are in the area that used to be the Vin de Pays Coteaux des Fenouillèdes (the name refers to the fennel that grows naturally on the hillsides), but the wines are all labeled as IGP Côtes de Catalanes. "The regulations for AOP are just too strict with regards to encépagement," Olivier says. There are three white cuvées and three red.

The entry-level wines, Mon P'tit Pithon, both red and white, come from purchased grapes: everything else comes from the estate. The top white wine, D18, is a blend of Grenache Gris and Blanc. The reds are the real heart of the domain, with Laïs based on a blend of Carignan and Grenache (it replaced two previous cuvées, La Coulée and Saturne); Le Pilou is a 100% Carignan from 100-year-old vines on calcareous terroir; and Le Clot (bottled only in magnums) is based on Grenache from schist. Olivier describes house style by saying, "The idea with the reds is to get elegance without aggressive tannins."

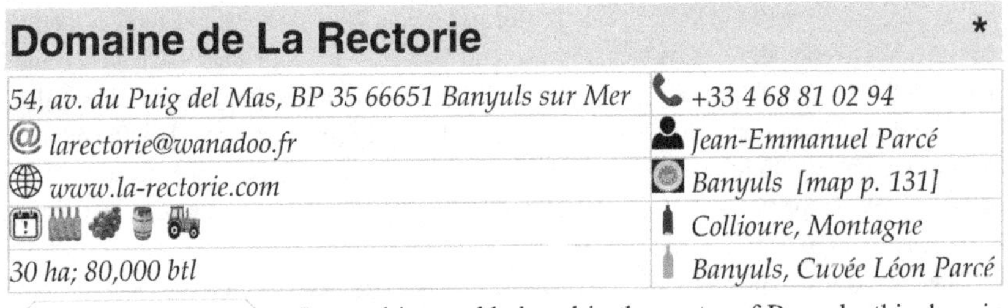

Domaine de La Rectorie *

54, av. du Puig del Mas, BP 35 66651 Banyuls sur Mer	*+33 4 68 81 02 94*
larectorie@wanadoo.fr	*Jean-Emmanuel Parcé*
www.la-rectorie.com	*Banyuls [map p. 131]*
	Collioure, Montagne
30 ha; 80,000 btl	*Banyuls, Cuvée Léon Parcé*

Located in an old chapel in the center of Banyuls, this domain goes back to the start of the nineteenth century. Grapes were sent to the coop until 1984, when Marc and Thierry Parcé decided to produce their own wine. Today Thierry runs the domain together with his son Jean-Emmanuel, while Marc runs an associated negociant, Les Vins Parcé-Frères. Vineyards are scattered in small plots all around the steep hills of Banyuls. Plantings focus on Grenache.

The sweet wines of Banyuls are only around 15% of production, with the main focus on dry red wines under the Collioure label. "It's often said that the wines of the south are too strong, too heavy, but we want to show they can have elegance," says Jean-Emmanuel. The red Collioure cuvées are L'Oriental (matured for a year in foudres, but with a modern impression), Côté Mer (matured in barriques and foudres, but fresh and approachable), and Montagne (the most complex assemblage and the most elegant impression, with the least Grenache, matured in barriques and foudres for 18 months).

Under the Banyuls label there are three cuvées of fortified wines: Thérèse Reig comes from an early harvest, with sweet, ripe, black fruits; Léon Parcé is harvested later from select parcels and has an intriguing mix of savory and sweet influences; and the new cuvée, Pierre Rapidol, is matured for six years before release to show an intense, oxidized style. Under the IGP Côte Vermeille there is a dry Rancio wine, the Pedro Soler cuvée.

Domaine Le Roc des Anges **

1 route de Montner, 66720 Latour de France	*+33 4 68 29 16 62*

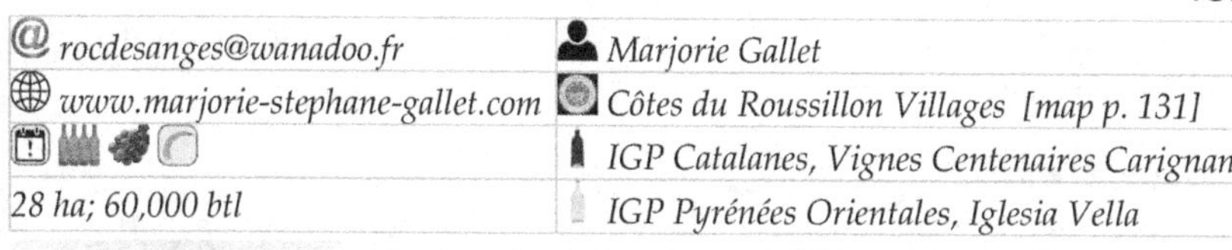

rocdesanges@wanadoo.fr	Marjorie Gallet
www.marjorie-stephane-gallet.com	Côtes du Roussillon Villages [map p. 131]
	IGP Catalanes, Vignes Centenaires Carignan
28 ha; 60,000 btl	IGP Pyrénées Orientales, Iglesia Vella

Coming from the northern Rhône after working at Yves Cuilleron and Pierre Gaillard, Marjorie Gallet cut short an apprenticeship at Domaine Gauby when the chance came to purchase her own vineyards in 2001. Roc des Anges started with 10 ha. Vineyards are around Montner, a village in the Agly valley in the far south of Roussillon. Originally located at Tautavel, a new cave was built at Montner in 2008, and her husband Stéphane came from nearby Mas Amiel to join Marjorie. (The name Montner derives from Monte Negro, reflecting the dark color of the schist; this was part of the Vin de Pays Coteaux Fenouillèdes before it was abolished.)

The focus is on traditional Mediterranean varieties (Carignan, Grenache, and Macabeo, supplemented by a little Syrah). Plantings are about two thirds black to one third white. Wines are matured in a mixture of concrete and old wood. Most whites are IGP Pyrénées Orientales, with Iglesia Vella coming from pure Grenache Gris, and the Vieilles Vignes coming from 70-year-old vines, mostly Grenache Gris. L'Oca Blanc comes from Macabeo. Most reds are AOP Côtes du Roussillon Villages. Segna de Cor comes from young vines; the Vieilles Vignes is a blend from old Grenache and Carignan (vines over seventy years old) plus some younger Syrah; and Vignes Centenaires Carignan cones from 3 ha of very old Carignan. There are also IGP des Côtes Catalanes in both red and white, as well as a rosé and passerillé dessert wine.

Profiles of Important Estates

Les Arabesques

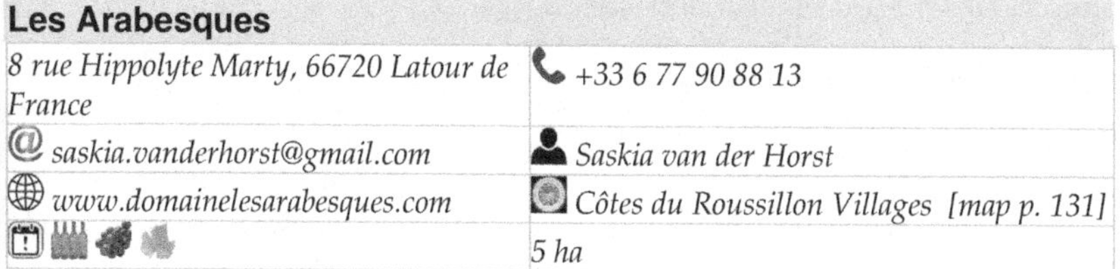

8 rue Hippolyte Marty, 66720 Latour de France	+33 6 77 90 88 13
saskia.vanderhorst@gmail.com	Saskia van der Horst
www.domainelesarabesques.com	Côtes du Roussillon Villages [map p. 131]
	5 ha

Saskia van der Horst was a sommelier in London before she studied oenology in Burgundy. She worked with 'natural' winemakers before starting her domain in 2013. Eight separate plots are in three villages, with soil types varying among schist in Montner, slate in Planèzes, and gneiss in Latour-de-France. Ocarina is a rosé from intermingled plantings of Syrah, Grenache, and Carignan. Elanion comes from intermingled Grenache Blanc, Grenache Gris, and Macabeu, fermented and aged in demi-muids. In reds, Lou Pal comes from young Syrah on calcareous clay, ages in vat, L'Estocade comes from the Lledoner Pelut sub-cultivar of Grenache, aged in old barriques from Burgundy for 9 months, Chopine comes from three parcels of Carignan, fermented by carbonic maceration, and aged in fiber-glass. Labels vary from Vin de France to IGP Côtes Catalanes to AOP Côtes du Roussillon.

Banyuls L'Etoile

26 Avenue Puig Del Mas, 66651 Banyuls sur Mer	*+33 4 68 88 00 10*
info@cave-letoile.com	*Xavier SAINT DIZIER*
www.banyuls-etoile.com	*Collioure [map p. 131]*
	108 ha; 250,000 btl

Founded in 1921 with only 12 members, this is the oldest cooperative in Banyuls, and remains quite small, with most of its members being descendants of the founders. It is known for the quality of its sweet wines, which remain the focus of production, with Banyuls in both modern (fruité) and oxidative style (traditionnel), Banyuls Grand Cru (aged in *bonbonnes* in the sun for two years and then in wood for at least ten years), and old vintages going as far back as 1945. There are also some dry wines under the Collioure and Roussillon AOPs.

Domaine of the Bee

La Bordé Neuve, 66720 Rasiguères	*+33 4 47 74 02 88*
worker@domaineofthebee.com	*Justin Howard-Sneyd*
www.domaineofthebee.com	*Côtes du Roussillon [map p. 131]*
	4 ha; 10,000 btl

Domaine of the Bee is an idiosyncratic operation, run by Justin Howard-Sneyd and his wife Amanda, who are based on London, but make wine from three small plots that they bought in 2003 in Maury. Grapes are also purchased from Domaine Lafage in Roussillon. Wines can be bought online or through a wine club. the plots vary from 60-100-years old, mostly Grenache, but with a hectare of Carignan. The main cuvée is a blend from all the plots. Les Genoux comes from the best lots from a field blend of 100-year-old vines in a 1.4 ha plot on black schist in Coume de Roy. There is a white wine, Field of the Bee, from Grenache Gris and Grenache Blanc. Tarona de Gris is an orange wine made from Grenache Gris as a partnership with Domaine Lafage.

Domaine de la Casa Blanca

16 Avenue de La Gare, 66650 Banyuls sur Mer	*+33 4 68 88 12 85*
domainedelacasablanca@orange.fr	*Hervé Levano*
domainedelacasablanca.e-monsite.com	*Banyuls [map p. 131]*
	7 ha; 21,000 btl

Laurent Escapa started making wine from a 1.5 ha family plot in 1980, then came to Casa Blanca to manage the vineyards in 1983. Hervé Levano became the winemaker and owner in 1995. The domain has been continually expanded by adding plots in new locations, and produces all styles of Banyuls: Les Ecumes is white from Grenache Blanc, Pineil is tradition (oxidative) style red from Grenache, the Hors d'Age is oxidative style from Grenache, and Rimage is the modern (nonoxidative) style from Grenache and Grenache Gris. There are two cuvées of dry red from Collioure: Calells is almost all Grenache, with just 5% Mourvèdre, and Illumari is a GSM blend. Production is about half Banyuls and half Collioure.

Domaine Boucabeille

Route Nationale, 66550 Corneilla La Rivière	*+33 6 09 06 37 88*
domaine@boucabeille.com	*Jean Boucabeille*
www.boucabeille.com	*Côtes du Roussillon Villages [map p. 131]*
	37 ha; 150,000 btl

The estate is on the steep schist slopes of the Forca Real hill, a few miles west of Perpignan, where viticulture was abandoned in the early twentieth century. René-Jean Camoi resurrected the vineyards with 12 ha of plantings on terraces at 150-400m altitude in 1976. Régis Boucabeille bought the property in 1990, and his son Jean made his first vintage in 2001. A new winery was built in 2008. Protective woods were planted around the vineyards in 1997, but burned down in 2015. The domain tries to be self-sustaining, and planted 650 cork trees in 2016. There are several red Côtes du Roussillon Villages Cuvées. Terrasses de Régis Boucabeille has equal Grenache and Syrah and ages in vat; Monte Nero has equal Grenache and Mourvèdre, and Orris has 70% Syrah with 15% each of Grenache and Mourvèdre, both aged in barriques. The white Terrasses has equal Grenache Blanc and Macabeu; the Orris white is 60% Grenache Blanc and 40% Roussanne, aged in barriques. There's a dry Muscat under IGP Côtes Catalanes, and also a Rancio Sec from Macabeu. A range from Rivesaltes includes Ambre, Tuilé, and Ambre Hors d'Age.

Domaine Boudau

6 Rue Marceau, 66600 Rivesaltes	*+33 4 68 64 45 37*
contact@domaineboudau.fr	*Véronique & Pierre Boudau*
www.domaineboudau.fr	*Roussillon [map p. 131]*
	60 ha; 200,000 btl

When brother and sister Pierre and Véronique took over from their parents in 1993, the domain produced only the fortified Vin Doux Naturel. Founded in the 1920s, the estate was largely planted with Grenache for Rivesaltes and there was also Muscat de Rivesaltes. Today the sweet wines are still made, but are only a small part of production, which focuses on dry red wines. The estate has almost doubled in size and falls into two parts. North of Rivesaltes, in the foothills of the Corbières Range, the single 23 ha parcel of Le Clos is planted with Grenache and Syrah, and makes Côtes du Roussillon or IGP Côtes de Catalanes. Under Côtes du Roussillon, the white is 80% Grenache Blanc and 20% Macabeu, aged briefly in barriques; and the reds are Patrimoine (70% Grenache and 30% Syrah, aged in cuve) and Padri (70% Mourvèdre, 20% Syrah, and 10% Grenache, aged in barriques). South of the town, on the plateau of Baixas where clay-calcareous soils are covered by large pebbles, a 27 ha parcel is planted mostly with old Grenache. Rivesaltes Grenat sur Grains is fortified Grenache, and the other dessert wine is Muscat de Rivesaltes.

Domaine le Casot des Mailloles

17 Avenue Puig Del, 66650 Banyuls sur Mer	*+33 6 15 61 45 00*
contact@casotdesmailloles.fr	*Jordi Perez*
www.casotdesmailloles.com	*Collioure [map p. 131]*
	5 ha; 12,000 btl

As evident from its own description as Artisans-Vignerons—Agro-écologie—Vins Vivant, this is an idiosyncratic domain. One of the smallest in Banyuls, it started in 1994 when Alain Castex made the first wine in an old Citroen garage. Jordi Perez took over the domain in 2015, and is continuing the focus on natural wine, with manual work in the vineyard, followed by vinification with no filtration, no fining, and no sulfur. Yields are very small, less than 20 hl/ha. All the wines are dry. The vineyards are in Collioure AOP, but in some years the wines were Vins de France, because they were denied the *agrément* for being atypical; most people think this means they were too good. Now the entry-level wines are Vins de France (vinified in cuve) and the rest are Collioure AOP (mostly vinified in old barrels). In whites, Obreptice is 100% Vermentino, and Blanc du Casot is a blend of Grenache Gris and Blanc with Vermentino and Roussanne. Rosé de Zara is 100% Syrah. In reds, Tererach is 100% Syrah, El Niño, perhaps the best known red, is a blend of Carignan, Syrah, and Mourvèdre, Soulà is a blend of Grenache and Mourvèdre, and Vi Sin Num comes from old vines where several varieties are intermingled.

Maison Cazes

4 rue Francisco Ferrer, 66602 Rivesaltes	*+33 4 68 64 08 26*
info@cazes-rivesaltes.com	*Emmanuel Cazes*
www.cazes-rivesaltes.com	*Rivesaltes [map p. 131]*
	220 ha; 800,000 btl

Founded in 1895 by Michel Cazes, and known for production of sweet wines, this is not only a large domain for the area, but is the largest biodynamic producer in France. In 2004 its sales arm was sold to major negociant JeanJean (now Advini); the Cazes family retained ownership of the property—fourth generation Emmanuel Cazes is the winemaker—but to all intents and purposes, it is part of Advini. In 2012, Advini purchased the Clos des Paulilles (see profile), the largest estate in the Collioure/Banyuls appellations, with another 63 ha. The combined estates have a dominant position in sweet wines, now including those from both Rivesaltes and Banyuls. Dry reds come from Fitou (under Cazes) and Collioure (under Paulilles).

Domaine des Chênes

7, rue Maréchal Joffre, 66600 Vingrau	*+33 4 68 29 40 21*
domainedeschenes@wanadoo.fr	*Alain Razungles*
www.domainedeschenes.fr	*Côtes du Roussillon Villages [map p. 131]*
	30 ha

François Razungles was making wine at the start of the twentieth century. His three sons purchased the Domaine des Chênes after the first world war. Vineyards are in the area of Maury, and they produced sweet fortified wines. Production had ceased before Alain Razungles (François's great grandson), persuaded his parents to restore the old cellars and start making wine in 1985. He now works with his daughter Marion. Vineyards are around Vingrau, where the limestone soils around the village are surrounded by calcareous cliffs; above the cliffs, there is a sandstone plateau. They started with Côtes du Roussillon Villages, Muscat, and Rivesaltes Tuilé, followed by a white. Today Côtes du Roussillon Villages Les Grand-Mères comes from 60% very old Carignan (with some carbonic maceration) and 30% Syrah (grown on limestone) and 10% Grenache (grown on sandstone). It ages in vat. There are two cuvées from Côtes du Roussillon Villages Tautavel, Le Mascarou with about a third of each variety, and La Carissa with 40% each of Grenache and Syrah and 10% each of Carignan and Mourvèdre. The Tautavel wines age in barriques. There are four white cuvées. Les Olivettes is IGP Côtes Catalanes (half each of Muscat and Macabeu, aged in stainless steel). The two Côtes du Roussillon white cuvées age in barriques: Les Sorbiers is about half Grenache Blanc and half Macabeu, and Les Magdaléniens (the original white cuvée) is more than half Roussanne, with the rest from Grenache Blanc. There's also a Rancio Côtes Catalanes from Macabeu, Muscat de Rivesaltes, and Ambré and Tuilé cuvées from Rivesaltes.

Domaine Clos del Rey

7 rue Henri Barbusse, 66460 Maury	*+33 4 68 59 15 08*
closdelrey@wanadoo.fr	*Jacques Montagné*
50 ha; 14,000 btl	*Maury [map p. 131]*

Jacques Montagné established the domain in 2001 and has been steadily buying vineyards ever since. Today he manages the vineyards and his son Julien is the winemaker. They make wine from only 8 ha; the majority of grapes go to the coop. The domain is in Maury, famous for its fortified dessert wines, but the Montagnés produce only dry wine under Côtes du Roussillon Villages. Le Sabina comes from 65% Grenache planted on schist, 25% Syrah planted on limestone, and 10% Carignan, aged in tank. The estate red is 60% Grenache and 40% Syrah. The domain started by using a lot of new oak, but later eased back. The oldest vines are Carignan, more than a century old, from which L'Aragone has been produced since 2012, aged 40% in new barriques and 60% in tank.

Le Clos de Paulilles

Baie-des-Paulilles, 66660 Port Vendres	*+33 4 68 81 49 79*
info@cazes.com	*Domaine Cazes*
www.lesclosdepaulilles.com	*Banyuls [map p. 131]*
	90 ha

This is the largest estate in Banyuls, family-owned until it was sold to the Maison Cazes (see profile) arm of Advini in 2013. The estate covers 90 ha, with about two thirds planted to vines. The facilities were renovated, and a restaurant was added overlooking the water as part of a focus on oenotourism. The white Collioure is 80% Grenache Blanc and 20% Grenache Gris, aged in vat. Cap Béar is 100% Grenache Gris, aged mostly in a huge concrete egg, but with some demi-muids. The red is 60% Grenache Noir, 30% Syrah, 10% Mourvèdre, aged in vat. Cap Béar red is 60% Grenache and 40% Syrah aged in 300-liter barrels. From Banyuls, the white is Grenache Blanc, the red Traditionnel is 95% Grenache, aged in glass bonbons for 20 months, the Grand Cru is 100% Grenache, aged in demi-muids for three years (mostly reductively), and there is also a Rimage.

Domaine Danjou-Banessy

1 bis, rue Thiers 66600 Espira de L'Agly	*+33 4 68 64 18 04*
contact@domainedanjou-banessy.com	*Sébastien & Benoît Danjou*
domainedanjou-banessy.com	*Côtes du Roussillon Villages [map p. 131]*
	17 ha; 40,000 btl

This old family estate expanded under Denis Banessy in the 1950s and focused on the sweet fortified wines of Rivesaltes. Benoît Danjou took over in 2001; joined five years later by his brother Sébastien, they introduced dry reds and whites to replace some of the traditional sweet wines. The dry wines are IGP Côtes Catalanes. Vineyards are dispersed in three locations: Les Terres Noires is northwest of the village and has black shale; Le Crest is to the northeast and has clay-limestone; Le Correc is to the south and has clay. La Truffière rouge (from 60-80-year old Carignan and Grenache) and blanc (Carignan Gris) come from Terres Noires, where the vines are 80-years old. Roboul is 80% Mourvèdre and 20% Grenache from calcareous terroir. Coste is a white from Macabeu (Viura). Supernova is an orange wine from Muscat, labeled as Vin de France. There are several varietal wines from old vines, in each case so old that the major variety is planted intermingled with other varieties: Myrs comes from 100-year old Carignan, Espuma from (mostly) 100-year old Cinsault, L'Estaca from 100-year old Grenache, and Mirandes from 60-year old Syrah. The wines age in old barriques or 500-liter barrels. There are also wines from Rivesaltes including sweet (VDN Muté sur Grains) and dry (Rancio Sec).

Domaine des Enfants

8bis rue Pierre Bascou, 66220 St.Paul de Fenouillet	*+33 9 62 32 35 58*
marcel@domaine-des-enfants.com	*Marcel Bühler*
www.domaine-des-enfants.com	*Maury [map p. 131]*
	23 ha

Founded in 2006, Domaine des Enfants takes a fairly extreme approach. "It's taking a step back into the past; regress as progress," says founder Marc Bühler. "We do not perform 'winemaking'. Our wines are the exact result of what the vineyards create; we try to intervene very little with the natural process." Vineyards are around Maury, on typical soils of schist, with some granite and gneiss. The dry wines are IGP Côtes Catalanes Plantings are more than half Grenache, with Carignan and Syrah and a little Mourvèdre. The white, Tabula Rasa (a clean start), comes from plots of Grenache Gris, Grenache Blanc, Carignan Blanc, and Macabeu scattered among the plantings of black grapes. Grapes are squeezed by foot-pressing and then pressed off into 400-liter barrels for fermentation and 12 months aging. The top red, La Larme de l'Âme (tears of the soul) comes from the best plots of Syrah (aged in barriques) and Grenache and Carignan (aged in 400-600-liter barrels). L'Enfant Perdu (the lost child) is the second wine, typically a third each of Syrah, Grenache, and Carignan, aged half in 300-600-liter barrels and half in concrete. Suit l'Étoile comes from the older plots of Carignan and Grenache with some Syrah, aged in 1-year barriques. There is also a Maury fortified wine.

Domaine Les Enfants Sauvages

10-12, rue Gilbert-Salamo, 11510 Fitou	*+33 4 68 45 69 75*
info@les-enfants-sauvages.com	*Nikolaus & Carolin Bantlin*
www.les-enfants-sauvages.com	*IGP Côtes Catalanes [map p. 131]*
	8 ha; 25,000 btl

Nikolaus and Carolin Bantlin are from Germany, where Caroline was an architect and Nikolaus had run his family business in leather. They bought a ruined sheep farm in 1999 and resurrected some abandoned vineyards. The first vintage in 2002 was made at Olivier Pithon's winery, and then by 2004 they had their own winery. The name is a translation into French of the title of The Doors' song, Wild Child. Vineyards are only a couple of miles from the Mediterranean, at 150m elevation, surrounded by the garrigue. The wines are all IGP Côtes Catalanes. The white, Cool Moon, is a blend of 80-90-year old vines of Grenache Gris and Blanc with Macabeu, and ages in barriques for 12 months. The red Ché Chauvio comes from young Syrah and Cinsault and ages in stainless steel; Enfant Sauvage is Carignan, Grenache, and Mourvèdre, aged in cement vats. Roi des Lézards is from 90-year-old Carignan and ages in foudre followed by stainless steel. There is also a Muscat de Rivesaltes.

Domaine du Clos des Fées

69, rue Maréchal Joffre 66600 Vingrau	*+33 4 68 53 40 00*
contact@closdesfees.com	*Hervé Bizeul*
www.closdesfees.com	*Côtes du Roussillon Villages [map p. 131]*
	30 ha; 100,000 btl

A well known sommelier and wine journalist, Hervé Bizeul (Best Sommelier in France in 1981) made his first vintage in 1988 using space in a cave borrowed from a friend. The following year he turned his garage into a cellar. By 2004, the domain reached 20 ha and he moved into a cave in the village. He now has 125 separate plots spread around the area and makes about 10 cuvées. The wines are eclectic. In conventional cuvées, Sorcières is a blend of 50% Syrah with 30% Grenache and 20-% Carignan, the Vieilles Vignes comes from 50-100-year old vines of Grenache, Lledoner Pelut with Carignan and Syrah, Clos des Fées itself is GSM and Carignan old vines from clay-limestone terroir, and La Petite Siberie is old vines Grenache from a single plot. De Battre Mon Coeur S'est Arrêté is from a tiny plot of Syrah on granite. Less conventionally, Un Faune Avec Son Fifre is mostly Cabernet Franc, and Images Derisoires is Tempranillo. Different cuvées age in cuve, in large old casks, or in new barriques. Prices range from $10 for Sorcières to $200 for La Petite Siberie.

Domaine Ferrer-Ribière

20, rue du Colombier, 66300 Terrats	*+33 4 68 53 24 45*
domferrerribiere@orange.fr	*Denis Ferrer & Bruno Ribière*
vinferrerribiere.plugwine.com	*Côtes du Roussillon [map p. 131]*
	44 ha; 144,000 btl

The domain started when Dennis Ferrer took over his family's vineyards in 1993 and partnered with Bruno Ribière, who had been involved with marketing the wines of Roussillon. Denis manages the vineyards and Bruno is the winemaker. Their wives joined also, making this a two-family venture. Vineyards are in many small plots a few miles west of Perpignan, at 100-250m altitude on the slopes of the Aspres range below the Canigous mountain. There are 23 ha of black varieties and 21 ha of white. There's a range of varietal wines in IGP Côtes Catalanes: G de Pierre is Grenache, SYRAHnosaurusrex is Syrah (aged in demi-muids), Empreinte Du Temps is Mourvèdre, and F is an equal blend of Carignan and Grenache. Côtes du Roussillon Tradition has 40% Syrah, 30% Grenache, 20% Carignan, and 10% Mourvèdre; Cana has 45% each of Syrah and

Mourvèdre and 10% of Grenache (aged in demi-muids). Whites include the F Côtes Catalanes (Macabeu, Grenache Blanc, and Muscat) and Grenache Blanc Vieilles Vignes (from 90-year-old vines). There's also Muscat de Rivesaltes.

Domaine Jolly Ferriol

66600 Rivesaltes	*+33 6 13 22 96 73*
jollyferriol@gmail.com	*Isabelle Jolly & Jean-Luc Chossart*
jollyferriol.fr	*Rivesaltes*
	7 ha; 20,000 btl

Domaine Ferriol dates from the seventeenth century, and was famous in the nineteenth century, but had been abandoned for fifty years when Isabelle Jolly & Jean-Luc Chossart bought the estate in 2005. The vineyards are surrounded by an arc of the Agly river, and have a variety of terroirs, mostly schist but including clay and pebbles. There were as much as 17 ha, but vineyards were cut back to maintain quality. The range was expanded by negociant wines under the label Jolly Nature (about 10% of production, coming from neighboring vineyards). They are well known for their Pet'Nat sparkling wine, which comes from Muscat and is made by the Méthode Ancestrale (single fermentation in the bottle to produce low pressure). On Passe au Rouge is varietal Grenache, Syrahre is of course Syrah, Va Nu Pieds is a blend of Carignan and Grenache. White Else? is a blend of Grenache Gris and Macabeu, and there is also a dry Muscat. From Rivesaltes, there is the appellation Muscat and also the Or du Temps cuvée, an ambré (Passe-Temps), and also the Au Fil du Temps Rancio Sec (labeled as Vin de France and considered a benchmark for the category). Yields are small, 20-25 hl/ha for most cuvées, and less than 10 hl/ha for the dessert wines. The vineyards were sold in 2018; the last vintage was 2018. Domaine Matassa (see profile) is now in the old Jolly-Ferriol cellars.

Domaine du Mas Blanc

Parcé et Fils, 9 Avenue du Général de Gaulle, 66650 Banyuls sur Mer	*+33 4 68 88 32 12*
jeaninfo@domaine-du-mas-blanc.com.com	*Jean-Michel Parcé*
www.domaine-du-mas-blanc.com	*Banyuls [map p. 131]*
	15 ha

This historic domain has belonged to the Parcé family since 1639 and was a major influence in the appellation under Dr. André Parcé, who died in 1998. The family background is in medicine, and André's son Jean-Michel was the first to focus entirely on wine. After Jean-Michel took over, the domain maintained its position, but in recent years has been generally felt to have slipped. Production is split more or less equally between Banyuls and Collioure. Banyuls include the traditional (oxidative style) of the Vieilles Vignes, the modernist style of the Rimage, the multivintage Cuvée Dr. Parcé, and the Hors d'Age Vieilli en Sostrera (Sostrera is Catalan for Solera) The dry cuvées from Collioure include Clos du Moulin (based on Mourvèdre), Cosprons Levants (cofermentation of Syrah, Mourvèdre, and Grenache), Terres de Schistes (based on Grenache), and Révérence André Parcé (based on a vineyard planted with Syrah cloned from pre-phylloxera vines).

Mas Janeil

66720 Tautavel	*+33 5 57 55 12 12*
laurent.dalzovo@francoislurton.com	*François Lurton*
masjaneil.com	*Maury [map p. 131]*
	24 ha

The Lurton family own several châteaux in Bordeaux, but François has broken out into interests worldwide, with vineyards in Chile, Argentina, and Spain, as well as France, where he rented Mas Janeil in Roussillon in 1996, and then purchased it in 2008. He also makes wine at Domaine de Nizas (see profile). A new cellar was built in 2011. The estate extends over 70 ha, and the vineyards are rich in 60-year-old Grenache. Hauts de Janeil is the entry-level line. Then there's a series of red cuvées representing different blends or plots, from Grenache, Carignan, and Syrah. Since 2012, the San Soufre cuvée (both red and rosé) has been made without sulfur except for a minimal dose at bottling. Whites come from Macabeo and Grenache Blanc and Gris.

Domaine Mas de Lavail

Route départementale 117, 66460 Maury	*+33 6 31 33 59 19*
info@masdelavail.com	*Nicolas Batlle*
masdelavail.com	*Maury [map p. 131]*
	80 ha; 200,000 btl

The Batlle family has been growing grapes in Maury for five generations, but it was only in 1999, when Nicolas joined his father Jean, that they bought this nineteenth century *mas* and started to bottle their own wine. Vineyards are on rock terraces of black schist. Plantings are all three varieties of Grenache and Syrah and Carignan. Under IGP Catalanes, there are Carignan Vieilles Vignes (from 50-year-old vines), Carignan Blanc Vieilles Vignes, and rosé, all aged in cuve. A cuvée without sulfur is a blend of Carignan and Syrah. A notch up, Le Sud is blend of old vines Grenache Blanc and Gris, aged in barriques. From Côtes du Roussillon, La Désirade is a blend of 50% Syrah with 25% each of Carignan and Grenache, given long maceration, while Ego is 80% Grenache and 20% Mourvèdre, both aged in barrique. Initiale is Maury Sec, from 70% Grenache and 10% each of Mourvèdre, Syrah, and Carignan, given slightly longer aging in barrique. The sweet fortified wines from Maury are the Blanc (from Grenache Blanc fermented and aged in new barriques), and Expression (from Grenache aged nonoxidatively for 12 months). There is also a Maury Ambré, from grapes harvested in 1999 when the domain was founded, and aged (oxidatively) for twenty years in barrique, and a Muscat de Rivesaltes.

Domaine Clos Massotte

D612, 66300 Trouillas	*+33 6 23 36 43 01*
pn@massotte.com	*Pierre-Nicolas Massotte*
www.massotte.com	*Côtes du Roussillon [map p. 131]*
	8 ha; 13,000 btl

Pierre-Nicolas Massotte was an engineer before he changed career to take over 8 ha of the 40 ha family domain in 2004. His plots include some very old vines. He follows 'natural' winemaking. In dry reds, Corail d'Automne is Côtes du Roussillon from equal Syrah and 100-year-old Grenache, and GAIA is 40% Syrah and 30% each of Grenache and Carignan; they have long (36-40 months) aging in barriques. The white Corail d'Automne is an IGP from equal Grenache Blanc and 80-year-old Grenache Gris; Ondine Blanc is a Vin de France from equal Grenache Gris and Grenache Blanc with 10%Muscat. They age for 12 months with half in barriques. Ondine rosé comes from equal Grenache Gris and Mourvèdre. Grand Roussillon is a VDN from Grenache. There is also an entry-level range in Vin de France.

Domaine de la Matassa

Mas Ferriol, 66600 Espira-de-l'Agly	*+33 4 68 64 10 13*
matassa@orange.fr	*Tom Lubbe*
www.matassawine.fr	*IGP Côtes Catalanes [map p. 131]*
	20 ha; 30,000 btl

Coming from New Zealand via South Africa, Tom Lubbe worked at Domaine Gauby (see profile) for three years from 1999. After marrying Gérard's sister, Nathalie, he started his own domain in 2003. The first vintage was made in his house; then in 2004 Gérard gave him the old Gauby cellar. Since 2019, the cellars have moved to the former Jolly Ferriol estate, near the original vineyard. The first vineyard, which he bought in 2001 in partnership with fellow New Zealander Sam Harrop, was 6 ha in the hills of the Coteaux du Fenouillèdes. Now vineyards include another 3 ha in Fenouillèdes and 6 ha around Calce from the Gauby family. Soils are on schist and marl. Tom believes that his intensive use of cover crops makes for better ripening, allowing him to harvest earlier, and like Gerard Gauby, he produces wines at lower alcohol than is common for the region, usually below 12%. Tom is allergic to sulfur, and most of the wines are made without adding sulfur, or using absolutely minimal amounts. The whites are all made by whole cluster pressing. Cuvée Nougé comes from 40% Macabeu, 30% Muscat, and 30% Viognier; Marguerite comes from old Viognier and Muscat; Alexandria is a dry Muscat; Matassa Blanc is 70-80% Grenache Gris at Calce and 20-30% Macabeu from St Paul de Fenouillet. In reds, Romanissa comes from schist at Calce and is 90% Grenache from vines up to 130-years old, with 10% Carignan; Matassa Rouge comes from the original vineyard in Fenouillèdes on granite, and is based on Carignan, including a field blend of old vines. Wines were initially labeled IGP Côtes de Catalanes, but then switched to Vin de France.

Château Nadal-Hainaut

RD37, 66270 Le Soler	*+33 4 68 92 57 46*
info@chateaunadalhainaut.com	*Martine Nadal*
www.chateaunadalhainaut.com	*Côtes du Roussillon [map p. 131]*
	53 ha

The domain is housed in a château built in 1826 on the site of twelfth century Cistercian priory of Santa Maria d'Eule; a chapel remains in the grounds. The Hainaut family bought the 125 ha estate in the early nineteenth century. Nadal was added to the name after Thérèse Hainaut married François Nadal in 1900. Trained as an oenologist, Martin Nadal took over from his father Jean in 1980. Located just west of Perpignan, most of the dry wines are IGP Côtes Catalanes, but there are also AOP Côtes du Roussillon. The entry-level IGP focuses on varietals, with Cabernet Sauvignon, the 3 Sources Syrah, and

La Centenaire Carignan ("the soul of the château"). Moving up a notch, there are several blends with 70% Syrah and 30% Grenache. In IGP, Terre de Quarante is a blend of the best Grenache and Syrah, and L'Hydre du Lac is a version without sulfur. In AOP, Signum, has some oak aging. Whites include Chardonnay, a Chardonnay-Macabeu blend, and a dry Muscat. In dessert wines, there are Muscat de Rivesaltes, and all categories of VDN from Rivesaltes.

Château de l'Ou

Route de Villenueve de la Raho, D8, 66200 Montescot	*+33 4 68 54 68 67*
contact@chateau-de-lou.fr	*Séverine Bourrier*
www.chateau-de-lou.com	*Côtes du Roussillon [map p. 131]*
	75 ha; 150,000 btl

The domain was founded in 1998 when Séverine and Philippe Bourrier bought a 30 ha property on the Plaine du Roussillon, planted with 36 ha of vines and 4 ha of olive trees. Séverine qualified in oenology in Bordeaux and is the winemaker. In 2009 they extended the domain by buying 8 h at Saint-Paul-de-Fenouillet (with terroir of schist at 325m altitude in the Agly valley) and 7 ha at Caudiès-de-Fenouillèdes (based on black schist at 385m altitude), followed in 2017 by 7 ha at Maury (planted with Grenache Noir and Gris), so now they have four separate areas. There are nine red cuvées. The Côtes du Roussillon cuvées are the entry-level here. One is a GSM blend aged in stainless steel; Compartir is GSM Côtes du Roussillon from Maury. Most of the cuvées are varietal Syrah in IGP Côtes de Catalanes. The range starts with Infiniment de l'Ou and l'Ove (Syrah from the Plaine), moving to Velours Noir (Syrah from black schist around Caudiès) and Secret de Schistes (Syrah from the Saint-Paul), and culminating in Ipso Facto (a selection of the best berries from all three terroirs) and Grenache Rhapsody (dry red from Maury). The unusual feature of the reds is that all except for the entry-level cuvée have vinification intégrale, with fermentation in open barriques, which are subsequently closed for aging. There are also whites, rosés, and fortified sweet wines.

Domaine Jean-Philippe Padié

11 Rue-des-Pyrénées 66600 Calce	*+33 6 99 53 07 66*
contact@domainepadie.com	*Jean-Philippe Padié*
www.domainepadie.com	*IGP Côtes Catalanes [map p. 131]*
	18 ha; 40,000 btl

Jean-Philippe Padié grew up in Burgundy, but his grandparents lived in the southwest, and he qualified in oenology in Montpellier. He worked at Mas Amiel and with Gérard Gauby before setting up his domain at Calce, where his vineyards are dispersed into 30 separate plots. He's known for the delicacy of his approach. Wines are Vins de France. Ciel Liquide is a blend of Grenache and Carignan plus some Syrah and Mourvèdre from plots around Calce, aged for two years in old barrels followed by one year in stainless steel. He describes Petit Taureau as a 'marriage of extremes in terms of terroir,' a blend of 50 % Carignan on calcareous clay with 50% Syrah on schist. It ages in concrete. Calice is an entry-level wine from Carignan on schist. Fleur de Cailloux is 50% Grenache Blanc, 30% Macabeu,. and 20% Grenache Gris from schist, aged in barrels with some new oak.

Domaine Paetzold

Lieu-dit Lous Sarradets, D38, 66720 Bélesta	*+33 5 57 83 85 90*
contact@domainepaetzold.com	*Michael Paetzold*
domainepaetzold.com	*Côtes du Roussillon Villages [map p. 131]*
	15 ha; 33,000 btl

Michael Paetzold qualified in oenology in Bordeaux and, after twenty years as an oenologist, established the domain in 2005. Originally called Domaine Mastrio, it was renamed as Domaine Patezold in 2015. Vineyards are on stony hillsides on gneiss, at elevations of 250-450m, and include 6 ha of Carignan more than a century old. Grapes from the best plots, planted before 1905, go into Mastrio. The Mastrio Blanc, introduced in 2009, comes from equally old vines of Carignan Blanc, blended with 15% Macabeu. Both come from plots facing north and northeast. Luxur comes from 30-60-year old Grenache on south-facing plots. Nagel comes from 30-year-old Syrah. All the wines age for 14 months in stainless steel. The only red blend is entry-level Le Cazotte, from all three varieties.

Domaine Pietri-Geraud

22 rue Pasteur, 66190 Collioure	*+33 4 68 82 07 42*
contact@domaine-pietri-geraud.com	*Laetitia Pietri-Geraud*
www.domaine-pietri-geraud.com	*Collioure [map p. 131]*
	20 ha; 45,000 btl

Located in the center of the old village of Collioure, the domain was founded at the end of the nineteenth century by Étienne Géraud. His granddaughter Maguy handed over to her daughter Laetitia in 2006. Wines are split between AOPs Collioure and Banyuls. Dry wines from Collioure include all three colors. Sine Nomine is an approachable wine from 60% Grenache, 20% Syrah, and 10% each of Mourvèdre and Carignan, aged in cuve. Moulin de La Cortine is more structured, with 70% Syrah, 15% Mourvèdre, and 15% Grenache. These age in cuve. Trousse Chemise ages in barriques for 24 months; initially a cuvée of Syrah, in 2016 it became Mourvèdre. In fortified sweet wines from Banyuls, Maguy is the white from Grenache Blanc, aged for 12 months in new barriques, Eléore is a rosé from all three colors of Grenache, aged in concrete, and Méditerranée is 90% Grenache and 10% Carignan, aged in mostly new barriques and topped up over four years. The traditional cuvée, Joseph Géraud, has the same blend, but ages in concrete for a year followed by six years in foudres, with a small part in barriques. Mademoiselle O is a modern style, Rimage cuvée.

Domaine Piquemal

RD 117 - KM 7 / Lieu dit della lo rec, 66600 Espira de L'Agly	*+33 4 68 64 09 14*
contact@domaine-piquemal.com	*Marie-Pierre Piquemal*
www.domaine-piquemal.com	*Côtes du Roussillon Villages [map p. 131]*
	48 ha; 180,000 btl

The Piquemal family founded the domain at the start of the twentieth century. and it is now in the hands of the third and fourth generations, Pierre Piquemal and his daughter Marie-Pierre. Pierre started estate bottling in 1983. Running along the Agly valley, terroirs vary between schist, round pebbles, and clay-limestone. There are wines from international varieties under IGP, dry reds and whites from AOP Côtes du Roussillon, and sweet wines from Rivesaltes and Muscat de Rivesaltes. The top wines are the Côtes du Roussillon Galatée (75% Grenache, 20% Syrah, 5% Carignan) and Pygmalion (75% Syrah, 20% Grenache, 5% Carignan), both aged in cuve.

Domaine du Possible

13 Avenue des Platanes 66720 Lansac	*+33 6 82 01 77 08*
loic.roure@laposte.net	*Loïc Roure*
www.domainedupossible.fr	*Côtes du Roussillon [map p. 131]*
	11 ha; 45,000 btl

Loïc Roure worked for Amnesty International in Lyon, then decided he wanted to open a wine bar. While interning as a sommelier in 1999, he worked for Thierry Allemand in Cornas, and became committed to the idea of making wine. After working at various estates in Alsace and the Rhône, he purchased 2.5 ha in the area of Fenouillèdes in 2003. Subsequent purchases all around the area brought the domain to its present size. The cellars are in the former cooperative in Lansac, which had been abandoned in 1990. Vineyards are mostly on volcanic rocks, including schist, gneiss, and granite, but there are some plots with calcareous clay. Plantings have 4.5 ha of Carignan, 2.6 ha Grenache, 1.3 ha of Syrah, and some Mourvèdre. Whites are mostly Macabeu. Most of the vines are old, 50-100 years. Most of the reds are made by semi-carbonic maceration (the technique of Beaujolais for making fruity wines without too much tannin). Couma Acò is an exception, a Syrah fermented and aged in old oak. Loïc also has a negociant activity called En Attendant La Pluie.

Domaine de Rancy

8 place du 8 mai 1945, 66720 Latour de France	*+33 6 87 11 15 18*
info@domaine-rancy.com	*Brigitte Verdaguer*
www.domaine-rancy.com	*Côtes du Roussillon Villages [map p. 131]*
	17 ha; 25,000 btl

The domain dates from the 1920s, and specialized from the start on Rancio. When Marcel Verdaguer took over in 1970, he focused on sweet VDNs from Rivesaltes, sold mostly in bulk, sending other grapes to the cooperative. His son Jean-Hubert took over in 1989 and introduced estate-bottling. He extended the range from Rivesaltes, focusing on Rancio, with plantings focused on Macabeu. The range includes monovarietal Rancio Sec cuvées from Macabeu, Carignan, and Syrah, all IGP Côtes Catalanes. The domain remains best known for its Rivesaltes Ambrés, with old vintages going back to 1919. After renovating the cellars, Jean-Hubert withdrew from the cooperative and started producing dry red wine in 2001. His daughter Delphine joined in 2006, and is now in charge of making the dry red wines, including monovarietals in IGP Côtes Catalanes from Carignan, Mourvèdre, and Grenache.

Vignoble Réveille

7 Rue des Corbières, 66720 Cassagnes	*+33 6 84 14 07 46*
france@vignoble-reveille.fr	*France Crispeels*
vignoble-reveille.fr	*Côtes du Roussillon [map p. 131]*
	11 ha

France Crispeels created the domain in 2006 when she purchased some old Carignan and Grenache planted on gneiss in the Agly valley. Since then she has expanded by buying other plots, with Syrah, Grenache, and Macabeu. She has moved increasingly towards 'natural' winemaking. Most of the cuvées are single varietals and labeled as IGP Côtes Catalanes; the AOP wines are Côtes du Roussillon. Aging is usually in concrete. In whites, White Spirit is Macabeu, and Vivre Sensible is Grenache Gris (aged in demi-muids). In reds, Tous des Oiseaux is Carignan, Ultra Violet is Syrah, Elan is Grenache, Franc Tireur is old Carignan from the original plot on gneiss at Cassagnes. Point Rouge is a blend of Carignan, Grenache, and Syrah.

Riberach

2 route de Caladroy, 66720 Bélesta	*+33 4 68 50 56 56*
cave@riberach.com	*Guilhem Soulignac*
www.riberach.com	*IGP Côtes Catalanes [map p. 131]*
	12 ha; 45,000 btl

Located below the medieval castle, this is a project in oenotourism to transfer an abandoned cooperative into a luxury hotel, Michelin-starred restaurant, and wine domain. The cooperative failed in 2006, and one of its leading members, Jean-Michel Mailloles, mobilized some associates to start a new enterprise. One of the four partners, Guilhem Soulignac explains that the name is a bit complicated. "The wine project is called Riberach, the tourism project is Domaine Riberach." Wines are all IGP Côtes Catalanes, ranging from conventional blends to monovarietals. Carignan is a dominant influence. Synthèse Gris is a rosé from Carignan. Parenthèse is a white from a Macabeu at Le Soula. The white Hypothèse comes from 1.5 ha of Carignan Gris that were part of Jean-Michel's vineyards. The red Hypothèse is Carignan from 100-year-old vines. The top red is Fou-Thèse, a blend of Carignan and Syrah from 60-year-old vines, made in the best years. Almost all aging is oak, usually in foudres.

Domaine Sant Jordi

5, Carrer Sant Jordi, 66650 Banyuls sur Mer	*+33 9 74 56 54 92*
zoe.holtzscherer@yahoo.fr	*Josy & Luc Holtzscherer*
www.domainesantjordi.com	*Collioure [map p. 131]*
	30 ha

René Holtscherer bought the family's first vineyards, but made wine in the cooperative movement, where he was an important figure. His son Riger was an agricultural engineer, and it was the next generation, Josy and Luc, who established the domain, now working with their children Manon and Zoé. From Collioure, the red is Mourvèdre and Grenache, the white is Grenache Blanc and Vermentino (both aged in oak), and the rosé is Grenache and Syrah. From Banyuls there is a Rimage from Grenache.

Clos Saint-Sébastien

Mas Xatard (winery) *10 avenue Pierre Fabre (shop), 66650 Banyuls sur Mer*	*+33 4 68 88 30 14*
r.peronne@clos-saint-sebastien.com	*Jacques Pirou & Romuald Peronne*
www.domaine-st-sebastien.com	*Banyuls [map p. 131]*
	20 ha

Clos Saint-Sébastien is a collaboration between Jacques Pirou (with a marine background) and Romuald Peronne (grandson of a vigneron in Roussillon), who bought Domaine Saint-Sébastien in 2008. In 2014 they bought another old domain, Clos Xatard, and joined the two domains together under the name of Clos Saint-Sébastien. They also run a restaurant in town, Le Jardin de St. Sébastien. The wines are made at Clos Xatard but there is a tasting room in town. The original estate of Domaine Saint-Sébastien is 14 ha; Clos Xatard added another 6 ha to the domain. Vineyards are dispersed and quite varied in plantings, ranging from modern plantings of single varieties to three plots dating from 1950 which were planted with intermingled varieties. There are three ranges. Empreintes comes from Grenache, Noir, Gris, or Blanc, with dry wines of all three colors from Collioure, and a white Banyuls and a red Banyuls Rimage. Inspirations represents the modern aspect of the domain. Minérale is a white from 90% Grenache Gris (4 ha of this relatively rare variety were recently planted at the estate) and 10% Grenache Blanc, with direct pressing followed by fermentation in stainless steel and aging in demi-muids. Collioure Marine is 90% Mourvèdre and 10% Grenache, while Céleste is 90% Grenache and 10% Carignan; both age for a year in foudres (new for Marine). Ardente is a Banyuls Tradition, aged oxidatively for 15-20 years in barriques. The top wines, labeled Collections, are selections from the best plots. Les Clos is a Collioure from 60 % Grenache, 20% Carignan, 10% Syrah, and 10% Mourvèdre. Les Clos Grande Réserve is 70% Syrah and 10% each of Mourvèdre, Carignan, and Grenache. For both cuvées, the individual varieties age separately in foudre for a year before assemblage. Banyuls Le Coeur ages oxidatively for 25 years before release.

Domaine des Schistes

1, rue Jean Lurcat 66310 Estagel	*+33 6 89 29 38 43*
sire-schistes@wanadoo.fr	*Mickaël Sires*
domainedesschistes.com	*Côtes du Roussillon Villages [map p. 131]*
	55 ha; 100,000 btl

The name of the domain reflects its location at the intersection of the Agly river with the villages of Estagel, Tautavel and Maury, where terroirs are based on black and gray schist. Vineyards are in 80 separate parcels, with most of the plots established in the 1940s. The family has been growing grapes here for generations, and Jacques Sires started estate-bottling in 1989; his son Mickaël has been expanding the domain since taking over ten years ago. There are about 12 cuvées, divided into four groups. IGP Côtes Catalanes comes mostly from younger vines around Estagel. The Côtes du Roussillon Villages Essencial red and white come from around Tautuvel. Wines from individual parcels are La Comeille (mostly Syrah from near Maury, aged in wood); Caune d'En Joffre is Carignan from 70-year old vines (aged in cement); and Devant le Mas is a blend of cofermented 70-year old Grenache and Lledoner Pelut (aged in wood). Sweet fortified wines include Muscat de Rivesaltes, Maury (100% Grenache), and Solera (from Grenache Gris). The domain has also made a name for its Rancio Sec, made by a solera system.

Domaine Semper

6 Route de Cucugnan, 66460 Maury	*+33 4 68 59 14 40*
domaine.semper@wanadoo.fr	*Paul Semper*
domaine.semper.over-blog.com	*Maury [map p. 131]*
	20 ha

This family domain has been handed from father to son for several generations. Located in the north of Roussillon, in the Vallée de l'Agly, its vineyards are divided equally between those on the schist terroir of Maury and those on the granite of Lesquerde. Several cuvées of Côtes du Roussillon Villages come from the granite: Lesquerde, Voluptas, and Famae. Another Côtes du Roussillon, cuvée Florent, is a selection from old vines on the schist, 60% Grenache, 30% Syrah, and 10% Carignan, with a quarter aged in barriques. There are also the white IGP, Regain (mostly Grenache Blanc), and the Muscat de Rivesaltes. The sweet dessert wines of Maury come from the schist, including Viatage, a 100% Grenache from a selection of old vines.

Domaine des Soulanes

Mas de Las Fredas, 66720 Tautavel	*+33 6 12 33 63 14*
daniel.laffite@nordnet.fr	*Daniel & Cathy Lafitte*
www.domaine-soulanes.com	*Côtes du Roussillon Villages [map p. 131]*
	17 ha; 30,000 btl

The Mas de Las Fredas was a family estate throughout the twentieth century. Daniel Laffite worked at the estate for 15 years with owner Jean Pull and then bought it in 2002, giving it the new name of Domaine des Soulanes. The name reflects the lie of the land: the estate has 18 separate parcels, all facing southeast, and a soulane is a hillside facing south-southeast. The property is close to the limestone cliffs of Tautavel. Kaya Blanc comes from 65-year old Grenache Gris and Blanc and Carignan Gris and Blanc, aged half in barrique and half in stainless steel. Kaya Rouge is Carignan and ages traditionally in concrete. Jean Pull is a blend of Grenache, Carignan, Mourvèdre, and Syrah, also aged in concrete. Sarrat del Mas is 50% Grenache and 25% each of Carignan and Syrah, aged in 2- and 3-year barriques. There's a series of sweet fortified wines from Maury, including white, Grenat, and Hors d'Age.

Les Terres de Fagayra

1, route de Montner, 66720 Latour de France	*+33 4 68 29 16 62*
rocdesanges@wanadoo.fr	*Stéphane Gallet*
www.marjorie-stephane-gallet.com	*Côtes du Roussillon Villages [map p. 131]*
	4 ha; 7,000 btl

Stéphane Gallet was at Mas Amiel (see profile) and then left to form his own domain, with his wife Marjorie Gallet of Roc des Anges (see profile), to make Vin Doux Naturel.

Most of the vineyards were planted in 1949. This small domain makes three sweet wines under AOP Maury. L'Energique is a white from Grenache Gris and Blanc, and Macabeo; Le Minéral comes from Grenache on calcareous schists, and Le Grand Classique is a blend of Grenache and Carignan from schist. The style is modern, and aims to preserve minerality; the wines are recognized as having an unusual elegance and precision for fortified wines of the appellation.

Terres des Templiers

8 Route du Mas Reig, 66650 Banyuls sur Mer	*+33 4 68 98 36 70*
info@templiers.fr	*Flavien Borgnon*
www.terresdestempliers.fr	*Collioure [map p. 131]*
	700 ha; 2,000,000 btl

The cooperative Cellier des Templiers was founded in 1921 and changed its name to Terre des Templiers in 2013. It represents 753 growers, with almost 700 ha of vines, and accounts for just over half the production of Banyuls. Its new cellars were built in 2011. It also owns the adjacent La Cave de l'Abbé Rous, a smaller cooperative created in 1950. There is a wide range of wines, with almost fifty cuvées of red, white, and rosé from Collioure, and almost twenty cuvées representing all styles of Banyuls.

Domaine la Tour Vieille

12, Route de Madeloc, 66190 Collioure	*+33 4 68 82 44 82*
info@latourvieille.com	*Vincent Cantie*
www.latourvieille.com	*Collioure [map p. 131]*
	13 ha; 70,000 btl

Vincent Cantié and Christine Campadieu took over their family domains in Collioure and Banyuls in 1981 and combined them under the name of La Tour Vieille. From Collioure, there are reds, rosé (Grenache and Syrah), and white (40% Grenache Gris and 30% Grenache Blanc, and other varieties). The major release from Collioure is La Pinède, 65% Grenache, 30% Mourvèdre, and 5% Carignan, with a short aging in tank. Collioure Puig Oriol is 70% Syrah, 25% Grenache and 5% Carignan. Puig Ambeille is 60% Mourvèdre and 40% Grenache, and a small part ages in demi-muids. There's a full range of fortified dessert wines from Banyuls, including nonoxidized Rimage and the traditional Reserva and Rancio. Vin de Méditation comes from old Grenache and Carignan. with very long aging in oak.

Domaine Val de Ray

44-46 Rue Gambetta, 66720 Tautavel	*+33 4 68 29 45 55*
contact@domainevalderay.com	*Raymond Hage*
www.domainevalderay.fr	*Maury [map p. 131]*
	20 ha; 36,000 btl

Raymond Hage made a change of career when he bought this domain with his wife Caroline in 2015. The first two vintages were assembled from wines that were already aging in the cellar; 2016 was the first vintage produced completely by Raymond. The cellars are just at the entrance to the village of Tautavel. Vineyards are on a variety of terroirs, including limestone, schist, and sandstone. There is one red cuvée from Côtes du Roussillon Villages and four from Côtes du Roussillon Villages Tautavel. The Tautavel cuvées Charme, Attraction, and Séduction have a majority of Grenache with Syrah (and Mourvèdre for Charme); Fusion is Syrah and Mourvèdre. Gouttes d'Or is white Roussillon Villages (70% Grenache Blanc, 30% Vermentino) and Désir has 50% Vermentino, 40% Grenache Blanc and 10% Macabeu. There are also Muscat de Rivesaltes and Rivesaltes Ambre and Grenat.

Domaine Vaquer

1 rue des écoles, 66300 Tresserre	*+33 4 68 38 89 53*
domainevaquer@gmail.com	*Frédérique Vaquer*
www.domaine-vaquer.com	*Côtes du Roussillon Villages Les Aspres [map p. 131]*
	18 ha; 33,000 btl

The estate was founded in 1912 and took its present name from the founder's son-in-law. The wine was sold to negociants until Fernand Vacquer started estate bottling in 1968. (He labeled the wines Roussillon des Aspres after the local area, but they were labeled as Vins de Table not AOP. Aspres became an AOP in Côtes de Roussillon Villages in 2017.) His son Bernard studied oenology in Beaune in 1985 before taking over, and after Bernard died in 2001, his wife Frédérique took over. Vineyards are at 200m altitude, kept fresh by exposure to the wind. Wines are labeled as Côtes du Roussillon Villages Les Aspres or IGP Côtes Catalanes. Bernard did not use oak, and most cuvées still age in vat, but barrels are now used for the top red and white cuvées. L'Exception is the one cuvée that Fernand originally labeled as AOP, a blend of Syrah aged in 2-3-year barriques with Grenache and Carignan aged in vat. It has now been joined by Epsilon, a selection of the best barriques with a similar blend. In IGP, Exigence is Grenache and L'Expression is Carignan. Bernard planted Roussanne in 1999, and this is the basis of Esquisse, together with Macabeu and Grenache Blanc. L'Exception is a blend under Côtes du Roussillon, 70% Grenache Blanc and Gris with 30% Macabeu, aged in demi-muids. In varietals, there is a 100% Macabeu. Fortified wines include Muscat de Rivesaltes, Ambré hors d'Age, and sometimes Rivesaltes Grenat.

Domaine Vial Magneres

Clos Saint André, 14, rue Edouard Herriot 66650 Banyuls sur Mer	*+33 4 68 88 31 04*
info@vialmagneres.com	*Olivier et Crystel Sapéras*
www.vialmagneres.com	*Banyuls [map p. 131]*
	10 ha; 30,000 btl

This family domain is now in its fourth generation. Olivier and Crystel Sapéras took over after the death of their father, Bernard, in 2013. Vineyards are all around the coastline near Banyuls. Grenache is the predominant variety here, with 65% of plantings, and another 25% Grenache Gris or Blanc. The average is 40-50 years. There's a wide range of wines including some unusual cuvées. Dry red, white and rosé are under Collioure AOP. From Banyuls there is the Rimage (modern, nonoxidative, sweet style), the Tradition (aged in wood under oxidative conditions for four years), the Gaby Vial (aged oxidatively for eight years), Al Tragou (aged for twenty years to produce a rancio style). Rivage is a modern-style white. Cuvée Bernard Sapéras is an Ambré, aged in solera. Ranfio Cino is aged under flor to produce a (non-fortified) Sherry-like wine. Ranfio Seco is a long-aged rancio, but is dry.

Domaine Yoyo

10 Chemin du Roi, 66760 Montesquieu-des-Albères	*+33 6 12 19 05 79*
yoyomk@aol.com	*Laurence Manya Krief*
domaineyoyo.fr	*Côtes du Roussillon* *[map p. 131]*
	7 ha; 14,000 btl

Laurence Manya Krief, known as Yoyo, has a tiny estate in the area of Banyuls where she makes 'natural' wines. She comes from a winemaking family, but went into fashion for ten years before deciding she really wanted to make wine. She works her 7 vineyard plots by hand, or with a horse or mule. All the wines are Vins de France, identified as Albères (from 3 ha) or Banyuls (from 4 ha within the AOP Banyuls area). Bateau Ivre comes from 30-year-old Grenache, La Négra is half Grenache and half Carignan, from 80-year-old vines. Vierge Rouge is 70% Grenache Gris, 20% Grenache, and 10% Grenache Blanc. Vent Debout is old Carignan grown on gneiss. KM31 is 80% Grenache Gris, 10% Grenache, and 10% Carignan from 100-year-old vines. Akoibon is 60% Grenache and 40% Mourvèdre. The white Restaké comes from 80-year-old Grenache Gris and Blanc, and 20% Carignan Gris and Blanc. The wines are made by carbonic maceration and mostly age in used barriques or demi-muids.

Glossary of French Wine Terms

Classification

There are three levels of classification, but their names have changed:

- *AOP* (Appellation d'Origine Protégée, formerly AOC or Appellation d'Origine Contrôlée) is the highest level of classification. AOPs are tightly regulated for which grape varieties can be planted and for various aspects of viticulture and vinification.
- *IGP* (Indication Géographique Protegée, formerly Vin de Pays) covers broader areas with more flexibility for planting grape varieties, and few or no restrictions on viticulture and vinification.
- *Vin de France* (formerly Vin de Table) is the lowest level of classification and allows complete freedom with regards to varieties, viticulture, and vinification.
- *INAO* is the regulatory authority for AOP and IGP wines.

Producers

- *Domaine* on a label means the wine is produced only from estate grapes (the vineyards may be owned or rented). *Château* in Bordeaux has the same meaning.
- *Maison* on the label means that the producer is a negociant who has purchased grapes (or wine).
- *Negociants* may purchase grapes and make wine or may purchase wine in bulk for bottling themselves. Some negociants also own vineyards.
- *Cooperatives* buy the grapes from their members and make the wine to sell under their own label.

Growers

- There is no word for winemaker in French. The closest would be *oenologue,* meaning a specialist in vinification; larger estates (especially in Bordeaux) may have consulting oenologues.
- A *vigneron* is a wine grower, who both grows grapes and makes wine.
- A *viticulteur* grows grapes but does not make wine.
- A *régisseur* is the estate manager at a larger property, and may encompass anything from general management to taking charge of viticulture or (commonly) vinification.

Viticulture

- There are three types of viticulture where use of conventional treatments (herbicides, insecticides, fertilizers, etc.) is restricted:
- *Bio* is organic viticulture; certification is by AB France (Agriculture Biologique).
- *Biodynamique* is biodynamic viticulture, certified by Demeter.
- *Lutte raisonnée* means sustainable viticulture (using treatments only when necessary). HVE (Haute Valeur Environmentale) is the best known certification.
- *Selection Massale* means that cuttings are taken from the best vines in a vineyard and then grafted on to rootstocks for replanting the vineyard.

- *Clonal selection* uses (commercially available) clones for replanting.
- *Vendange Vert* (green pruning) removes some berries during the season to reduce the yield.

Winemaking

- *Vendange entière* means that grapes are fermented as whole clusters.
- *Destemming* means that the grapes are taken off the stems and individual berries are put into the fermentation vat.
- *Vinification intégrale* for black grapes means the wine ferments in a barrique standing up open without an end piece. After fermentation, the end is inserted and the wine ages in the same barrique in which it was fermented.
- During fermentation of red wine, grape skins are pushed up to the surface to form a cap. There are three ways of dealing with it:
    - *Pigeage* (*Punch-down*) means using a plunger to push the cap into the fermenting wine.
    - *Remontage* (pump-over) means pumping up the fermenting wine from the bottom of the vat to spray over the cap.
    - *Délestage* (rack-and-return) means running the juice completely out of the tank, and then pouring it over the cap (which has fallen to the bottom of the vat)
- *Chaptalization* is the addition of sugar before or during fermentation. The sugar is converted into alcohol, so the result is to strengthen the alcoholic level of the wine, not to sweeten it.
- A *cuve* is a large vat of neutral material—old wood, concrete, or stainless steel.
- *Cuvaison* is the period a wine spends in contact with the grape skins.
- *Battonage* describes stirring up the wine when it is aging (usually) in cask.
- *Soutirage* (racking) transfers the wine (without the lees) from one barrique to another.
- *Élevage* is the aging of wine after fermentation has been completed.
- *Malo* is an abbreviation for malolactic fermentation, performed after the alcoholic fermentation. It reduces acidity, and is almost always done with red wines, and often for non-aromatic white wines.
- A *vin de garde* is a wine intended for long aging.

Aging in oak

- A *fût* (*de chêne*) is an oak barrel of unspecified size.
- A *barrique* (in Bordeaux or elsewhere) has 225 liters or 228 liters (called a *pièce* in Burgundy).
- *Tonneau* is an old term for a 900 liter container, sometimes used colloquially for containers larger than barriques, most often 500 or 600 liter.
- A *demi-muid* is a 600 liter barrel.
- A *foudre* is a large oak cask, round or oval, from 20-100 hl.

Sweet wines

- *Moelleux* is medium-sweet wine.

- *Liquoreux* is fully sweet dessert wine.
- *Doux* is sweet (usually not botrytized) still or sparkling wine.
- *Mutage* is addition of alcohol to stop fermentation and produce sweet wine. The style is called Vin Doux Naturel (VDN).
- *Passerillage* leaves grapes on the vine for an extended period so that sugar concentration is increased by desiccation.
- *Botrytis,* also known as *noble rot,* means grapes have been infected with the fungus Botrytis cinerea, which concentrates the juice and causes other changes.

Index of Estates by Rating

Index of Organic and Biodynamic Estates

Château Massamier la Mignarde
Domaine Clos Massotte
Domaine de la Matassa
Domaine Mirabel
Domaine de Montcalmès
Mas Montel - Mas Granier
Domaine Mylène Bru
Château Nadal-Hainaut
Domaine Thierry Navarre
Château de la Négly
Clos des Nines
Domaine de Nizas
Domaine Ollier-Taillefer
Mas Onésime
Clos d'Ora
Château de l'Ou
Domaine Jean-Philippe Padié
Domaine Paetzold
Les Païssels
Domaine du Pas de l'Escalette
Château de Pech Latt
Château Pech Redon
Château de Perdiguier
Domaine Peyre Rose
Domaine Olivier Pithon
Romain Portier
Domaine du Possible
Prieuré Saint Jean de Bébian
Domaine de la Prose
Mas des Quernes
Domaine de Rancy
Domaine de Ravanès
Le Clos des Reboussiers
Vignoble Réveille
Riberach
Domaine Rimbert
Domaine Le Roc des Anges
Domaine Saint-Daumary
Domaine Sainte-Marie des Crozes
Domaine Saumarez
Château la Sauvageonne
Domaine des Schistes
Domaine Jean-Baptiste Senat
Le Mas de la Séranne
Mas du Soleilla
Domaine le Sollier
Domaine des Soulanes
Abbaye de Sylva Plana
Terre des Dames
Les Terres de Fagayra
Domaine de La Tour Boisée
La Traversée
Turner Pageot
Domaine Val de Ray
Château Vieux Moulin
Les Vignes Oubliées
Villa Symposia
Villa Tempora
Verena Wyss
Domaine Yoyo

Producers Making Natural Wines or Wines With No Sulfur

Les Arabesques
Château Auzias
Château La Baronne
Domaine Léon Barral
Domaine le Casot des Mailloles
Maison Cazes
Clos du Gravillas
Domaine Les Enfants Sauvages
Domaine Ludovic Engelvin
La Graine Sauvage
Château Guilhem
Domaine Jolly Ferriol
Mas Foulaquier
Mas Janeil
Domaine Mas de Lavail
Domaine Clos Massotte
Domaine de la Matassa
Château Nadal-Hainaut
Domaine Jean-Philippe Padié
Domaine du Possible
Vignoble Réveille
Riberach
Domaine Terre Inconnue
Domaine Val de Ray
Château Vieux Moulin
Verena Wyss
Domaine Yoyo

Index of Estates by Appellation

Domaine Ollier-Taillefer
Mas Onésime
Abbaye de Sylva Plana

Fitou

Domaine Bertrand-Bergé
Le Mas Des Caprices
Château Champ des Soeurs
Domaine les Mille Vignes
Château de Nouvelles
Domaine de la Rochelierre

Grès de Montpellier

Abbaye de Valmagne
Domaine Belles Pierres
Clos de l'Amandaie
Domaine Ellul-Ferrières
Château de L'Engarran
Domaine Mylène Bru
Clos des Nines
Domaine Peyre Rose
Château Saint Martin de la Garrigue
Domaine Saumarez
Domaine Terre Inconnue

IGP Cévennes

Mas d'Espanet

IGP Côtes Catalanes

Domaine Les Enfants Sauvages
Domaine Gauby
Domaine de la Matassa
Domaine Jean-Philippe Padié
Domaine Olivier Pithon
Riberach

IGP Gard

Roc d'Anglade
Domaine Ludovic Engelvin

IGP Pays d'Hérault

Mas Cal Demoura
Domaine de Clovallon
Mas de Daumas Gassac
Le Mas de l'Écriture
Domaine de La Grange des Pères
Mas Combarèla
Mas Conscience
Mas Jullien
Château de Perdiguier
Domaine La Terrasse d'Élise
Villa Symposia

IGP Pays d'Oc

Domaine Gayda

La Clape

Château d'Anglès
Château d'Aussières
Château L'Hospitalet
Château des Karantes
Château de la Négly
Château Pech Céleyran
Château Pech Redon
Château Rouquette-sur-Mer
Domaine Sarrat de Goundy
Mas du Soleilla

Languedoc

Château Le Thou
Terre des Dames

Languedoc Saint Drézéry

Château Puech Haut

Languedoc Saint Georges d'Orques

Domaine Henry
Domaine de la Prose

Languedoc Saint-Christol

Domaine de la Coste Moynier
Château des Hospitaliers

Languedoc Sommières

Domaine d'Aigues Belles
Domaine Mirabel
Mas Montel - Mas Granier

Languedoc-Montpeyroux

Domaine de L'Aiguelière
Domaine d'Aupilhac
Domaine Alain Chabanon
Mas des Quernes

Languedoc-Pézenas

Domaine Les Aurelles
Domaine Le Conte des Floris
Domaine De La Font Des Ormes
Mas Gabriel
Domaine de Nizas
Domaine Pech Rome
Prieuré Saint Jean de Bébian
Turner Pageot
Villa Tempora
Verena Wyss

Limoux

Maison Antech
Domaine de Baronarques
Domaine Jean-Louis Denois
Domaine J. Laurens
Château de Martinolles
Domaine de Mouscaillo

Domaine Rosier
Sieur d'Arques

Lunel

Domaine Le Clos de Bellevue
Les Vignerons du Muscat de Lunel

Malepère

Domaine Girard
Château Guilhem

Maury

Domaine Clos del Rey
Domaine des Enfants
Domaine du Mas Amiel
Mas Janeil
Domaine Mas de Lavail
Domaine Semper
Domaine Val de Ray

Minervois

Domaine Pierre Cros
Château la Grave
Anne Gros & Jean-Paul Tollot
Château Massamier la Mignarde
Château d'Oupia
Domaine Jean-Baptiste Senat
Domaine de La Tour Boisée
Domaine Vordy

Minervois La Livinière

Domaine des Aires Hautes
Domaine Borie de Maurel
Clos Centeilles
Château de Cesseras
Domaine la Combe Blanche
Combes Cachées
Château Sainte-Eulalie
Château de Gourgazaud
Château Maris
Clos d'Ora
Domaine de L'Ostal
Domaine L'Oustal Blanc
Domaine Piccinini

Muscat de Mireval

Domaine de la Belle Dame

Pic Saint Loup

Bergerie du Capucin
Mas Bruguière
Château de Cazeneuve
Domaine Clavel
Ermitage du Pic Saint-Loup
Domaine de L'Hortus
Château de Lancyre
Château de Lascaux
Château de L'Euzière
Clos Marie
Mas Foulaquier
Le Clos des Reboussiers
Domaine Saint-Daumary

Rivesaltes

Maison Cazes
Domaine Jolly Ferriol

Roussillon

Domaine Boudau

Saint Chinian

Clos Bagatelle
Borie La Vitarèle
Domaine Canet Valette
Château de Castigno
Mas Champart
Domaine Les Eminades
Domaine La Grange Léon
Domaine Laurent Miquel
Domaine La Lauzeta
Domaine la Madura
Domaine Thierry Navarre
Les Païssels
Domaine Rimbert

St. Jean-de-Minervois

Clos du Gravillas

Terrasses du Larzac

Clos de la Barthassade
Mas des Brousses
Domaine Caujolle-Gazet
Mas des Chimères
Clos Maïa
Mas Haut-Buis
Domaine l'Hermas
Domaine de Malavieille-Mas de Bertrand
Domaine de Montcalmès
Domaine du Pas de l'Escalette
La Pèira
Romain Portier
Château Saint Jean d'Aumières
Domaine Saint Sylvestre
Château la Sauvageonne
Le Mas de la Séranne
La Traversée
Domaine Vaïsse
Les Vignes Oubliées

Index of Estates by Name

Made in the USA
Las Vegas, NV
08 January 2022